From the test kitchens of
Better Homes and Gardens—
an all-occasion

CASSEROLE COOKBOOK

Wonderful one-dish answers to every mealtime
situation you face . . .

● **Everyday family casseroles**—a big collection
in a flavor range to suit everyone's taste

● **Entrees for entertaining**—from casual to
elegant, including a host of cook-at-the-table
specialties; recipes and shopping tips to help
you cater to a crowd

● **Speedy suppers**—a variety of delicious
combinations that go together quickly and
cook the same way, in the oven or on the range,
plus a choice selection for pressure-cooking

Bantam Cookbooks
Ask your bookseller for the books you have missed

AMERICA'S FAVORITE RECIPES FROM BETTER HOMES AND GARDENS®

THE ART OF FISH COOKING

THE ART OF FRENCH COOKING

THE ART OF GERMAN COOKING

THE ART OF INDIAN COOKING

THE ART OF ITALIAN COOKING

THE ART OF JEWISH COOKING

THE ART OF SALAD MAKING

THE BETTER HOMES AND GARDENS® BARBECUE BOOK

THE BETTER HOMES AND GARDENS® CALORIE COUNTERS COOKBOOK

THE BETTER HOMES AND GARDENS® CASSEROLE COOKBOOK

THE BETTER HOMES AND GARDENS® MEAT COOKBOOK

BLEND IT SPLENDID: THE NATURAL FOODS BLENDER BOOK

THE COMPLETE BOOK OF MEXICAN COOKING

THE COMPLETE BOOK OF ORIENTAL COOKING

THE COMPLETE BOOK OF PASTA

THE COMPLETE BOOK OF VEGETABLE COOKERY

THE COMPLETE BOOK OF WINE COOKERY

COOKING WITHOUT A GRAIN OF SALT

THE DESSERT LOVERS' COOKBOOK

THE DOCTOR'S QUICK WEIGHT LOSS DIET COOKBOOK

THE DRINKING MAN'S DIET COOKBOOK

THE ENTERTAINING WOMAN'S COOKBOOK

THE FANNIE FARMER BOSTON COOKING SCHOOL COOKBOOK

THE FANNIE FARMER JUNIOR COOKBOOK

THE FRENCH CHEF COOKBOOK

GIRL SCOUT COOKBOOK

THE GRAHAM KERR COOKBOOK

HAZEL MEYER'S FREEZER COOKBOOK

AN HERB AND SPICE COOKBOOK

HOME BAKEBOOK OF NATURAL BREADS & GOODIES

HORS D'OEUVRE AND CANAPES

THE INTERNATIONAL CHAFING DISH COOKBOOK

THE INTERNATIONAL FONDUE COOKBOOK

THE LIVE LONGER COOKBOOK: COOKING WITH NATURAL FOODS

THE LOW BLOOD SUGAR COOKBOOK

MAKING YOUR OWN BABY FOOD

THE NO-BEEF COOKBOOK

THE ONE POT DINNER

SMART SHOPPER'S COOKBOOK

THE SOUP AND SANDWICH COOKBOOK

THE SPANISH COOKBOOK

THE TUESDAY SOUL FOOD COOKBOOK

WHOLE EARTH COOKBOOK

YOGA NATURAL FOODS COOKBOOK

# BETTER
# HOMES
# and
# GARDENS®
# CASSEROLE
# COOKBOOK

BANTAM BOOKS · TORONTO · NEW YORK · LONDON

BETTER HOMES & GARDENS® CASSEROLE COOKBOOK

*A Bantam Book / published by arrangement with
Meredith Corporation*

*Bantam Cookbook Shelf edition published August 1969*

| | |
|---|---|
| 2nd printing .. September 1970 | 8th printing ... August 1972 |
| 3rd printing ..... March 1971 | 9th printing . September 1972 |
| 4th printing ...... April 1971 | 10th printing ...... May 1972 |
| 5th printing .... October 1971 | 11th printing ... October 1973 |
| 6th printing .... January 1972 | 12th printing ... January 1974 |
| 7th printing ... February 1972 | 13th printing ...... May 1974 |

*Bantam Books are published by Bantam Books, Inc. Its trade-
mark, consisting of the words "Bantam Books" and the por-
trayal of a bantam, is registered in the United States Patent
Office and in other countries. Marca Registrada. Bantam
Books, Inc., 666 Fifth Avenue, New York, New York 10019.*

PRINTED IN THE UNITED STATES OF AMERICA

# Contents

Every recipe in the CASSEROLE COOKBOOK is tested and endorsed by the Better Homes and Gardens Test Kitchens as measuring up to high standards of family appeal, practicality, and consistently fine taste.

# EVERYDAY MEALS

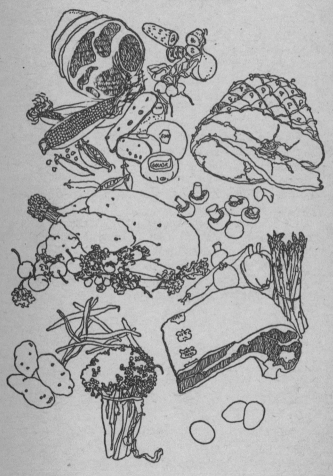

Looking for new and interesting ways to spark everyday meals? What could be easier to serve than a casserole or one-dish meal?

New and old combinations with every kind of meat, poultry, fish, and seafood are included—both for using leftovers and for starting from scratch.

Look what you can do with vegetables baked in a casserole. They double either as main dishes or as accompaniments for oven meals.

Or try an easy-on-the-budget main dish using cheese, eggs, or noodles. Turn to page 86, then to page 98, for recipe ideas which cover them all.

Leftovers are no longer a problem. With just a little ingenuity and ideas from the chart on page 106, turn them into appetizing everyday main dishes.

# HEARTY BEEF

## JUMBO CORNBURGER

1½ pounds ground beef
2 slightly beaten eggs
1 8-ounce can tomato sauce
¾ teaspoon salt
  Dash pepper
1 teaspoon Worcestershire sauce
1 12-ounce can whole kernel corn
½ cup medium-coarse cracker
  crumbs
1 slightly beaten egg

¼ cup diced green pepper
¼ cup chopped onion
2 tablespoons chopped canned
  pimiento
½ teaspoon salt
¼ teaspoon rubbed sage
1 medium tomato, peeled and
  cut in wedges
2 ounces sharp process American
  cheese, shredded (½ cup)

Combine beef with next 5 ingredients and spread *half* of mixture in 8¼x1¾-inch round ovenware cake dish or 8x8x2-inch baking dish. Combine remaining ingredients except tomato and cheese; spoon over meat. Cover with remaining meat mixture. Bake at 375° for 1 hour. Last 5 minutes, arrange tomato on top; sprinkle with cheese. Serves 6.

## SALMAGUNDI BAKE

Combine one 8-ounce can tomato sauce, ¾ cup uncooked long-grain rice, 1 cup water, 1 cup chopped onion, ½ cup chopped green pepper, 1 teaspoon salt, and dash pepper. Turn into a 2-quart casserole. Layer 1 pound uncooked ground beef on top. Sprinkle with 1 teaspoon salt and ½ teaspoon monosodium glutamate. Evenly spread over beef one 12-ounce can whole kernel corn, drained. Add 1 to 2 teaspoons chili powder to one 8-ounce can tomato sauce; pour mixture over corn.

Cover and bake in moderate oven (375°) for 1 hour; uncover and bake 10 minutes longer or till rice is tender. Garnish with crisp bacon curls, if desired. Makes 6 to 8 servings.

## MEATBALL VEGETABLE BAKE

1½ pounds ground beef
1 slightly beaten egg
1 cup soft bread crumbs
¼ cup milk
2 tablespoons **dry** onion soup mix
   Dash pepper
2 tablespoons salad oil
1 1-pound can tomatoes
¼ cup cold water
2 tablespoons all-purpose flour
1 tablespoon beef-flavored gravy base
1½ cups carrot, sliced lengthwise and cut in thirds
2 medium onions, quartered
1 cup bias-sliced celery chunks

Thoroughly combine meat, egg, bread crumbs, milk, soup mix, and pepper. Shape into 8 to 10 meatballs. Brown lightly in hot oil in large skillet. Remove meatballs and drain off excess fat; add tomatoes. Blend water, flour, and gravy base; stir into tomatoes.

Cook till mixture thickens and bubbles. Add meatballs, carrots, onions, and celery. Cover; simmer 15 minutes. Pour into 2-quart casserole. Cover; bake at 350° for 1 hour or till vegetables are tender. Serves 4 or 5.

## VEGETABLE MEATBALL SOUP

Rinse 1 cup large dry lima beans. In a large saucepan combine lima beans and 5 cups water; boil 2 minutes. Cover and let stand 1 hour. In a skillet cook ½ cup chopped onion in 1 tablespoon butter till tender but not brown. Add onion to soaked lima beans with one 8-ounce can tomatoes, 1 cup sliced celery, 1 cup diced carrot, 1 bay leaf, and 2 teaspoons salt. Cover and cook slowly 2 hours.

Mix ¾ pound ground lean beef, ¼ cup fine dry bread crumbs, 3 tablespoons milk, ½ teaspoon salt, and ¼ teaspoon Worcestershire sauce. Shape into 1-inch balls; add to soup. Simmer 15 minutes longer. Serves 6.

---

## TEST KITCHEN TIPS

### Extend ground beef in a casserole

*A pound of ground beef will make four regular-size patties or two giant ones. A casserole made from the same amount usually makes 4 to 6 servings.*

---

# HAMBURGER BISCUIT BAKE

| | |
|---|---|
| 1 pound ground beef | 3 tablespoons snipped parsley |
| ¼ cup chopped onion | 1½ cups packaged biscuit mix |
| 4 ounces sharp process American cheese, shredded (1 cup) | ½ cup milk |
| ¼ cup mayonnaise or salad dressing | Vegetable Sauce |

Cook beef and onion till meat is browned; drain excess fat. Stir in cheese, mayonnaise, and parsley. Combine biscuit mix and milk and stir till moistened; turn out onto floured surface and knead 8 to 10 times. Divide in half; roll into two 8-inch circles. Press one circle into well-greased 8¼ x 1¾-inch round ovenwear cake dish. Spread meat mixture over biscuit. Top with second biscuit. Bake at 375° for 20 to 25 minutes. Cut wedges and serve with Vegetable Sauce. Serves 6.

*Vegetable Sauce:* Heat one 10¾-ounce can of condensed cream of vegetable soup with ⅓ cup milk and ¼ teaspoon monosodium glutamate.

## TEST KITCHEN TIPS

### Ground beef—how to choose and use

HAMBURGER: Ground beef with a fairly high proportion of suet, and a low price per pound. Good for full-flavored patties.
GROUND CHUCK: Meat from the shoulder containing less fat than hamburger. It shrinks less in cooking and is well-suited for most ground beef dishes.
GROUND ROUND STEAK: This is the leanest ground meat of all. You may add a little suet to the meat for juicier patties.

## BEEF PATTIES PARMESAN

1 pound ground beef
½ cup packaged biscuit mix
⅓ cup tomato juice
¼ cup finely chopped green pepper
1 slightly beaten egg
1 small clove garlic, minced
1 teaspoon salt
½ teaspoon dried oregano, crushed
Dash pepper
½ teaspoon Worcestershire sauce
3 tablespoons shredded Parmesan cheese
Cooked buttered noodles

In a bowl combine beef, biscuit mix, tomato juice, green pepper, egg, garlic, salt, oregano, pepper, and Worcestershire sauce; mix lightly. Shape into 4 patties and place in greased shallow baking pan. Bake in hot oven (400°) for 20 minutes. Remove from oven; sprinkle patties with Parmesan cheese. Garnish with green olive slices, if desired. Serve on a bed of buttered noodles. Makes 4 servinge.

## BARBECUED MEATBALLS

1 pound ground beef
½ cup quick-cooking rolled oats
1 slightly beaten egg
½ cup milk
1 teaspoon salt
Dash pepper
2 tablespoons all-purpose flour
1 teaspoon paprika
½ teaspoon salt
2 tablespoons shortening
½ cup chopped onion
½ cup bottled barbecue sauce
½ cup water
1 1-pound can (2 cups) whole kernel corn, drained

Combine meat and next 5 ingredients; let stand 15 minutes.
Shape into 18 balls. Combine flour, paprika, and ½ teaspoon
salt. Roll meatballs in flour mixture. Brown in hot shortening;
drain. Place in 1½-quart casserole.

Cook onion in shortening till tender but not brown. Stir
in remaining ingredients and heat to boiling; add to meatballs
in casserole. Cover and bake in moderate oven (350°) for 35
to 40 minutes. Makes 6 servings

## VEGETABLE BEEF BAKE

1½  pounds beef, cut in 1-inch
       cubes
  2  tablespoons all-purpose flour
  2  teaspoons paprika
  1  to 1½ teaspoons chili powder
1½  teaspoons salt
  ¼  teaspoon pepper

  2  tablespoons shortening
  1  1-pound can (2 cups) tomatoes
  2  or 3 carrots, sliced lengthwise
  2  cups water
  1  cup coarsely chopped onion
  1  cup sliced celery
1½  cups uncooked mostaccioli

Coat meat with flour and seasonings. In skillet, brown meat
in shortening. Stir in tomatoes; add carrots, cover, and cook
over low heat 30 minutes. Add 2 cups water, onion, celery,
mostaccioli, and ½ teaspoon salt; bring to boiling. Pour meat
mixture into 3-quart casserole. Cover.

Bake in moderate oven (350°), stirring occasionally, 1 hour
or till vegetables and meat are tender. Makes 6 to 8 servings.

## MEATBALL GARDEN SKILLET

Preheat electric skillet to 325° or use regular skillet over low
heat. Cook ¼ cup chopped onion in 1 tablespoon butter or
margarine till tender but not brown. In a bowl, combine ½
pound ground beef and ½ pound ground veal with 2 tablespoons flour, 1 teaspoon salt, dash pepper, 1 egg, and ¼ cup
milk. Beat with fork thoroughly till light and fluffy. Add cooked
onion and form into 1-inch balls.

Brown meatballs lightly in 1 tablespoon butter in 350°
skillet or over medium heat. Push meatballs to one side. Blend
2 tablespoons flour into butter in skillet; add one 10½-ounce
can condensed beef broth and ⅔ cup water. Cook, stirring
constantly, till mixture thickens and bubbles.

Add 6 medium potatoes, quartered, 6 medium carrots,

quartered, and 5 or 6 green onions, cut in pieces. Sprinkle vegetables lightly with salt and pepper. Cover skillet; reduce heat and simmer till vegetables are tender, about 30 to 35 minutes. Pour boiling water over one 10-ounce package frozen peas to separate them; drain. Add peas; cover and simmer 5 minutes longer. Serves 6.

## STUFFED MANICOTTI

1 pound ground beef
½ cup chopped onion
1 large clove garlic, minced
2 6-ounce cans (1⅓ cups) tomato paste
2 cups water
2 tablespoons chopped parsley
1 tablespoon dried basil, crushed
1½ teaspoons salt
Dash pepper

. . .

⅔ cup grated Romano or Parmesan cheese

1½ pounds (3 cups) fresh ricotta, or cream-style cottage cheese, drained
2 slightly beaten eggs
¼ cup snipped parsley
½ teaspoon salt

. . .

Dash pepper
8 manicotti shells
½ cup grated Romano or Parmesan cheese

In large saucepan brown meat lightly. Drain off excess fat. Add onion, garlic, tomato paste, water, parsley, crushed basil, 1½ teaspons salt, and dash pepper. Simmer uncovered about 30 minutes, stirring occasionally. Meanwhile, combine ricotta *or* cottage cheese, ⅔ cup Romano *or* Parmesan cheese, eggs, parsley, ½ teaspoon salt, and dash pepper.

Cook manicotti shells in boiling salted water till just tender; drain. Rinse shells in cold water. Stuff manicotti with cheese mixture. Use a small spoon or cut the shells lengthwise with scissors; open to fill.

Pour *half* the tomato-meat sauce into 12x7½x2-inch baking dish. Arrange stuffed manicotti in a row. Top with remaining sauce. Sprinkle with ½ cup Romano *or* Parmesan cheese. Bake in moderate oven (350°) for 30 to 35 minutes. Makes 6 to 8 servings.

## CORNED BEEF SQUARES

In a bowl combine 1 cup milk, 2 eggs, 1 cup fine cracker crumbs (20 to 22 crackers), ½ cup chopped onion, 1 tablespoon prepared horseradish, and 1 teaspoon dry mustard. Add two 12-ounce cans corned beef, chopped (4 cups), and mix well.

Turn into 10x6x1½-inch baking dish. Bake in moderate oven (375°) for 30 to 35 minutes. Cut in squares. Serve with 1 medium head cabbage, cut in 6 to 8 wedges and cooked. Pass Dill Sauce. Makes 6 to 8 servings.

*Dill Sauce:* In medium saucepan combine one 10½-ounce can condensed cream of mushroom soup, ½ cup milk, 1 teaspoon dried dillweed, and 1 teaspoon dry mustard. Cook, stirring frequently, over medium heat till mixture is smooth and bubbly.

## CORNED BEEF 'N NOODLES

4 ounces noodles
3 tablespoons butter or
  margarine
3 tablespoons all-purpose flour
2¼ cups milk
1 tablespoon prepared
  horseradish

1 teaspoon prepared mustard
1 10-ounce package frozen peas
1 12-ounce can corned beef,
  cut in 6 slices

Cook noodles according to package directions; drain. In saucepan melt butter; stir in flour. Add milk; cook quickly, stirring constantly, till mixture thickens and bubbles. Stir in horseradish, mustard, 2 teaspoons salt, and dash pepper. Add noodles and thawed peas; turn into 10x6x1½-inch baking dish. Arrange corned beef slices on noodle mixture. Bake at 350° for 30 minutes. Serves 5 or 6.

## ROUND STEAK SAUERBRATEN

1½ pounds round steak, ½ inch
  thick
1 envelope brown gravy mix
1 tablespoon instant minced
  onion
1 tablespoon brown sugar

2 tablespoons wine vinegar
1 teaspoon Worcestershire sauce
¼ teaspoon ground ginger
1 bay leaf
  Hot buttered noodles

Cut meat in 1-inch squares. Brown meat in 1 tablespoon hot shortening. Remove meat from skillet; add gravy mix and 2 cups water. Bring to boiling, stirring constantly. Stir in next

6 ingredients, ½ teaspoon salt, and ¼ teaspoon pepper. Add meat. Turn into 1½-quart casserole. Cover; bake at 350° for 1½ hours. Remove bay leaf. Serve on noodles. Makes 5 or 6 servings.

## SAUCED CORNED BEEF ROLL

Combine one 12-ounce can corned beef, broken up, one 8-ounce can potatoes, drained and diced, 1 slightly beaten egg, ¼ cup milk, and 2 tablespoons chopped onion. Combine 2 cups biscuit mix and ⅔ cup milk. Knead 5 to 10 strokes on lightly floured surface. Roll to a 12-inch square.

Spread corned beef mixture on dough, to within ½ inch of edges. Roll up jelly roll fashion, sealing edges together. Place, seam side down, on greased baking sheet. Cut slits in top of roll. Bake at 425° for about 25 minutes. Cover lightly with foil for last few minutes if crust browns too quickly. Let cool 5 minutes before removing to serving platter.

Serve with Fluffy Mustard Sauce: Combine ½ cup dairy sour cream, ½ cup mayonnaise, and 1 tablespoon prepared mustard; heat through. Makes 6 servings.

## SWEDISH CABBAGE ROLLS

1 egg
1 teaspoon salt
Dash pepper
1 teaspoon Worcestershire sauce
¼ cup finely chopped onion
⅔ cup milk
½ pound ground beef
½ pound ground pork

¾ cup cooked rice

. . .

6 large cabbage leaves
1 10¾-ounce can condensed tomato soup
1 tablespoon brown sugar
1 tablespoon lemon juice

In a bowl combine egg, salt, pepper, Worcestershire sauce, onion, and milk; mix well. Add ground beef, ground pork, and cooked rice; beat together with fork. Immerse cabbage leaves in boiling water for 3 minutes or just till limp; drain. Heavy center vein of leaf may be slit about 2½ inches. Place ½ cup meat mixture on each leaf; fold in sides and roll ends over meat. Place rolls in 12x7½x1-inch baking dish.

Blend together soup, brown sugar, and lemon juice; pour over cabbage rolls. Bake in moderate oven (350°) for 1¼ hours. Baste once or twice with sauce. Makes 6 servings.

## BEEF GOULASH AND NOODLES

2 pounds beef chuck, cut in
  ¾-inch cubes
⅓ cup shortening
1 cup chopped onion
1 tablespoon all-purpose flour
1 tablespoon paprika
1 8-ounce can (1 cup) tomato
  sauce

1 1-pound can (2 cups) tomatoes
1 or 2 cloves garlic, minced
  Bouquet garni*
6 ounces medium egg noodles
2 tablespoons poppy seed
2 tablespoons butter or margarine

In large saucepan brown *half* the beef cubes in *half* the shortening; repeat. Add onion; cook till tender. Stir in flour, paprika, and 1 teaspoon salt. Add tomato sauce, tomatoes, garlic, and bouquet garni. Cover, simmer over low heat till meat is tender, about 1½ hours. Remove bouquet garni.

Cook noodles in boiling salted water; drain. Add poppy seed and butter. Serve Goulash over noodles. Serves 6 to 8.

*Bouquet garni: In cheesecloth, tie 1 bay leaf, 1 stalk celery, cut up, 2 tablespoons parsley, and ¼ teaspoon thyme.

## CURRIED BEEF CUBES

2 pounds beef chuck, cut in
  ¾-inch cubes
⅓ cup all-purpose flour
⅓ cup shortening
1 large onion, sliced
2 8-ounce cans tomato sauce

1 clove garlic, minced
2 to 3 teaspoons curry powder
1 9-ounce package frozen
  cut green beans
Hot cooked rice or noodles

Coat beef cubes with flour. In skillet brown meat in shortening. Add onion and cook till tender. Combine tomato sauce, 1½ cups water, garlic, 1 teaspoon salt, and ¼ teaspoon pepper; pour over meat. Cover and cook slowly over low heat till meat is tender, about 1½ hours. Stir in curry powder. Add green beans and cook till tender, about 15 minutes, separating beans with fork as they heat. Serve over hot rice or noodles. Makes 6 to 8 servings.

## CHILI CON CARNE

1 pound ground beef
1 large onion, chopped (1 cup)
1 green pepper, chopped (¾ cup)
1 1-pound can (2 cups) tomatoes,
  broken up

1 8-ounce can tomato sauce
1 1-pound can (2 cups) red
  kidney beans, drained
1 teaspoon salt
1 to 2 teaspoons chili powder
1 bay leaf

. . .

In heavy skillet cook meat, onion, and green pepper till meat is lightly browned and vegetables are tender, Stir in tomatoes, tomato sauce, kidney beans, salt, chili powder, and bay leaf. Cover and simmer for 1 hour. Remove bay leaf. Makes 4 servings.

## YAKAMISH

| | |
|---|---|
| ¼ cup chopped onion | 2 tablespoons butter or |
| 2 tablespoons butter or | margarine |
| margarine | 1½ cups shredded raw carrot |
| . . . | 2 cups cooked rice |
| 1 pound sirloin steak, 1 inch | Soy sauce |
| thick, cut in very thin strips | |

In a skillet cook onion in 2 tablespoons butter or margarine till tender. Remove from skillet. Combine *half* the meat and 2 tablespoons butter or margarine in skillet; season lightly with salt and pepper. Brown quickly. Remove meat; brown and season remaining meat. Stir in cooked onion, carrot, and cooked rice; toss till heated through. Pass soy sauce. Makes 4 or 5 servings.

## ORIENTAL BEEF SKILLET

| | |
|---|---|
| 1 pound round steak, ½ inch | 1 10½-ounce can condensed |
| thick, cut in very thin strips | cream of mushroom soup |
| Instant unseasoned meat | 2 tablespoons soy sauce |
| tenderizer | 1 cup drained canned bean |
| 2 tablespoons shortening | sprouts |
| 1 cup bias-cut celery slices | 3 cups fresh spinach, torn in |
| ½ cup coarsely chopped onion | pieces |
| ⅔ cup water | Hot cooked rice |

Tenderize meat according to label directions. Quickly brown meat, *half* the amount at a time, in hot shortening. Remove meat; add celery and onion. Cook and stir till tender-crisp, 2 to 3 minutes. Stir in soup, water, and soy sauce; heat to boiling. Add bean sprouts and spinach; heat through. Serve over hot cooked rice. Pass soy sauce. Makes 5 servings.

# EGGPLANT SKILLET

1 pound ground beef
¼ cup chopped onion
¼ cup chopped celery
1 8-ounce can (1 cup) tomato
   sauce
½ cup water
½ to ¾ teaspoon dried oregano,
   crushed

½ to ¾ teaspoon chili powder
1 small eggplant (about 1 pound),
   cut in ½-inch slices
4 ounces sharp process American
   cheese, shredded (1 cup)
Paprika
Shredded Parmesan cheese

Cook beef, onion, and celery till meat is browned. Drain off excess fat. Stir in tomato sauce, water, oregano, and chili powder. Season eggplant slices with salt and pepper. Arrange on top of meat sauce. Cover and simmer till eggplant is tender, 15 to 20 minutes. Top with shredded process American cheese and sprinkle with paprika. Serve with Parmesan cheese. Makes 4 or 5 servings.

---

## TEST KITCHEN TIPS

### Chopped, diced or minced—there is a difference

*To chop is to cut food into pieces about the size of peas. Diced food is cut in small cubes of uniform size and shape. Minced means very finely chopped.*

---

## TURKISH ZUCCHINI DOLMAS

1 pound ground beef
⅓ cup uncooked packaged
   precooked rice
¾ cup milk
½ cup chopped onion
1 teaspoon chopped fresh mint
   leaves, or ¼ teaspon dried
   mint, crushed, or 1 teaspoon

chopped fresh dillweed, or
   ¼ teaspoon dried dillweed
¼ teaspoon pepper
2 pounds (5 medium) zucchini
   squash
2 8-ounce cans tomato sauce
½ teaspoon salt

Combine ground beef, rice, milk, onion, 1 teaspoon salt, mint
*or* dillweed, and pepper; mix well. Cut both ends from zucchini. With apple corer, scoop out centers. (Chop centers and
reserve.) Fill zucchini loosely with meat mixture. Make balls
from leftover mixture.

In a large skillet combine tomato sauce, salt, and reserved
chopped zucchini centers; heat. Add zucchini and meatballs.
Cover and simmer 30 minutes or till squash are tender. Serve
with sauce. Makes 4 to 6 servings.

---

## TEST KITCHEN TIPS

### How much spaghetti and sauce to prepare

*One pound uncooked spaghetti will make 6 to 8 servings as
a main dish with sauce. Allow ¾ to 1 cup sauce per serving.*

---

## ITALIAN MEAT SAUCE

| | |
|---|---|
| 1 pound ground beef | 1 tablespoon brown sugar |
| 1 cup chopped onion | 1½ teaspoons ground oregano |
| 2 cloves garlic, minced | 1 teaspoon salt |
| 1 1-pound 14-ounce can tomatoes, cut up | ½ teaspoon monosodium glutamate |
| 1 1-pound can tomatoes, cut up | ¼ teaspoon dried thyme, crushed |
| 1 6-ounce can tomato paste | 1 bay leaf |
| ¼ cup snipped parsley | |

In large saucepan or Dutch oven, combine meat, onion, and
garlic; brown lightly. Drain off excess fat. Add 2 cups water
and remaining ingredients. Simmer uncovered 3 hours or
till sauce is thickened; stir occasionally. Remove bay leaf.
Serve over hot cooked spaghetti. Pass bowl of shredded Parmesan cheese. Makes 6 servings.

## BEEF AND SPAGHETTI

Cut 1 pound round steak in cubes. Coat meat with 2 tablespoons all-purpose flour; brown in 2 tablespoons hot shortening. Add ½ cup chopped onion; cook till tender but not

brown. Add 1 clove garlic, minced, one 3-ounce can broiled chopped mushrooms with liquid (⅔ cup), one 10¾-ounce can condensed tomato soup, 1 tablespoon Worcestershire sauce, 3 drops bottled hot pepper sauce, ½ teaspoon salt, and dash pepper; mix well.

Cover and simmer till tender, about 1¼ hours, stirring occasionally. Stir in 1 cup dairy sour cream and ¼ cup water; heat through (do not boil). Spoon meat mixture over individual servings of hot spaghetti. Sprinkle with Parmesan cheese. Makes 6 servings.

## SPAGHETTI AND MEATBALLS

| | |
|---|---|
| ¾ cup chopped onion | 1½ teaspoons salt |
| 1 clove garlic, minced | ½ teaspoon pepper |
| 3 tablespoons salad oil | 1½ teaspoons dried oregano, |
| 2 1-pound cans tomatoes, cut up | crushed |
| 2 6-ounce cans (1⅓ cups) | 1 bay leaf |
| tomato paste | Italian Meatballs |
| 2 cups water | Hot cooked spaghetti |
| 1 teaspoon sugar | |

Cook onion and garlic in hot oil till tender but not brown. Stir in tomatoes, tomato paste, water, sugar, salt, pepper, oregano, and bay leaf. Simmer uncovered 30 minutes; remove bay leaf. Add Italian Meatballs and continue cooking loosely covered about 30 minutes longer. Serve over hot spaghetti. Pass grated Parmesan cheese. Makes 6 servings.

## ITALIAN MEATBALLS

| | |
|---|---|
| 4 slices bread | 2 tablespoons snipped parsley |
| ½ cup water | 1 teaspoon salt |
| 2 eggs | ¼ teaspoon dried oregano, crushed |
| . . . | Dash pepper |
| 1 pound ground beef | 2 teaspoons salad oil |
| ¼ cup grated Parmesan cheese | |

Soak bread in water 2 to 3 minutes; add eggs and mix well. Combine with ground beef, Parmesan cheese, parsley, salt, oregano, and pepper. With wet hands, form into small balls (about 24). Brown slowly in hot salad oil. Add meat balls to spaghetti sauce; simmer loosely covered for 30 minutes as directed for Spaghetti and Meatballs. Makes 6 servings.

## MONDAY MEAT PIE

½ cup chopped onion
1 tablespoon shortening
2 to 3 cups cooked beef, cut in
  ½-inch cubes
2 medium carrots, cooked and
  sliced (1 cup)
4 ounces sharp process American
  cheese, shredded (1 cup)

2 cups cubed cooked potatoes
½ cup mayonnaise or salad
  dressing
1 10¾-ounce can (1¼ cups)
  beef gravy
1 14-ounce package corn bread
  mix

In saucepan cook onion in hot shortening till tender but not
brown. Add beef, potatoes, carrots, *half* the cheese, mayonnaise, and beef gravy. Heat to bubbling; pour into a 9x9x2-
inch baking dish. Prepare corn bread mix according to package directions adding remaining cheese. Spoon over hot meat
mixture. Bake at 400° for 25 minutes or till bread is browned.
Makes 6 to 8 servings.

## HAMBURGER PIE

1 pound ground beef
½ cup chopped onion
1 1-pound can (2 cups) cut green
  beans, drained

1 10¾-ounce can condensed
  tomato soup
Potato Fluff Topper

In skillet combine meat, onion, ½ teaspoon salt, and dash
pepper. Brown meat lightly. Add drained beans and soup.
Pour into 1½-quart casserole. Drop Potato Fluff Topper in
mounds over meat. If desired, sprinkle potatoes with 2 ounces
process American cheese, shredded (½ cup). Bake in moderate oven (350°) for 25 to 30 minutes Makes 6 servings.

*Potato Fluff Topper:* Mash 5 medium cooked potatoes*
while hot; add ½ cup warm milk and 1 beaten egg. Season
with salt and pepper. Drop in mounds over casserole.

*For speed, use packaged instant mashed potatoes. Prepare
enough for 4 servings, according to package directions, but
reserve the milk. Add egg to potatoes. Season with salt and
pepper. Slowly add enough reserved milk to make potatoes
hold shape.

# VEGETABLE MEAT PIE

1 8-ounce can (1 cup) tomatoes
¼ cup finely chopped onion
1 tablespoon chopped green
  pepper
1 tablespoon butter or margarine

1 pound ground beef
1 cup soft bread crumbs
  (1½ slices)

½ teaspoon salt
1 small bay leaf, crushed
  Dash dried thyme, crushed
1 beaten egg
1 10-ounce package frozen mixed
  vegetables, cooked and
  drained
¼ teaspoon garlic salt

Drain tomatoes reserving ½ cup juice. In skillet cook onion
and green pepper in butter till tender but not brown. Combine with beef, bread crumbs, seasonings, egg, and the ½ cup
reserved tomato juice; mix well. Press into 9-inch pie plate
building up edges.

Bake in moderate oven (350°) for 10 minutes. Season
vegetables with garlic salt; pour into meat shell. Spoon on
drained tomatoes. Bake an additional 20 minutes with cookie
sheet under pie plate to catch any spill-over. Let stand 5 minutes. Makes 4 or 5 servings.

# SAUCED MOSTACCIOLI

In large skillet brown 1 pound ground beef; remove and reserve. In same skillet cook ½ cup chopped onion and 2 cloves
garlic, minced, in 2 tablespoons hot shortening until crisp-
tender. Add one 1-pound 12-ounce can (3½ cups) tomatoes,
cut up, one 8-ounce can (1 cup) tomato sauce, one 6-ounce
can tomato paste, and 1 teaspoon salt. Simmer covered 1
hour. Add reserved beef, ¼ pound pepperoni, thinly sliced,
and ½ pound mushrooms, sliced*; continue cooking 30 minutes longer; drain off fat.

Meanwhile, add 2 tablespoons salt to large amount of
rapidly boiling water. Gradually add 12-ounces mostaccioli**.
Cook uncovered, stirring occasionally, until tender; drain. Toss
with meat sauce. Pass grated Parmesan cheese. Makes 8 to 10
servings.

*Or use one 3-ounce can sliced mushrooms, drained
(½ cup).

**Or use 12 ounces elbow macaroni.

## OLD-TIME STUFFED PEPPERS

6 to 8 green peppers
1 pound ground beef
¼ cup chopped onion
1 12-ounce can whole kernel
  corn, drained
1 8-ounce can (1 cup) tomato
  sauce
½ teaspoon Worcestershire sauce

½ teaspoon salt
¼ teaspoon monosodium glutamate
4 ounces sharp process American
  cheese, shredded (1 cup)
½ cup soft bread crumbs
2 teaspoons butter or margarine,
  melted

Cut off tops of green peppers; remove seeds and membranes. Precook pepper cups in 2 quarts boiling salted water about 5 minutes; drain.* Sprinkle insides very lightly with salt.

In skillet brown meat and onion; add corn, tomato sauce, Worcestershire sauce, ½ teaspoon salt, and monosodium glutamate. Simmer till heated through, about 5 minutes. Add cheese and stir till melted.

Stuff peppers; stand upright in 12x7½x2-inch baking dish. Combine bread crumbs and melted butter. Sprinkle with buttered crumbs. Fill baking dish with water to ½ inch. Bake uncovered in moderate oven (350°) for 40 minutes or till heated through. Makes 6 to 8 servings.

*For crisp peppers, omit precooking.


## BEEF AND NOODLE BAKE

Rinse 3 ounces (1 cup) snipped dried beef with hot water; drain. In saucepan melt 2 tablespoons butter; blend in 2 tablespoons all-purpose flour, ½ teaspoon salt, and ¼ teaspoon pepper. Stir in 1½ cups milk. Cook and stir till mixture thickens and bubbles. Mix in dried beef, 1 teaspoon prepared mustard, ¼ cup chopped celery, 2 tablespoons chopped green pepper, 2 hard-cooked eggs, chopped, and 2 ounces (1 cup) medium noodles, cooked. Turn into 1-quart casserole, or divide among four 8-ounce individual casseroles. Mix 1 cup soft bread crumbs with 2 tablespoons melted butter; sprinkle atop.

Bake in moderate oven (350°) for 15 to 20 minutes for individual casseroles or 30 to 35 minutes for 1-quart casserole. Serves 4.

# YANKEE RED-FLANNEL HASH

⅓ cup finely chopped onion
¼ cup shortening or salad oil
1½ cups finely chopped cooked corned beef
3 cups finely chopped cooked potatoes

1 1-pound can (2 cups) beets, finely chopped
⅓ cup milk
½ teaspoon salt
Dash bottled hot pepper sauce

In skillet cook onion in hot shortening till tender but not brown. Lightly toss together with remaining ingredients. Spread hash evenly over bottom of skillet. Cook over medium heat till bottom of hash is brown and crusty. Makes 4 servings.

# SKILLET HASH

In skillet cook ⅓ cup finely chopped onion in 2 tablespoons butter or margarine till tender but not brown. Add 2 cups diced or ground cooked beef roast, 2 or 3 medium raw potatoes, diced or ground, ½ cup beef broth or leftover gravy, and ½ teaspoon salt; mix well. Cover; cook over low heat, stirring often, till potatoes are tender, about 15 minutes. Makes 4 servings.

# BEST OVEN HASH

1 cup coarsely ground cooked beef
1 cup coarsely ground cooked potatoes
¼ cup coarsely ground onion
1 teaspoon salt
Dash pepper

¼ cup snipped parsley
2 teaspoons Worcestershire sauce
1 6-ounce can (⅔ cup) evaporated milk
¼ cup fine dry bread crumbs
1 tablespoon butter, melted

Lightly mix first 8 ingredients. Turn into 1-quart casserole. Mix bread crumbs and melted butter; sprinkle over top. Bake in moderate oven (350°) for 30 minutes or till heated through. Makes 4 servings.

# Beef stew

## BURGER SKILLET STEW

In a bowl combine 1 pound ground beef, ⅓ cup fine dry bread crumbs, ⅓ cup milk, 1 slightly beaten egg, and 3 tablespoons mix from 1 envelope spaghetti sauce mix. Form meat mixture into 12 balls; brown in 1 tablespoon hot shortening.

Blend remaining spaghetti sauce mix with one 10¾-ounce can (1¼ cups) beef gravy and ¼ cup water. Add to meat balls with ½ cup chopped green pepper, 4 medium carrots, pared and cut in 1-inch pieces, and 1 medium onion, quartered. Simmer covered 50 to 60 minutes. Makes 4 to 6 servings.

## SWEET-SOUR STEW

¼ cup all-purpose flour
1 teaspoon salt
 Dash pepper
2 pounds beef stew meat, cubed
¼ cup shortening

. . .

1 cup water
½ cup catsup

¼ cup brown sugar
¼ cup vinegar
1 tablespoon Worcestershire sauce
1 cup chopped onion
6 large carrots, cut in ¾-inch pieces (3 cups)

Combine flour, 1 teaspoon salt, and pepper in a plastic or paper bag. Add meat; shake to coat. In large skillet brown meat well in hot shortening. Combine water, catsup, brown sugar, vinegar, Worcestershire sauce, and 1 teaspoon salt. Stir into browned meat; add onion. Cover and cook over low heat for 45 minutes, stirring once or twice. Add carrots; cook 45 minutes more or till meat and carrots are tender. Makes 6 to 8 servings.

## PIONEER BEEF STEW

| | |
|---|---|
| 1 cup large dry lima beans | 1 small bay leaf |
| 1 teaspoon salt | Dash ground allspice |
| ¼ cup all-purpose flour | 1 medium onion, quartered |
| 1 teaspoon salt | 3 medium carrots, cut in 1-inch |
| ¼ teaspoon pepper | slices |
| 1 pound beef stew meat, cubed | 3 stalks celery, cut in 1-inch |
| 2 tablespoons shortening | slices |
| ½ cup chopped onion | 1 recipe Pastry Topper |
| 1½ cups tomato juice | (see Index) |
| 1 teaspoon salt | |

Add beans to 2½ cups water and 1 teaspoon salt and soak overnight. (Or bring mixture to a boil; boil 2 minutes. Remove from heat; let stand covered 1 hour.) Combine flour, 1 teaspoon salt, and pepper in a plastic bag; add meat and shake. Brown meat in hot shortening. Add chopped onion, tomato juice, 1 teaspoon salt, bay leaf, and allspice. Cover tightly and simmer 30 minutes. Add beans with liquid, onions, carrots, and celery. Cover and simmer 45 minutes or till vegetables are tender. Remove bay leaf. Thicken stew if desired. Arrange Pastry Topper on hot stew. Serves 6.

## BAVARIAN-STYLE STEW

Brown 2 pounds beef chuck, cut in 1-inch cubes, in 2 tablespoons hot shortening. Add 3 cups water, 2 medium onions, sliced, 1 tablespoon salt, ¼ teaspoon pepper, 1 bay leaf, and 1½ teaspoons caraway seed. Cover; simmer 1 hour. Add ½ cup vinegar and 2 tablespoons sugar. Cut 1 small head red cabbage in thin wedges; place atop meat.

Cover; simmer 45 minutes or till tender. Remove cabbage to platter. Add ½ cup broken gingersnaps to liquid; bring to boiling, stirring constantly. Makes 6 to 8 servings.

## OLD-TIME OXTAIL STEW

| | |
|---|---|
| 2 pounds oxtail, cut in 1½-inch | 1 1-pound can (2 cups) tomatoes |
| lengths | 8 small onions, halved |
| 1 medium onion, sliced | 4 potatoes, pared and quartered |
| 1 10½-ounce can condensed beef | 4 carrots, pared and quartered |
| broth | |

Coat meat with flour. In Dutch oven brown meat in 2 table-spoons hot shortening. Add onions, tomatoes, broth, 1½ teaspoons salt, and ¼ teaspoon pepper. Cover; simmer 2 hours or till meat is just tender. Add vegetables; cover; simmer 1 hour. Skim off fat. Remove meat and vegetables. Thicken broth.

*Pressure pan:* Coat meat with flour; brown in 2 tablespoons hot shortening. Add sliced onion, tomatoes, broth, 1½ tea-spoons salt, and ¼ teaspoon pepper. Cook at 15 pounds pres-sure 35 minutes. Reduce pressure under cold running water. Add vegetables; return to 15 pounds pressure; cook 10 minutes. Reduce pressure under cold running water. Skim off fat. Re-move meat and vegetables. Thicken broth. Makes 6 servings.

---

## TEST KITCHEN TIPS

### A hint when cooking with garlic cloves

*Before adding garlic to cooking liquid, slash cloves several times. Spear each clove with a wooden pick to hold it to-gether. Come serving time, it's a snap to find and remove the garlic.*

---

## CHUCK WAGON STEW

Cut 2 pounds lean beef chuck in 1½-inch cubes. In Dutch oven, brown meat slowly in 2 tablespoons hot shortening. Add 2 cups water*, 1 medium onion, sliced, 1 clove garlic, minced, 1 tablespoon salt, 1 teaspoon sugar, ¼ teaspoon dried thyme, crushed, and 1 teaspoon Worcestershire sauce. Cover; simmer 1½ hours, stirring occasionally to prevent meat from sticking.

Add ½ cup celery sliced in ½-inch pieces, 6 carrots, cut in 1-inch slices, and ½ pound small white onions *or* one 1-pound can onions, drained, and 3 potatoes, pared and quartered; cook covered 20 minutes. Add 2 or 3 tomatoes, cut in wedges *or* one 1-pound can tomatoes, drained (reserve liquid). Cook

15 minutes or till meat and vegetables are tender. Skim fat from stew. Thicken, if desired. Serves 6 to 8.

   *If canned tomatoes are used, use drained juice as part of the liquid.

## TEST KITCHEN TIPS
### Best way to brown beef cubes

*In Dutch oven or deep heavy kettle, brown meat cubes slowly in hot shortening. It takes about 20 minutes to develop color and flavor. If kettle is too crowded, brown part of the meat at a time. Turn cubes often for even browning.*

## GRAVY FOR BEEF STEW

Skim most of fat from stew liquid. For 3 cups liquid blend ½ cup cold water with 2 to 3 tablespoons flour. Mixture must be *smooth*. Add flour mixture slowly to meat stock, stirring constantly till gravy thickens and bubbles all over. Cook and stir 5 minutes longer. Makes 6 to 8 servings.

## SHORT-RIB STEW

| | |
|---|---|
| 2 pounds beef short ribs | 1 tablespoon Worcestershire |
| ¼ cup all-purpose flour |    sauce |
| 2 teaspoons salt | 4 to 5 carrots, sliced |
| ¼ teaspoon pepper | 2 medium onions, sliced |
| 2 tablespoons shortening | 1 medium potato, diced |
| 2 1-pound cans (4 cups) | 1½ teaspoons salt |
|    tomatoes |    Dash pepper |
| 2 cloves garlic, minced |    Parsley Dumplings |

Cut short ribs in serving pieces. Combine flour, 2 teaspoons salt, and ¼ teaspoon pepper; coat ribs with flour mixture. In Dutch oven or large kettle brown meat in hot shortening. Combine tomatoes, garlic, and Worcestershire sauce; pour over ribs. Cover and simmer 1½ hours.

   Add carrot, onion, and potato to meat. Simmer 45 minutes longer, or till meat and vegetables are tender. Skim off fat. Season with salt and pepper. Thicken slightly, if desired. Drop Parsley Dumpling mixture from tablespoon atop bubbling stew. Cover tightly; bring to boiling. Reduce heat (don't lift cover) and simmer 15 minutes. Serves 4 or 5.

## FLUFFY DUMPLINGS

1 cup sifted all-purpose flour          ½ cup milk
2 teaspoons baking powder               2 tablespoons salad oil
½ teaspoon salt

Sift together dry ingredients. Combine milk and salad oil;
add to dry ingredients, stirring just till moistened. Drop from
tablespoon atop bubbling stew. Cover tightly; bring to boil.
Reduce heat (don't lift cover); simmer 15 minutes or till
done. Makes 9 or 10 dumplings.

## PARSLEY DUMPLINGS

Prepare Fluffy Dumplings adding ¼ cup snipped parsley to
the sifted dry ingredients. Continue directions for Fluffy
Dumplings.

---

## TEST KITCHEN TIPS

### A slick trick—snip don't chop parsley

*Have the indispensable kitchen scissors ready. Rinse parsley
thoroughly. Cut off stems; put the tops in measuring cup
(glass for easy measuring). Hold kitchen scissors with points
down in cup of parsley. Snip-snip till leaves are finely cut.*

---

## EASY DUMPLINGS

¾ cup milk                              2 cups packaged biscuit mix

Add milk to packaged biscuit mix all at once; stir just till mixture is moistened. Drop by rounded tablespoon atop hot,
bubbling stew. Cook uncovered over low heat 10 minutes.
Cover and cook 10 minutes longer, or till done. Makes 10 to
12 dumplings.

## TEST KITCHEN TIPS

### Getting good results with dumplings

*When stew is done, drop dumplings atop meat and vegetables from a tablespoon. The dumplings will slide off the spoon easily if the spoon is dipped into the stew liquid each time.*

*Cover with a tight lid. Do not lift cover or dumplings will fall. Cook about 12 minutes or till dumplings are done. Remove dumplings and stew to serving platter. To thicken liquid for gravy, see Gravy for Beef Stew.*

# PORK–FRESH AND SMOKED

## PORK CHOP OVEN DINNER

| | |
|---|---|
| 6 pork chops, about ¾ inch thick | 1 tablespoon snipped parsley |
| 3 tablespoons all-purpose flour | 1 bay leaf |
| ¾ teaspoon salt | 6 small carrots, pared and halved lengthwise |
| ¼ teaspoon garlic salt | |
| ½ cup water | 6 small potatoes, pared and halved |
| ¼ cup dry sherry | |
| ⅛ teaspoon ground cloves | 1 medium onion, thinly sliced |
| Dash pepper | |

Trim fat from chops. Heat fat in skillet. When about 2 tablespoons melted fat accumulates, remove trimmings. Combine
flour, salt, dash pepper, and garlic salt; dip chops in mixture.
Brown chops well, about 15 minutes per side.

In 3-quart casserole, combine water and next 5 ingredients.
Sprinkle carrots and potatoes generously with salt; place *in
the liquid*. Arrange chops atop; add onion slices. Cover. Bake
at 350° for 1¼ hours or till vegetables and meat are tender,
basting once or twice. Skim off excess fat; remove bay leaf.
Trim with parsley. Makes 6 servings.

## PORK AND RICE BAKE

Place ¾ cup uncooked long-grain rice in a 13x9x2-inch baking dish. Add one 1-pound 13-ounce can tomatoes, ¼ cup
chopped green pepper, 1 teaspoon monosodium glutamate, ½
teaspoon chili powder, ½ teaspoon salt, and dash pepper. Mix
well, breaking up larger pieces of tomato.

Arrange five ½-inch thick pork chops over top of rice
mixture; sprinkle chops with 1 teaspoon salt. Top each chop
with an onion slice. *Cover tightly* with foil. Bake at 325° for
1¼ hours. Remove foil. Sprinkle with 4 ounces sharp natural
Cheddar cheese, shredded (1 cup). Place a green pepper ring
and mushroom crown on each onion-topped chop. Return to
oven 10 to 15 minutes longer. Serves 5.

## RIBS AND KRAUT WITH STUFFING BALLS

| | |
|---|---|
| 3 pounds pork spareribs, cut in serving pieces | 2 tablespoons brown sugar |
| 2 teaspoons salt | 2 teaspoons caraway seed |
| ¼ teaspoon pepper | • • • |
| 1 1-pound 11-ounce can sauerkraut | ⅔ cup water |
| | ¼ cup butter or margarine |
| 1 unpared tart apple, finely chopped | 1½ cups packaged herb-seasoned stuffing mix |
| 1½ cups tomato juice | 1 slightly beaten egg |

Season ribs with salt and pepper. Place in large saucepan or
Dutch oven. Combine sauerkraut (including liquid) with
apple and next 3 ingredients; spoon over ribs. Simmer, covered, 1½ to 2 hours, or till ribs are done, basting kraut with
juices several times.

Meanwhile, heat water with butter; add stuffing mix and
toss until stuffing is moistened. Stir in egg. Shape stuffing
into 6 balls.

When ribs are tender, pull ribs to surface of kraut. Drop
balls onto ribs in saucepan. Increase heat to create more steam,
cover tightly, and cook 15 minutes longer (don't lift cover).
Makes 6 servings.

# FRUIT STUFFED PORK

Sprinkle salt and pepper over 8 double rib pork chops with pockets cut in them. Combine 2 cups small dry bread cubes, 1 cup finely chopped unpared apple, 1 cup shredded sharp process American cheese, ¼ cup light raisins, ¼ cup butter or margarine, melted, ¼ cup orange juice, ½ teaspoon salt, and ¼ teaspoon ground cinnamon. Stuff into pockets in chops. Press edges of pockets together to seal. Bake at 350° for 1½ hours, or till chops are tender. Makes 8 servings.

## SOUTHERN PORK CHOPS

4 to 6 pork chops, about ¾ inch thick

1 envelope **dry** cream of mushroom soup mix

⅓ to ½ cup peanut butter

2 cups water

1 medium onion, sliced

½ green pepper, sliced in strips

Trim excess fat from chops; heat fat in skillet until about 1 tablespoon drippings accumulates; remove trimmings. Brown pork chops well in the hot fat; remove chops from skillet.

Blend soup mix and peanut butter into pan drippings. Gradually add water, stirring till smooth; bring to boiling. Reduce heat and add pork chops, onion slices, and green pepper strips. Simmer covered (*don't boil*) 45 to 50 minutes or till tender. Serve right from electric skillet or remove chops to warm platter; sprinkle with paprika. Spoon off any excess fat from gravy; add a little kitchen bouquet sauce, if desired, for rich color, then season lightly. Serve with chops. Serves 4 to 6.

## SMOKED PORK CHOP AND LIMA SKILLET

2 10-ounce packages frozen lima beans

. . .

5 or 6 smoked pork loin chops

1 teaspoon liquid chicken-flavored gravy base

1 tablespoon all-purpose flour

½ teaspoon dried basil, crushed

¾ cup water

Cook lima beans according to package directions omitting salt in cooking water; drain.

In skillet brown chops over medium heat. Remove chops from skillet. Pour off all but about 1 tablespoon of the drippings. Add chicken-flavored gravy base to skillet. Blend in flour and crushed basil. Add water; cook and stir over medium heat till sauce thickens and boils. Add limas to skillet; stir to coat with sauce. Arrange chops over the limas. Cover and cook over low heat about 5 minutes or till heated through. Serves 5 or 6.

## CANADIAN BACON-BEAN BAKE

Combine one 1-pound can pork and beans in tomato sauce with 1 tablespoon instant minced onion, ¼ cup catsup, 2 teaspoons *each* prepared horseradish and prepared mustard, and 1 teaspoon Worcestershire sauce. Pour into a 10x6x1½-inch baking dish. Bake at 350° for 45 minutes. Arrange 4 orange slices, ¼ inch thick, and 8 slices Canadian-style bacon, about ¼ inch thick, on top. Sprinkle with ⅓ cup brown sugar; dot with 2 tablespoons butter. Bake for 30 minutes more. Makes 4 servings.

## HAWAIIAN HAM PIE

Pastry for 1-crust pie (see Index)
1 pound ground cooked ham
⅓ cup fine dry bread crumbs
1 beaten egg
2 tablespoons sliced green onion
½ cup milk
1 tablespoon prepared mustard
1 1-pound 4½-ounce can crushed pineapple, well drained (1½ cups)
¼ cup brown sugar

Prepare pastry. Flatten ball on lightly floured surface. Roll from center to edge till dough is ⅛ inch thick. Fit pastry into 9-inch pie plate; trim ½ to 1 inch beyond edge; fold under and flute.

Thoroughly combine ham, crumbs, egg, milk, onion, mustard, and ½ *cup* of the pineapple. Spread ham mixture into pastry shell. Combine remaining pineapple and brown sugar; arrange on ham mixture in a spoke pattern. Bake in moderate oven (350°) for 45 minutes. Makes 6 to 8 servings.

## HAM 'N CHEESE DELIGHT

Cook ½ cup finely chopped onion in 1 tablespoon butter till tender. Combine with 2 cups finely chopped cooked ham, 3 slightly beaten eggs, 4 ounces sharp process American cheese, shredded (1 cup), ⅔ cup finely crushed crackers (about 15), 1½ cups milk, and dash pepper. Mix well. Pour into 10x6x1½-inch baking dish. Bake at 350° for 45 to 50 minutes or till a knife inserted just off center comes out clean. Makes 6 servings.

## LIMA BEAN-HAM CHOWDER

| | |
|---|---|
| 1½ cups large dry lima beans | 2 tablespoons butter or |
| 1 quart water | margarine |
| • • • | • • • |
| 1 pound meaty ham hocks | 1 8¾-ounce can (1 cup) |
| 1 teaspoon salt | cream-style corn |
| 1 cup chopped onion | 2 cups milk |
| ½ cup chopped green pepper | |

In kettle, cover beans with 1 quart water; bring to boiling; simmer 2 minutes. Remove from heat and let stand covered for 1 hour. Add ham hocks; cover and simmer till tender, about 1½ hours. Add salt during last 30 minutes of cooking.

Remove ham hocks. With potato masher, mash beans slightly. Remove ham from bones and shred. Cook onion and green pepper in butter or margarine till tender. Add to mashed limas along with the corn, shredded ham, and milk. Heat thoroughly but do not boil. Add salt to taste. Makes 4 to 6 servings.

## SWISS HAM PIE

| | |
|---|---|
| Pastry for 1-crust pie (see Index) | 1½ cups milk |
| | • • • |
| • • • | 4 ounces process Swiss cheese, |
| 2 tablespoons butter or | shredded (1 cup) |
| margarine | 3 slightly beaten eggs |
| 2 tablespoons all-purpose flour | 1 cup diced cooked ham |
| ⅛ teaspoon ground nutmeg | |

Prepare pastry. Flatten ball on lightly floured surface. Roll from center to edge till dough is ⅛ inch thick. Fit pastry into a 9-inch pie plate; trim ½ to 1 inch beyond edge; fold under and flute.

In medium saucepan melt butter or margarine; blend in flour and nutmeg. Add milk all at once; cook and stir till thick and bubbly. Add cheese; stir till melted. Cool slightly; stir small amount of cheese sauce into eggs. Return egg mixture to cheese sauce; add ham. Pour into pastry shell.

Bake in moderate oven (375°) for 25 to 30 minutes. Trim with slices of Swiss cheese cut in triangles, if desired. Let pie cool 10 minutes. Makes 6 servings.

## HAWAIIAN SWEET-SOUR HAM

2 cups cooked ham cut in julienne strips
1 tablespoon salad oil
1 8¾-ounce can (1 cup) pineapple tidbits
2 tablespoons brown sugar
1 teaspoon monosodium glutamate

1½ tablespoons cornstarch
3 to 4 teaspoons vinegar
2 teaspoons prepared mustard
¾ cup water
1 green pepper, cut in ½-inch squares
2 cups cooked rice

Brown ham in hot oil. Drain pineapple, reserving syrup. Mix brown sugar, cornstarch, monosodium glutamate, vinegar, and mustard; stir in reserved syrup and water; add to skillet. Cook and stir till mixture thickens and bubbles. Cover; simmer 10 minutes.

Add pineapple tidbits and green pepper; simmer 3 to 5 minutes. Salt to taste. Serve with hot cooked rice. Makes 4 servings.

## HAM-POTATOES AU GRATIN

¼ cup chopped green onion
¼ cup chopped green pepper
2 tablespoons butter or margarine
1 tablespoon all-purpose flour
Dash pepper
1 cup milk

4 ounces sharp process American cheese, shredded (1 cup)
¼ cup mayonnaise or salad dressing
3 medium potatoes, cooked and diced (3 cups)
1 pound cooked ham, diced (2 cups)

. . .

Cook onion and green pepper in butter till tender. Stir in flour and pepper. Add milk all at once and bring to boil stirring constantly. Reduce heat; add cheese and mayonnaise; stir till cheese melts. Combine potatoes and ham with sauce. Bake in a 10x6x1½-inch baking dish in moderate oven (350°) for 30 to 35 minutes. Makes 4 to 6 servings.

# BACON ORIENTAL

1 pound sliced bacon
1 medium onion, sliced
1 cup chopped celery
1 6-ounce can broiled sliced
   mushrooms (1⅓ cups)
2 tablespoons cornstarch

½ teaspoon salt
Dash pepper
1 tablespoon soy sauce
1 cup chopped green pepper
1 1-pound can bean sprouts,
   drained

Cook bacon till crisp; remove from pan. Drain off all but 1 tablespoon of the drippings. Cook onion and celery in drippings till tender-crisp but not brown. Drain mushrooms, reserving liquid; add water to liquid to make 1½ cups. Dissolve cornstarch in ¼ cup cold water; combine with mushroom liquid, salt, pepper, and soy sauce. Add to onion and celery. Cook and stir till mixture thickens and bubbles. Stir in mushrooms, green pepper, and bean sprouts; heat through. Crumble bacon over top. Serve with hot rice. Makes 6 to 8 servings.

# CANTONESE CASSEROLE

1 10-ounce package frozen
   French-style green beans
1 tablespoon butter or margarine
1 tablespoon all-purpose flour
¾ cup milk
2 tablespoons soy sauce

1 cup dairy sour cream
2 cups cubed cooked ham
1 5-ounce can water chestnuts,
   drained and thinly sliced
1 cup buttered soft bread crumbs
Paprika

Pour boiling water over beans to separate; drain well. In saucepan melt butter or margarine; blend in flour. Stir in milk and soy sauce; cook and stir over medium heat till thick and bubbly. Stir in sour cream, cubed ham, the beans, and water chestnuts.

Pour into greased 10x6x1½-inch baking dish. Sprinkle buttered bread crumbs over top. Dash generously with paprika. Bake in moderate oven (350°) for 30 minutes, or till just heated through. Makes 6 servings.

# CALIFORNIA CURRY PLATTER

2 hard-cooked eggs
¾ cup light raisins
2 cups cooked rice
2 tablespoons finely chopped
   onion

2 tablespoons cornstarch
1 teaspoon curry powder
1 teaspoon monosodium
   glutamate
¼ teaspoon salt

1 tablespoon snipped parsley
¼ teaspoon salt
   Dash pepper
3 tablespoons butter or
   margarine

3 cups milk
12 slices packaged (or 6 extra-
   thick slices) chopped ham
   Baked Chutney Peaches

Chop eggs, reserving 1 egg yolk to sieve for garnish. Combine the chopped eggs, raisins, rice, onion, parsley, salt, and pepper. In a saucepan melt butter. Stir in mixture of cornstarch, curry powder, monosodium glutamate, and salt. Add milk; cook and stir till mixture thickens and bubbles. Add *half* the curry sauce to the rice mixture; blend. Spoon rice mixture into large oval or 13x9x2-inch baking dish, leaving space at one side to add peaches later.

Using 2 slices chopped ham for each (or 1 extra-thick slice), place meat over rice, tucking sides of meat into rice mixture. Pour remaining sauce over rolls. Bake at 350° for 25 minutes. Arrange Chutney Peaches beside rice. Bake 10 to 15 minutes longer, or till peaches are heated through. Garnish ham rolls with sieved egg yolk. Serves 6.

## BAKED CHUTNEY PEACHES

6 canned peach halves
6 tablespoons chutney

1 tablespoon butter or margarine,
   melted

Place drained peaches, cut side up, on cake rack. Brush with melted butter or margarine. Spoon 1 tablespoon chutney into center of each peach half. Place in baking dish with curried chopped ham rolls and rice. Bake in moderate oven (350°) 10 to 15 minutes or till heated through. Serve hot.

## HAM SUCCOTASH

Add two 9-ounce packages frozen cut green beans to boiling salted water; return just to boiling and drain; set aside. Combine two 1-pound cans whole kernel corn, drained, two 1-pound cans cream-style corn, 2 cups soft bread crumbs, 2 beaten eggs, 1 tablespoon instant minced onion, 2 teaspoons *each* dry mustard and dried basil, crushed, 1 teaspoon salt, and dash pepper. Cut ½ pound boneless cooked ham, sliced ½ inch thick, into cubes; cut 1 pound cooked ham into serving pieces (reserve pieces). Stir ham cubes into corn mixture.

Stir in green beans and one 6-ounce can sliced mushrooms, drained. Turn into 3-quart casserole. Bake uncovered at 350° for 1 hour. Arrange ham pieces atop corn. Bake uncovered 30 minutes more. Serves 12.

## YANKEE BACON BAKE

½ pound sliced bacon
½ cup cornmeal
2 cups milk
½ cup sifted all-purpose flour
1 tablespoon sugar

1 teaspoon baking powder
½ teaspoon salt
3 well-beaten egg yolks
3 stiffly beaten egg whites

Quarter bacon slices; cook till crisp; drain. Mix cornmeal with 1 *cup* of the milk; cook till thickened; remove from heat. Sift together dry ingredients; blend into cornmeal. Mix in remaining milk and egg yolks; fold in egg whites and bacon. Bake in greased 2-quart casserole at 325 ° about 1 hour. Serves 6.

# TEMPTING LAMB

## LAMB EGGPLANT CASSEROLE

1½ pounds cubed lamb
1 tablespoon salad oil
½ cup chopped onion
1 1-pound can (2 cups) tomatoes
1 clove garlic, minced

¼ teaspoon dried thyme, crushed
¼ teaspoon dried basil, crushed
1 medium eggplant, peeled and
   cubed (about 4½ cups)
½ cup uncooked long-grain rice

Brown lamb in hot oil; add onion and cook till tender but not brown. Add tomatoes, garlic, 1 cup water, 2 teaspoons salt, and seasonings. Cover and simmer 15 minutes. Stir in eggplant and rice. Pour mixture into a 2½-quart casserole. Cover and bake at 350° for 1 hour, stirring occasionally. Makes 6 to 8 servings.

## SHEPHERD'S PIE

Packaged instant mashed
  potatoes (enough for 4
  servings)
½ cup finely chopped celery
2 tablespoons chopped onion
2 tablespoons butter or margarine
2 tablespoons all-purpose flour
1 cup milk

¾ cup beef or lamb broth
2 cups cooked lamb, cut in cubes
1 tablespoon snipped parsley
⅛ teaspoon dried dillweed
  (optional)
¼ teaspoon kitchen bouquet sauce
¼ cup shredded sharp process
  American cheese

Prepare mashed potatoes according to package directions. In
a skillet cook celery and onion in butter till tender but not
brown. Blend in flour. Add milk and broth all at once. Cook
and stir till mixture thickens and bubbles. Stir in lamb, parsley,
½ teaspoon salt, ⅛ teaspoon pepper, dillweed, and kitchen
bouquet sauce. Pour meat mixture into a 1½-quart casserole
and top evenly with potatoes; sprinkle with cheese. Bake at
400° for 20 to 25 minutes or till brown. Serves 6.

## LAMB SKILLET SUPPER

4 lamb shoulder chops, about ½
  inch thick
1 teaspoon monosodium glutamate
½ teaspoon garlic salt
1 8-ounce can (1 cup) spaghetti
  sauce with mushrooms

½ teaspoon paprika
1 cup sliced carrots
1 1-pound can (2 cups) whole
  new potatoes, drained
1 1-pound can (2 cups) cut green
  beans, drained

Trim fat from chops. In 10-inch skillet cook fat till about
2 tablespoons drippings accumulate. Discard trimmings.
Sprinkle chops with seasonings; brown in drippings. Remove
chops; drain off excess fat. Add spaghetti sauce and carrots;
return chops to skillet.

Cover and simmer 45 minutes. Add drained potatoes and
beans to skillet, arranging meat atop vegetables. Cover and
simmer 15 minutes more. Makes 4 servings.

## LAMB WITH VEGETABLES

4 lamb shoulder chops
¾ teaspoon salt
¼ teaspoon pepper
¼ teaspoon celery salt
¼ cup sliced green onion

¼ pound (about 1¼ cups) sliced
  fresh mushrooms
½ cup water
1 medium tomato

Trim fat from lamb chops; cook fat till about 2 tablespoons drippings accumulate. Season chops with salt, pepper, and celery salt; brown in drippings. Drain off excess fat. Add onion and sliced mushrooms; cook 5 minutes. Add water; cover and simmer 30 minutes. Cut tomato in quarters and top each chop with tomato piece. Cover and cook till heated through. Makes 4 servings.

## SPRING LAMB STEW

2 pounds boneless lamb
   shoulder, cut in 1-inch cubes
¼ cup all-purpose flour
1 tablespoon shortening
1 1-pound 12-ounce can
   tomatoes
1½ teaspoons salt

¼ teaspoon pepper
¼ teaspoon dried thyme, crushed
1 10-ounce package frozen or
   1 pound fresh cut
   green beans
2 medium onions, cut in ½-inch
   slices

Coat meat with flour. In Dutch oven brown meat in hot shortening. Add tomatoes and seasonings. Cover; simmer 1½ hours or till meat is almost tender; stir occasionally. Add beans and onions. Cover; simmer 20 to 25 minutes. Serves 6 to 8.

## LAMB STEW 'N DUMPLINGS

Combine ¼ cup all-purpose flour, 2 teaspoons salt, 1 teaspoon paprika, and ¼ teaspoon pepper. Cut 2 pounds boneless lamb shoulder in 1-inch cubes; coat with seasoned flour. Brown meat in 2 tablespoons hot shortening. Add 2 cups water, one 8-ounce can (1 cup) tomato sauce, 1 clove garlic, minced, ½ teaspoon dried thyme, crushed, and ½ teaspoon dried marjoram, crushed.

Cover and simmer 1 hour or till meat is almost tender. Add one 10-ounce package frozen baby limas, 6 medium carrots, cut in ½-inch pieces, and 6 small whole onions; cover and simmer 20 minutes or till tender.

Top with 10 to 12 small Dumplings: To 1 cup packaged biscuit mix add ⅓ cup milk. Mix well; spoon onto hot bubbling stew. Cook uncovered over low heat 5 minutes. Cover and cook 10 minutes. Serves 6 to 8.

# PLEASING VEAL

## HERBED RIBLETS AND LIMAS

¼ cup all-purpose flour
2 teaspoons salt
Dash pepper
3 pounds veal riblets
2 tablespoons shortening
2 tablespoons wine vinegar

1 teaspoon brown sugar
¼ teaspoon dried thyme, crushed
¼ teaspoon dried marjoram, crushed
1 10-ounce package frozen lima beans

Combine flour, salt, and pepper in a plastic bag. Add riblets, a few at a time, and coat with flour. Reserve excess flour. Brown riblets in shortening in large skillet. Add 1 cup water, vinegar, brown sugar, thyme, and marjoram. Cover and simmer 1½ hours.

Add lima beans; cover, and simmer 20 to 25 minutes longer (stir occasionally to break up beans). Remove riblets and stir reserved flour mixture into beans. Cook till sauce thickens; serve with riblets. Serves 4 or 5.

## VEAL OLIVE SAUTE

2 pounds veal shoulder, cut in
    ¾-inch cubes
¼ cup all-purpose flour
3 tablespoons shortening
1 large onion, thinly sliced
1 clove garlic, minced
1 8-ounce can (1 cup) tomato
    sauce

2 chicken bouillon cubes
¼ cup snipped parsley
½ teaspoon salt
¼ teaspoon dried rosemary,
    crushed
25 pitted ripe olives, halved
    (¾ cup)

Coat veal with flour; brown in shortening in skillet. Add
onion and garlic; cook till tender. Dissolve bouillon cubes in
1½ cups boiling water. Add to meat with tomato sauce,
parsley, ½ teaspoon salt, and rosemary. Cover; simmer till
tender, about 45 minutes. Add olives; heat through. Serve
over cooked fusilli or medium egg noodles. Serves 6.

## VEAL PARMESAN SUPPER

¼ cup fine dry bread crumbs
¼ cup grated Parmesan cheese
½ teaspoon salt
    Dash pepper
½ teaspoon garlic salt
½ teaspoon paprika
4 veal chops, ¾ inch thick
1 beaten egg
3 tablespoons olive or salad oil

1 pound (about 12) tiny new
    potatoes, scraped or
    4 medium potatoes, peeled
    and quartered
1 8-ounce can (1 cup) tomato
    sauce
1 teaspoon dried oregano,
    crushed
4 thin slices mozzarella cheese

Combine bread crumbs, Parmesan cheese, and seasonings.
Dip chops in egg, then in crumb mixture. Brown slowly on
both sides in hot oil; arrange potatoes around meat. Combine tomato sauce, 1 cup water, and crushed oregano. Pour
around meat and potatoes.

Cover; simmer 45 to 50 minutes, or till meat and potatoes
are done. Last few minutes place a slice of cheese atop each
chop. Serves 4.

## VEAL CHOP DINNER

Coat four ½-inch-thick veal chops with 2 tablespoons all-
purpose flour. In large skillet brown chops slowly on both
sides in 2 tablespoons hot shortening or salad oil.

Combine ⅓ cup grated Parmesan cheese, ¼ teaspoon salt,
and ⅛ teaspoon pepper. Sprinkle 2 *tablespoons* of the mixture

over the meat. Cover with 4 medium potatoes, thinly sliced (about 4 cups). Sprinkle with 2 tablespoons additional cheese mixture. Add 2 medium onions, thinly sliced (about 2 cups). Sprinkle remaining cheese mixture atop.

Dissolve 3 beef bouillon cubes in ¾ cup boiling water. Add 1 tablespoon lemon juice and pour over meat. Cover; simmer about 40 minutes, or till tender. Thicken remaining juices in pan with a mixture of 1 tablespoon all-purpose flour and 2 tablespoons cold water. Trim with parsley. Makes 4 servings.

## VEAL AND CARROTS

Cut 1½ pounds ¾-inch-thick veal round steak into ¾-inch cubes. Combine 2 tablespoons all-purpose flour, 1 teaspoon salt, and ⅛ teaspoon pepper. Coat meat evenly with mixture. In large skillet brown meat on all sides in 2 tablespoons hot shortening. Add ¾ cup tomato juice, 1 cup diced pared carrots, and ½ cup finely chopped onion.

Cover skillet and simmer 1 hour or till meat and vegetables are tender. Serve over hot buttered noodles. Makes 5 or 6 servings.

## VEAL STEW WITH RAVIOLI

Combine 3 tablespoons all-purpose flour, 1 teaspoon salt, and dash pepper. Coat 1 pound veal stew meat, cut in 1-inch cubes, with all the flour mixture. Brown in 4 teaspoons hot shortening. Add ¼ cup chopped onion and 1 small clove garlic, minced. Cook 4 to 5 minutes. Add 1½ cups water; cover and simmer 1 hour or till meat is tender. Add one 10-ounce package frozen peas, one 1-pound can ravioli, 2 tablespoons snipped parsley, and ¼ teaspoon dried oregano, crushed. Cook 15 minutes; stir occasionally. Makes 4 servings.

## VEAL NOODLE BAKE

| | |
|---|---|
| 1 pound veal cutlets, diced | 1 8-ounce can tomatoes, cut up |
| ½ teaspoon salt | 3 tablespoons grated Parmesan |
| 3 tablespoons butter or margarine | cheese |
| ¼ cup chopped onion | ¼ teaspoon dried basil, crushed |
| 1 clove garlic, minced | ⅛ teaspoon dried oregano, crushed |
| 1 10½-ounce condensed cream | 4 ounces noodles, cooked and |
| of mushroom soup | drained |

Sprinkle veal with salt; brown in butter or margarine in skillet. Reduce heat; simmer, covered, 30 minutes. Add onion and garlic; cook till tender. Blend in soup and tomatoes; bring to boiling. Stir in cheese and herbs; add noodles. Turn into 1½-quart casserole. Bake uncovered at 350° for 30 minutes. Serves 4.

## TUFOLI STUFFED WITH VEAL

1 cup tomato juice
1 8-ounce can (1 cup) tomato sauce
1 1-pound can tomatoes, cut up
½ cup chopped onion
1 clove garlic, crushed
¼ teaspoon dried thyme, crushed
¼ teaspoon dried marjoram, crushed
1 bay leaf

1 teaspoon Worcestershire sauce
4 ounces tufoli or large tubular macaroni
1 pound ground veal
¼ cup milk
1 slightly beaten egg
¼ cup chopped onion
½ teaspoon dried oregano, crushed
1 teaspoon salt

In a 3-quart saucepan combine first 9 ingredients. Bring to a boil; reduce heat and simmer, uncovered, for 30 minutes. Cook tufoli noodles in boiling salted water till tender. Drain and cool. Combine remaining ingredients and dash pepper; stuff into tufoli. Pour *half* the sauce into a 12x7½x2-inch baking dish. Arrange stuffed tufoli over sauce; cover with remaining sauce. Cover; bake at 350° for 1 hour. Makes 6 to 8 servings.

# POPULAR CHICKEN AND TURKEY

## CHICKEN CHIP BAKE

2 cups cubed cooked chicken
2 cups sliced celery
¾ cup mayonnaise or salad dressing
⅓ cup toasted slivered almonds
2 teaspoons grated onion
2 tablespoons lemon juice

½ teaspoon monosodium glutamate
½ teaspoon salt
2 ounces process American cheese, shredded (½ cup)
1 cup crushed potato chips

Combine all ingredients except cheese and potato chips. Pile lightly in 1½-quart casserole. Sprinkle with cheese, then with potato chips. Bake in hot oven (435°) 20 minutes or till heated through. Serves 5 or 6.

## CHICKEN DINNER BAKE

› envelope **dry** turkey-noodle
    soup mix
  3-ounce can broiled sliced
    mushrooms, drained (reserve
    liquid)
› 6-ounce can (⅔ cup)
    evaporated milk
    . . .
⅓ cup butter or margarine
¼ cup chopped onion

⅓ cup all-purpose flour
¼ teaspoon salt
  Dash pepper
3 5-ounce cans boned chicken,
    diced, **or** 2 cups diced cooked
    chicken
½ 10-ounce package frozen peas,
    broken apart (1 cup)
¼ cup chopped canned pimiento

Combine soup mix and 1½ cups water; bring to boil, reduce heat, and simmer 5 minutes. Add mushroom liquid and milk. In large skillet, melt butter; cook onion till tender but not brown. Blend in flour, salt, and pepper. Add soup mixture; cook and stir till thick and bubbly. Add mushrooms, chicken, peas, and pimiento. Pour into 1½-quart casserole. Bake at 350° for 45 minutes. Serves 8.

## CHICKEN WITH NOODLES

Cook 4 ounces medium noodles in boiling salted water till tender; drain. Cook 1 cup sliced celery and ¼ cup diced green pepper in 2 tablespoons butter till tender. Add one 10½-ounce can condensed cream of chicken soup and ⅔ cup milk. Heat, stirring constantly. Add 1½ cups shredded sharp process American cheese; stir still melted. Add 2 cups cubed cooked chicken, ½ cup slivered toasted almonds, and ¼ cup diced canned pimiento. Combine with noodles; pour into 1½-quart casserole. Top with 1 cup buttered bread crumbs. Bake uncovered at 350° for 30 to 35 minutes. Serves 6.

## CHICKEN A LA KING BAKE

¼ cup chopped onion
3 tablespoons butter or
    margarine
3 tablespoons all-purpose flour
½ teaspoon salt
1½ cups chicken broth
2 cups cubed cooked chicken

1 cup cooked or canned peas
1 3-ounce can sliced mushrooms,
    drained (½ cup)
1 cup cooked sliced carrots
2 tablespoons chopped pimiento
1 package refrigerated biscuits

Cook onion in butter till tender. Blend in flour and salt. Add broth all at once; cook and stir till thickened and bubbly. Add chicken and vegetables; heat till bubbly. Pour into 1½-quart casserole.

Make *Biscuit Snippers:* With scissors, snip 6 biscuits in quarters; arrange in ring, rounded side down, atop *hot* chicken. (Bake remaining biscuits on baking sheet.) Bake casserole at 425° for 8 to 10 minutes or till biscuits are done. Makes 6 servings.

---

## TEST KITCHEN TIPS

### How much to buy for diced or sliced cooked chicken

One 3½-pound ready-to-cook chicken yields about 3 cups diced cooked chicken.

Two whole chicken breasts (10 ounces each) yield 1½ to 2 cups diced cooked chicken or 12 thin slices cooked chicken.

To slice cooked chicken breasts: Chill chicken breasts well, but do not freeze. Carefully remove meat from bone (meat will split in half). Lay each piece flat on cutting board. Hold in place; with sharp knife, slice chicken breasts lengthwise parallel to board. Each breast half will yield about three thin slices.

---

## STEWED CHICKEN

| | |
|---|---|
| 1 5- to 6-pound ready-to-cook stewing chicken, cut up, **or** 2 large broiler-fryer chickens, cut up | 4 stalks celery with leaves |
| | 1 carrot, sliced |
| | 1 small onion, cut up |
| | 2 teaspoons salt |
| | ¼ teaspoon pepper |
| · · · | Raisin Dumplings |
| 2 sprigs parsley | |

Place chicken pieces in Dutch oven or large kettle with enough water to cover (about 2 quarts). Add remaining ingredients. Cover; bring to boiling and cook over low heat about 2½ hours, or till tender. Leave chicken on bones in liquid for

chicken with dumplings. Or, remove meat from bones. This
will yield about 5 cups diced cooked chicken.

*Raisin Dumplings:* Sift together 1 cup all-purpose flour, 3
teaspoons baking powder, and 1 teaspoon salt. Cut 1 tablespoon shortening into dry ingredients. Add ½ cup raisins and
I cup coarse dry bread crumbs. Combine 1 beaten egg, ¾ cup
milk, and 2 teaspoons grated onion. Add to raisin mixture;
mix just to moisten.

Drop from tablespoon atop stewed chicken in boiling
stock. Cover tightly (don't lift cover); simmer 20 minutes.
Remove chicken and dumplings; thicken broth.

## CHINESE CHICKEN

1 medium green pepper, cut in      ⅓ cup water
  strips                          2 tablespoons soy sauce
1 cup bias cut celery
2 tablespoons butter or margarine      . . .
1 10½-ounce can condensed          2 cups cubed cooked chicken
  cream of chicken soup              1 1-pound can (2 cups) chop suey
                                      vegetables, drained

In a saucepan, cook green pepper and celery in butter till
crisp-tender. Stir in soup, water, and soy sauce. Add chicken
and chop suey vegetables; heat through. Serve with hot
cooked rice. Pass soy sauce. Makes 6 servings.

## CHICKEN UPSIDE-DOWN PIE

1 10¾-ounce can chicken gravy       Dash pepper
1 3-ounce can sliced mushrooms,     2 5-ounce cans boned chicken,
  drained (½ cup)                     diced
2 tablespoons sliced pimiento-      1 teaspoon dried sage, crushed
  stuffed green olives               2 cups prepared biscuit mix

Reserve ⅔ cup gravy. In a saucepan, combine remaining
gravy with mushrooms, olives, and pepper; stir in chicken.
Bring to boiling. Turn into shallow 8- or 9-inch round baking
dish. Add sage to biscuit mix. Prepare biscuit dough according to package directions, *but use the ⅔ cup reserved gravy
for liquid.*

Roll out on waxed paper to fit baking dish; flip biscuit
over *hot* sauce. Bake at 450° for 15 minutes. Loosen edge
with knife. Invert on deep platter (sauce will run down sides
of biscuit). Trim with parsley. Cut in wedges. Serve with an

extra 10¾-ounce can chicken gravy as sauce, if desired. Serves 6.

# SWEET POTATO CHICKEN PIE

2 1-pound cans sweet potatoes, drained

2 tablespoons butter or margarine, melted

⅛ teaspoon ground nutmeg

⅛ teaspoon ground allspice

¼ teaspoon salt

½ cup chopped onion

2 tablespoons butter or margarine

1 10½-ounce can condensed cream of mushroom soup

2 cups diced cooked chicken

1 3-ounce can broiled sliced mushrooms, undrained (⅔ cup)

Mash sweet potatoes; beat in 2 tablespoons melted butter, nutmeg, allspice, and salt. Line a 9-inch pie plate with sweet potato mixture, building up the edges about ½ inch high. In skillet cook onion in 2 tablespoons butter till tender but not brown. Add soup, chicken, mushrooms, and dash pepper. Heat, stirring occasionally. Turn mixture into prepared sweet potato crust. Bake at 350° for 30 minutes or till heated through. Makes 6 servings.

# CHICKEN RICE CASSEROLE

1 cup uncooked long-grain rice

½ cup chopped onion

¼ cup butter or margarine, melted

. . .

2¼ cups chicken broth

½ cup chopped green pepper

½ cup diced celery

1½ cups cut-up cooked chicken

1 3-ounce can sliced mushrooms, drained (½ cup)

. . .

2 slices sharp process American cheese, halved diagonally

Sliced ripe olives

In medium skillet brown rice and onion in butter over medium heat, stirring occasionally. Add chicken broth; cover and cook 10 minutes. Add green pepper and celery; cook, covered, 10 to 15 minutes longer, or till rice is tender, stirring occasionally. Add chicken and sliced mushrooms; mix well. Transfer to 1½-quart casserole. Bake, covered, in moderate oven (350°) 15 to 20 minutes, or till heated through. Remove casserole from oven, top with halved cheese slices, forming a pinwheel design, and return to oven for a few minutes till cheese begins to melt. Garnish with sliced ripe olives. Makes 5 or 6 servings.

## CHICKEN POT PIE

1 3-pound ready-to-cook stewing
   chicken, cut up
1 medium onion, quartered
3 celery leaves
3 sprigs parsley
1 bay leaf
10 whole black peppercorns

1 teaspoon monosodium glutamate
¼ teaspoon dried rosemary,
   crushed
7 carrots, pared and cut up
½ cup milk
1 10-ounce package frozen peas
1 recipe Pastry for 1-crust pie
   (see Index)

In large kettle, combine first 8 ingredients. Add 2 quarts
water and 2 teaspoons salt. Bring to boiling; simmer, covered till chicken is tender—about 2 hours. Remove chicken.
Strain stock. In 2 cups of the stock, cook carrots, covered, till
tender. Remove bones; cube chicken; turn into 2-quart
casserole.

Combine ¼ cup flour, 1 teaspoon salt, dash pepper, and
milk. Quickly stir into stock with carrots. Add thawed peas.
Bring to boil, stirring constantly. Simmer till peas are tender.
Pour over chicken in casserole; toss.

Roll pastry to fit top of casserole with ½ inch overhang.
Turn edge under; seal and crimp. Slash vents in top. Bake at
425° for about 20 minutes. Makes 6 to 8 servings.

## SPANISH-STYLE CHICKEN

1 2½- to 3-pound ready-to-cook
   broiler-fryer chicken, cut up
1 teaspoon salt
¼ teaspoon pepper
½ teaspoon monosodium glutamate
3 tablespoons shortening
½ cup chopped onion

1 clove garlic, minced
1 cup tomato juice
2 cups chicken broth
1 cup uncooked long-grain rice
1 10-ounce package (2 cups)
   frozen peas, broken apart
¼ cup chopped canned pimiento

Season chicken with salt, pepper, and monosodium glutamate.
In skillet brown chicken in hot shortening. Add onion and
garlic; cook till onion is tender but not brown. Add tomato
juice and ½ *cup* of the chicken broth. Cover; simmer 20
minutes.

Add rice and remaining broth. Simmer covered 20 minutes.
Add peas and pimiento. Simmer 5 minutes more or till peas
are tender, stirring once or twice. Serves 4.

# TURKEY CHOP SUEY

½ cup sliced onion
2 tablespoons butter or margarine
2 cups diced cooked turkey
2 cups chicken broth
1 cup sliced celery
1 5-ounce can water chestnuts,
   drained and thinly sliced

½ cup water
3 tablespoons soy sauce
¼ cup cornstarch
¼ teaspoon monosodium glutamate
1 1-pound can bean sprouts,
   drained

In saucepan cook onion in butter till tender but not brown.
Add turkey, broth, celery, and water chestnuts; heat to boiling.
Combine water, soy sauce, cornstarch, and monosodium
glutamate; stir into turkey mixture. Cook and stir till thick
and bubbly.

Add bean sprouts and heat through. Serve on hot rice
sprinkled with toasted slivered almonds, if desired. Pass additional soy sauce. Makes 4 to 6 servings.

# FRANKFURTERS AND SAUSAGES

## FRANK AND KRAUT STEW

1 large onion, sliced (1 cup)
½ cup chopped green pepper
2 tablespoons shortening
1 1-pound can (2 cups) sauerkraut
1 1-pound can (2 cups) tomatoes
3 potatoes, pared and cubed
   (3 cups)

2 medium carrots, thinly
   sliced (about ½ cup)
½ cup water
2 tablespoons brown sugar
1 teaspoon salt
¼ teaspoon pepper
1 pound frankfurters, quartered

In Dutch oven or large kettle, cook onion and green pepper in shortening till tender. Add remaining ingredients except franks. Simmer covered about 35 minutes or till vegetables are tender. Add frankfurters; simmer 10 minutes longer. Makes 5 or 6 servings.

## WIENIE-LOTTAS

8 to 10 frozen tortillas
2 10½-ounce cans chili without
   beans
1 tablespoon instant minced onion
6 to 8 drops bottled hot pepper
   sauce

1 pound (8 to 10) frankfurters
1 8-ounce can tomato sauce
¼ cup seeded and chopped canned
   green chili peppers
4 ounces sharp natural Cheddar
   cheese, shredded (1 cup)

Cook tortillas in water according to package directions. Combine next three ingredients. Place a frank on each tortilla; top each with 2 tablespoons chili mixture (reserve remaining). Roll tortillas around franks. Arrange, seam side down, in 12x7½x2-inch baking dish. Combine remaining chili mixture and tomato sauce; pour over tortillas. Sprinkle with chili peppers. Bake at 350° for 25 to 30 minutes. Top with cheese. Serves 4 or 5.

## SUPPER SKILLET FRANKS

1 small onion, chopped (½ cup)
2 tablespoons butter or margarine
1 pound (8 to 10) frankfurters,
   cut in ½-inch pieces
1 1-pound can tomatoes, cut up
1 cup tomato juice
1 clove garlic, minced

1 teaspoon salt
   Dash pepper
½ teaspoon dried marjoram,
   crushed
¼ teaspoon dried basil, crushed
4 ounces medium noodles
1 green pepper, cut in strips

Cook onion in butter till just tender. Add next 8 ingredients; bring to boiling. Add noodles; simmer covered, for 10 minutes. Add green pepper; simmer covered, 3 to 5 minutes or till noodles are tender. Makes 6 servings.

## SAVORY FRANK-NOODLE BAKE

Cook 4 ounces (1 cup) medium noodles in boiling salted water about 7 minutes or till tender; drain. In small skillet cook ½ cup chopped onion in 1 tablespoon butter or margarine till tender but not brown. Thinly slice crosswise ½ pound frankfurters (4 or 5), setting aside a few slices for garnish.

Combine sliced frankfurters, cooked noodles, 3 slightly beaten eggs, 1 cup dairy sour cream, ½ cup cream-style cottage cheese, ½ teaspoon salt, and dash pepper. Pour mixture into greased 9-inch pie plate. Mix ½ cup cornflake crumbs and 1 tablespoon butter or margarine, melted; sprinkle over top.

Bake in moderate oven (375°) 20 minutes. Top with reserved frankfurter slices; bake 5 minutes more. Let stand 10 minutes; cut in wedges. Makes 4 to 6 servings.

## CORNBREAD FRANKS

1 14-ounce package corn muffin mix
¼ cup chopped onion
2 tablespoons chopped green pepper
1 10-ounce package frozen chopped spinach

1 pound (8 to 10) frankfurters
1 10½-ounce can condensed cream of mushroom soup
2 tablespoons butter or margarine
1 teaspoon instant minced onion
1 teaspoon prepared mustard
¼ teaspoon salt

Mix corn muffin mix according to package directions. Stir in chopped onion and green pepper. Turn into greased 12x7½ x 2-inch baking dish. Halve frankfurters lengthwise and score; arrange atop muffin mixture. Bake in moderate oven (375°) for 25 minutes.

Serve with *Spinach Sauce:* Cook spinach according to package directions; drain. Add mushroom soup, butter, onion, mustard, and salt. Heat to boiling, stirring frequently. Makes 5 or 6 servings.

## HOT FRANK POTATO SALAD

½ pound bacon (about 10 slices)
½ cup chopped onion
2 tablespoons all-purpose flour
2 tablespoons sugar
1½ teaspoons salt
1 teaspoon celery seed
Dash pepper

½ cup vinegar
6 cups sliced or diced cooked potatoes
1 pound (8 to 10) frankfurters, halved crosswise
2 hard-cooked eggs, sliced
2 tablespoons snipped parsley

In skillet cook bacon till crisp; drain and crumble. Drain off all but about 4 tablespoons drippings from skillet. Add onion, cook till tender but not brown. Blend in flour, sugar, salt, celery seed, and pepper. Add vinegar and 1 cup water; cook and stir till thick and bubbly. Remove from heat; stir in crumbled bacon and potatoes, toss lightly.

Place part of salad in center of 8¼ x1¾ -inch round baking

dish. Stand frankfurter halves upright around sides; fill center with remaining salad. Bake at 350° for 20 minutes, or till hot through. Trim with slices of egg. Sprinkle with parsley. Makes 5 or 6 servings.

## WIENER-BEAN BAKE

1 10-ounce package frozen limas
1 1-pound can (2 cups) pork and beans in tomato sauce
1 1-pound can kidney beans, drained
½ cup chili sauce
¼ cup molasses
½ to 1 teaspoon dry mustard
½ teaspoon Worcestershire sauce
½ envelope **dry** onion soup mix
1 pound (8 to 10) frankfurters, cut in 1-inch pieces

Cook limas according to package directions; drain. Mix with pork and beans and drained kidney beans. Stir in remaining ingredients. Turn into 2-quart casserole or bean pot. Bake covered in moderate oven (350°) for 1 hour. Uncover; stir and continue baking 30 minutes. Makes 6 servings.

## SAUSAGE EGG CASSEROLE

4 hard-cooked eggs
¼ cup butter or margarine, melted
¼ cup sifted all-purpose flour
½ teaspoon salt
Dash pepper
2 cups milk

1 pound bulk pork sausage, cooked and drained
1 1-pound can (2 cups) whole kernel corn, drained

. . .

1 cup soft bread crumbs (1½ slices)

. . .

Slice 2 *of the hard-cooked eggs* into 1½ quart casserole. In sancepan melt butter or margarine; blend in flour, salt, and pepper. Add milk all at once. Cook, stirring constantly, till mixture thickens and bubbles. Stir in sausage and corn. Pour over sliced eggs.

Slice remaining 2 hard-cooked eggs. Arrange eggs over top of sausage mixture. Sprinkle with soft bread crumbs. Bake in moderate oven (375°) for 20 to 25 minutes or till heated through. Pass relishes. Makes 6 servings.

# CREOLE SAUSAGE-BEAN BAKE

1 pound sausage links, cut in
    thirds
¼ cup water
    . . .
½ cup chopped onion
¼ cup chopped green pepper
2 1-pound cans (4 cups) kidney
    beans, drained

1 medium clove garlic, minced
2 8-ounce cans or 1 15-ounce can
    (2 cups) tomato sauce
¼ cup water
1 teaspoon sugar
1 bay leaf, crumbled
    Dash bottled hot pepper sauce

To skillet add sausages with ¼ cup water. Cover and cook over low heat for 5 minutes; drain. Uncover and brown sausages lightly. To skillet add onion, green pepper, and garlic; cook till tender but not brown. Stir in kidney beans, tomato sauce, ¼ cup water, sugar, crumbled bay leaf, and bottled hot pepper sauce. Bring to boil.

Pour mixture into 2-quart casserole. Bake uncovered in moderate oven (350°) for 45 minutes. Makes 6 servings.

# SAUSAGE STRATA

6 slices white bread
1 pound bulk pork sausage
1 teaspoon prepared mustard
4 ounces process Swiss cheese,
    shredded (1 cup)

3 slightly beaten eggs
1¼ cups milk
¾ cup light cream
1 teaspoon Worcestershire sauce

Fit bread into bottom of greased 12x7½x2-inch baking dish. Brown sausage; *drain off all excess fat.* Stir in mustard. Spoon sausage evenly over bread; sprinkle with cheese. Combine eggs, milk, cream, Worcestershire, ½ teaspoon salt, dash pepper, and dash ground nutmeg; pour over cheese. Bake at 325° for 30 minutes or till set. Makes 6 servings.

# SAUSAGE SQUASH SPECIAL

1 pound bulk pork sausage
1 clove garlic, crushed
4 cups sliced summer squash
½ cup fine dry bread crumbs
½ cup grated Parmesan cheese

½ cup milk
1 tablespoon snipped parsley
½ teaspoon dried oregano, crushed
½ teaspoon salt
2 beaten eggs

Cook sausage and garlic till meat is brown; *drain off excess fat*. Cook squash, covered, in small amount of water till tender; drain. Stir squash and next 6 ingredients into meat; carefully fold in eggs. Turn into 10x6x1½-inch baking dish. Bake in slow oven (325°) for 25 to 30 minutes. Makes 4 to 6 servings.

# FISH AND SEAFOOD

## TUNA ITALIAN

½ cup chopped onion
1 10½-ounce can condensed
   cream of mushroom soup
1 6-ounce can evaporated milk **or**
   ⅔ cup light cream
⅓ cup grated Parmesan cheese
1 6½- or 7-ounce can tuna,
   drained

1 3-ounce can sliced mushrooms,
   drained (½ cup)
¼ cup chopped ripe olives
2 tablespoons snipped parsley
2 teaspoons lemon juice
4 ounces noodles, cooked and
   drained (about 2 cups)

Cook onion in small amount of butter till tender but not brown. Add soup, milk, and cheese; heat and stir. Break tuna in chunks; add with remaining ingredients. Pour into 2-quart casserole. Sprinkle with additional Parmesan and paprika. Bake at 350° for 25 to 30 minutes. Top with additional snipped parsley and ripe olive slices. Serves 6.

# TUNA A LA KING

¼ cup chopped green pepper
1 tablespoon minced onion
3 tablespoons butter or margarine
3 tablespoons all-purpose flour
2 cups milk
1 6½- or 7-ounce can tuna,
   drained

1 cup cooked peas
1 3-ounce can sliced mushrooms,
   drained (½ cup)
2 tablespoons chopped canned
   pimiento
½ teaspoon salt
¼ teaspoon paprika

In a 2-quart saucepan cook green pepper and onion in butter till just tender, stirring frequently. Blend in flour; stir in milk. Cook and stir till thick and bubbly.

Break tuna into large pieces; add with peas, mushrooms, pimiento, and seasonings to creamed mixture. Heat through. Serves 4.

# TUNA NOODLE CASSEROLE

6 ounces medium noodles
1 6½- or 7-ounce can tuna,
   drained
½ cup mayonnaise or salad
   dressing
1 cup sliced celery
⅓ cup chopped onion
¼ cup diced green pepper

¼ cup chopped canned pimiento
. . .
1 10½-ounce can condensed
   cream of celery soup
½ cup milk
4 ounces sharp process American
   cheese, shredded (1 cup)
½ cup toasted slivered almonds

Cook noodles in boiling salted water till tender; drain. Combine noodles, next 6 ingredients, and ½ teaspoon salt.

Blend soup and milk; heat through. Add cheese; heat and stir till cheese melts. Add to noodle mixture. Turn into 2-quart casserole. Top with almonds. Bake uncovered in hot oven (425°) about 20 minutes. Serves 6.

# SWEET-SOUR TUNA

Drain one 8¾-ounce can (1 cup) pineapple tidbits, reserving syrup. In saucepan combine ⅓ *cup* of the pineapple syrup, pineapple tidbits, 1 cup green pepper strips, 1 vegetable bouillon cube, and ½ cup water. Heat to boiling; simmer 5 minutes.

Mix 1 tablespoon cornstarch with remaining pineapple syrup, 3 tablespoons sugar, 1 tablespoon vinegar, and 1 teaspoon soy sauce; stir into pineapple mixture. Cook, stirring constantly, till thick and bubbling. Add one 6½- or 7-ounce can tuna, drained, and 1 tablespoon butter. Heat through. Warm one 3-ounce can chow mein noodles. Serve tuna mixture over noodles. Serves 3 or 4.

## TUNA VEGETABLE PIE

Cook 1½ cups sliced carrots and 1½ cups cubed pared potatoes in small amount of boiling salted water till tender. Drain, reserving liquid. Add enough milk to make 2 cups.

Melt ¼ cup butter or margarine in saucepan; add ¼ cup chopped onion; cook till tender but not brown. Blend in 2 tablespoons all-purpose flour, ½ teaspoon salt, dash pepper, and ¼ teaspoon dried rosemary, crushed. Add milk mixture all at once. Cook, stirring constantly, till mixture thickens and bubbles.

Add carrots, potatoes, one 8-ounce can peas, drained, and two 6½- or 7-ounce cans tuna, drained and flaked. Turn into a 10x6x1½-inch baking dish. Prepare 1 stick pie crust mix according to package directions. Roll out; cut into 6 triangles. Place around edge of tuna mixture. Bake at 425° for 30 to 35 minutes, or till lightly browned. Serves 6.

## BAKED TUNA SUPREME

1 10-ounce package frozen broccoli
1 9-ounce can tuna, drained
1 10½-ounce can condensed cream of mushroom soup
¼ cup milk
½ cup cubed sharp process American cheese
1 cup soft bread crumbs
1 tablespoon butter or margarine, melted

Cook broccoli according to package directions, *omitting salt in cooking water;* drain. Arrange in a 10x6x1½-inch baking dish. Flake tuna and place over broccoli. Combine soup, milk, and cheese; heat till cheese is melted. Pour over tuna. Combine crumbs and butter; sprinkle over top. Bake in moderate oven (350°) for 20 to 25 minutes. Makes 6 servings.

## RICE AND TUNA PIE

For rice shell, combine 2 cups cooked rice, 2 tablespoons butter or margarine, melted, 1 tablespoon chopped onion, ¼ teaspoon dried marjoram, crushed, and 1 slightly beaten egg. Press into bottom and sides of lightly buttered 10-inch pie plate or 10x6x1½-inch baking dish. Layer one 9-ounce can tuna, drained and flaked, evenly over rice shell.

Combine 3 beaten eggs, 1 cup milk, 4 ounces process Swiss cheese, shredded (1 cup), 1 tablespoon chopped onion, ¼ teaspoon salt, dash pepper, and ¼ teaspoon dried marjoram, crushed. Pour over tuna.

Bake in a moderate oven (350°) for 50 to 55 minutes, or till knife inserted just off center comes out clean. Garnish with pimiento, if desired. Makes 6 servings.

## TUNA 'N RICE SOUFFLE

1 10½-ounce can condensed
   cream of mushroom soup
1 6½- or 7-ounce can tuna,
   drained and flaked

1 cup cooked rice
¼ cup chopped canned pimiento
2 tablespoons snipped parsley
4 eggs

In saucepan heat and stir soup. Add tuna, rice, pimiento, and parsley; heat through. Remove from heat. Separate eggs. Beat whites till stiff. Beat yolks till thick and lemon-colored; gradually stir in tuna mixture. Pour slowly onto beaten egg whites, folding together thoroughly. Turn into ungreased 2-quart casserole. Bake at 350° for 30 to 35 minutes or till mixture is set in center. Serve immediately. Pass lemon wedges. Serves 6.

## SHRIMP CREOLE

½ cup chopped onion
½ cup chopped celery
1 clove garlic, minced
3 tablespoons shortening
1 1-pound can (2 cups) tomatoes
1 8-ounce can (1 cup) tomato
   sauce
1½ teaspoons salt
1 teaspoon sugar

1 tablespoon Worcestershire
   sauce
½ to 1 teaspoon chili powder
Dash bottled hot pepper sauce
2 teaspoons cornstarch
12 ounces frozen shelled shrimp,
   thawed
½ cup chopped green pepper

In skillet cook onion, celery, and garlic in shortening till tender but not brown. Add tomatoes, tomato sauce, and next 5 ingredients. Simmer uncovered 45 minutes. Mix cornstarch with 1 tablespoon cold water; stir into sauce. Cook and stir till mixture thickens and bubbles. Add shrimp and green pepper. Cover; simmer 5 minutes. Serve with Parsley Rice Ring. Serves 6.

# PARSLEY RICE RING

3 cups hot cooked rice                    ¼ cup snipped parsley

Combine hot cooked rice with parsley; pack into an ungreased 5½-cup ring mold. Turn out at once on warm platter. Serves 6.

# PACIFIC CHOWDER

4 slices bacon
¼ cup chopped onion
2 tablespoons chopped green
   pepper

1 10¼-ounce can frozen condensed cream of potato soup
2 cups milk
1 6½- or 7-ounce can tuna, drained and broken in chunks

Cook bacon till crisp. Drain, reserving 2 tablespoons drippings. In drippings, cook onion and green pepper till tender. Add soup and milk; heat just to boiling. Add tuna and crumbled bacon. Heat. Serves 4.

# HEARTY OYSTER STEW

½ cup finely diced carrots
½ cup finely diced celery
½ cup butter or margarine
2 tablespoons all-purpose flour
1½ teaspoons salt
1 teaspoon Worcestershire sauce

Dash bottled hot pepper sauce
2 10-ounce cans (2¼ cups) oysters
4 cups milk, scalded, or 3 cups milk and 1 cup light cream, scalded

In large saucepan cook carrots and celery in ¼ *cup butter* until tender. Add a smooth mixture of flour, seasonings, and 2 tablespoons water. Add oysters and the liquor. Return to boiling; simmer over very low heat 3 to 4 minutes, stirring gently. Add hot milk. Remove from heat. Cover; let stand 15 minutes.

Place remaining ¼ cup butter in tureen. Reheat stew to serving temperature. Pour into tureen; dash with paprika. Serves 4 to 6.

# MANHATTAN CLAM CHOWDER

Wash 2 dozen medium-sized quahog clams (*or* use two 7½-ounce cans clams *or* 1 pint fresh shucked clams, finely diced, reserving ½ cup liquor). Cover quahogs with salt water (⅓ cup salt to 1 gallon cold water); let stand 15 minutes; rinse. Repeat twice.

Place quahogs in large kettle; add 1 cup water. Cover and steam just till shells open, 5 to 10 minutes. Remove clams from shells; dice finely. Strain liquor, reserving ½ cup.

Partially cook 3 slices bacon, finely diced. Add 1 cup finely diced celery and 1 cup chopped onion; cook till tender. Add 3 cups water, ½ cup clam liquor, one 1-pound can tomatoes, cut up, 2 cups diced pared potatoes, 1 cup finely diced carrots, 1½ teaspoons salt, ¼ teaspoon dried thyme, crushed, and dash pepper. Cover; simmer 35 minutes. Blend 2 tablespoons flour with 2 tablespons cold water. Stir in; cook and stir to boiling. Add clams; heat. Serves 6 to 8.

# DOUBLE SHRIMP CASSEROLE

| | |
|---|---|
| 4 ounces ( 3 cups) medium noodles | ¼ cup diced celery |
| 1 10-ounce can frozen condensed cream of shrimp soup | ¼ teaspoon salt |
| ¾ cup milk | . . . |
| ½ cup mayonnaise or salad dressing | ⅓ cup shredded natural Cheddar cheese |
| 1 tablespoon chopped green onion | 1 cup cooked shrimp |
| | . . . |
| | ¼ cup chow mein noodles |

Cook noodles according to package directions; drain. Thaw soup; combine with milk, mayonnaise, onion, celery, and salt; mix well. Stir in cheese, shrimp, and cooked noodles. Turn into 1½-quart casserole.

Bake uncovered in a moderate oven (350°) for 30 to 35 minutes. Top with chow mein noodles; bake 10 minutes longer. Serves 4 to 6.

## HAWAIIAN SHRIMP PLATTER

| | |
|---|---|
| 1 10-ounce package frozen breaded shrimp | 2 tablespoons cornstarch |
| | 2 tablespoons vinegar |
| ½ cup chopped onion | 1 tablespoon soy sauce |
| ¼ cup chopped green pepper | 1 1-pound 4½-ounce can |
| 2 tablespoons butter or margarine | (2½ cups) pineapple tidbits |
| • • • | • • • |
| 2 tablespons sugar | 3 cups hot cooked rice |

Cook shrimp according to package directions. Set aside, keeping shrimp warm.

Cook chopped onion and green pepper in butter or margarine till tender but not brown. Combine sugar, cornstarch, vinegar, and soy sauce. Stir into onion mixture. Drain pineapple, reserving syrup. Add syrup to onion mixture. Cook and stir till mixture thickens and boils; cook 1 minute longer. Stir in pineapple; heat to boiling. Serve over rice, with the shrimp. Makes 4 servings.

## SAUCY SHRIMP SQUARES

Combine 3 well-beaten eggs and 1½ cups milk; stir in 3 cups soft bread crumbs, two 4½-or 5-ounce cans shrimp, drained, 2 tablespoons *each* minced parsley and onion, 1 tablespoon lemon juice, ¼ teaspoon salt, and dash pepper. Turn into well-greased 10x6x1½-inch baking dish. Bake at 350° for 35 to 40 minutes, or till set. Cut into 6 servings.

Serve with *Cheese Sauce:* Melt 1 tablespoon butter; stir in 1 tablespoon flour and ¼ teaspoon salt. Add 1½ cups milk all at once. Cook quickly, stirring constantly, till thickened. Remove from heat; stir in 4 ounces sharp process American cheese, shredded (1 cup).

## SALMON CASSEROLE

Cook ¼ cup *each* chopped onion and celery in 1 tablespoon butter till tender. Combine one 7¾-ounce can salmon, boned and flaked (with liquid), one 10½-ounce can condensed cream of mushroom soup, ½ cup shredded sharp process American cheese, and 2 cups cooked rice. Turn into 1-quart casserole; sprinkle ½ cup buttered soft bread crumbs atop. Bake at 350° for 30 minutes. Serves 4.

## TEST KITCHEN TIPS
### How shrimp measures up in ounces and cups

| SHRIMP IN 1 POUND . . . | |
| --- | --- |
| Size | Number of raw shrimp in shell from 1 pound |
| Jumbo-size | *15 to 18* |
| Average-size | *26 to 30* |
| Tiny | *60 or more* |

| BUY IN SHELL OR SHELLED | |
| --- | --- |
| Amount needed | Amount to buy |
| For each 1 cup cleaned cooked shrimp | *12 ounces raw shrimp in shell* or *7 or 8 ounces frozen shelled shrimp* or *1 4½- or 5-ounce can shrimp* |

| SHRIMP IN CASSEROLE OR SAUCE | |
| --- | --- |
| Servings | Amount needed |
| For 4 servings of casserole or creamy sauce (approximate) | *1 pound shrimp in shell* or *1⅓ cups cleaned cooked shrimp* or *1 or 2 4½- or 5-ounce cans (1 or 2 cups) shrimp* |

## HERBED FISH BAKE

1 pound frozen fish fillets,
  partially thawed
⅓ cup chopped onion
1 small clove garlic, minced
2 tablespoons butter or margarine

½ teaspoon dried tarragon,
  crushed
¼ teaspoon dried thyme, crushed
¼ teaspoon salt
  Dash pepper
¼ cup cornflake crumbs

Place fillets in greased 10x6x1½-inch baking dish. Cook onion and garlic in butter till tender. Stir in seasonings; cook 1 minute. Spread over fish. Top with crumbs. Bake at 500° for 12 minutes or till fish flakes easily with a fork. Makes 4 servings.

## FISH IN CHEESE SAUCE

1 pound fish steaks or fillets, cut
  in serving pieces
1 tablespoon butter or margarine
1 10-ounce package frozen cut
  asparagus

1 11-ounce can condensed
  Cheddar cheese soup
¼ cup milk
1 cup soft bread crumbs
2 tablespoons butter, melted

Place fish in greased 10x6x1½-inch baking dish; dot with butter; sprinkle with ¼ teaspoon salt and dash pepper. Bake at 350° about 30 minutes. Meanwhile, cook asparagus according to package directions; drain. Place asparagus atop fish. Combine soup and milk; pour over all. Combine crumbs and melted butter; sprinkle atop. Return to oven till lightly browned, 10 minutes. Serves 4.

## FISH AND CHIPS

Dip 2 pounds fish fillets, cut in serving pieces, in ¼ cup milk, then in a mixture of 1 cup crushed potato chips, ¼ cup grated Parmesan cheese, and ¼ teaspoon dried thyme, crushed. Place fish in greased baking dish. Sprinkle with any extra crumbs. Drizzle ¼ cup melted butter over top. Bake in extremely hot oven (500°) for 12 to 15 minutes. Serves 6.

# LUSCIOUS VEGETABLES

## TOMATO-ZUCCHINI SCALLOP

2 small zucchini squash, sliced
1 medium onion, thinly sliced
2 small tomatoes, peeled and
   sliced
1 cup plain croutons

1 teaspoon salt
  Pepper
1 tomato, cut in wedges
4 ounces sharp natural Cheddar
   cheese, shredded (1 cup)

In a 1½-quart casserole, layer *half* of the zucchini, onion, sliced tomatoes, and croutons. Season with ½ teaspoon salt and dash pepper. Repeat layers. Top with tomato wedges. Cover and bake in moderate oven (350°) for 1 hour. Uncover and sprinkle with cheese. Return to oven till cheese melts. Serve in sauce dishes. Makes 6 servings.

# STUFFED ACORN SQUASH

3 medium acorn squash
1 slightly beaten egg
1 chicken bouillon cube
⅓ cup boiling water
¼ cup chopped onion

2 tablespoons butter or margarine
½ cup crushed herb-seasoned
    stuffing mix
½ teaspoon salt
Dash pepper

Cut squash in half lengthwise; remove seeds. Place cut side down on baking sheet. Bake at 400° for 30 minutes, or till tender. Scoop squash from shells (reserve shells); mash squash. Add egg. Dissolve bouillon cube in water; add to mashed squash. (Add additional water if needed to make mixture quite soft.)

Cook onion in butter till tender but not brown. Stir in stuffing mix. Reserve ¼ cup stuffing mixture; add remainder to mashed squash. Add seasonings. Mix well. Fill shells (squash mixture will be thin). Sprinkle with reserved stuffing. Bake at 400° for 25 to 30 minutes or till lightly browned. Serves 6.

# ELEGANT EGGPLANT

Pare and thinly slice 1 large eggplant (1¾ pounds). Dip into 2 well-beaten eggs, then in 1½ cups finely crushed cracker crumbs (about 36 crackers). Brown slowly in hot shortening. Place *one-fourth* of the eggplant slices in bottom of 2-quart casserole; top with *one-fourth* of one 8-ounce package sliced sharp process American cheese.

Combine two 8-ounce cans (2 cups) tomato sauce, ½ teaspoon Worcestershire sauce, and 1 teaspoon dried oregano, crushed. Spoon *one-fourth* of the sauce (about ½ cup) over cheese. Repeat layers till all ingredients are used, ending with sauce. Cover and bake at 350° for 50 to 60 minutes or till eggplant is tender. Snip parsley over top. Serves 8.

# SPINACH-STUFFED ZUCCHINI

3 zucchini squash (about 1 pound)
1 10-ounce package frozen
    chopped spinach, cooked and
    well drained
2 tablespoons all-purpose flour

½ cup milk
⅓ cup shredded natural
    Cheddar cheese
4 slices bacon, crisp-cooked,
    drained and crumbled

Trim off ends of zucchini; cook, whole, in boiling water 10 to 12 minutes. Drain thoroughly. Halve zucchini lengthwise. Scoop out centers; chop and add to spinach. Reserve zucchini shells to stuff.

In saucepan blend flour and milk; add spinach mixture. Cook and stir till thickened. Place zucchini halves in shallow baking dish; sprinkle cavities with salt. Spoon spinach mixture into zucchini shells. Top with cheese and bacon. Bake in moderate oven (350°) 15 to 20 minutes. Makes 6 servings.

## OVEN SPANISH RICE

½ cup chopped onion
½ cup chopped green pepper
2 tablespoons shortening or
    salad oil

1 cup uncooked long-grain rice
½ teaspoon salt
½ cup water

. . .

1 envelope spaghetti sauce mix
2 1-pound cans (4 cups) tomatoes

2 ounces sharp process American
    cheese, shredded (½ cup)

In saucepan cook onion and green pepper in shortening or salad oil till tender but not brown. Stir in spaghetti sauce mix, tomatoes, uncooked rice, salt, and water. Simmer 10 minutes, stirring frequently.

Pour into a greased 1½-quart casserole; cover and bake in moderate oven (350°) 30 minutes or till rice is done. Sprinkle with shredded sharp cheese. Makes 4 to 6 servings.

## HOT GERMAN RICE SALAD

1 cup uncooked long-grain rice
8 slices bacon

. . .

⅓ cup sugar
⅓ cup vinegar
2 tablespoons chopped green
    pepper

2 tablespoons water
2 tablespoons chopped canned
    pimiento
1 tablespoon chopped onion
½ teaspoon celery seed
½ teaspoon salt
1 hard-cooked egg, sliced

Cook rice according to package directions. Cook bacon till crisp; drain and crumble. In saucepan combine ¼ cup of the bacon drippings, the cooked rice, sugar, vinegar, water, green pepper, pimiento, onion, celery seed, and salt. Cook and stir till liquid is absorbed. Add bacon (reserve some for garnish); toss. Top with reserved bacon and hard-cooked egg slices. Serve hot. Makes 6 servings.

# MINTED RICE CASSEROLE

2 teaspoons salt
2 cups water
1 cup uncooked long-grain rice
¼ cup butter or margarine

. . .

Dash garlic salt
Dash monosodium glutamate

1 13¾-ounce can (1¾ cups)
   chicken broth (not condensed) **or** 2 chicken bouillon
   cubes dissolved in 1¾ cups
   boiling water
½ teaspoon dried mint leaves,
   crushed
¼ cup toasted slivered almonds

Add the 2 teaspons salt to water; bring to boiling. Remove from heat; add uncooked rice. Cover; let stand 30 minutes. Rinse rice with cold water and drain well.

Melt butter or margarine in skillet. Add rice and cook over medium heat, stirring frequently, till butter is almost absorbed, about 5 minutes. Turn rice into 1-quart casserole; sprinkle with garlic salt and monosodium glutamate. Pour chicken broth over rice.

Bake covered in slow oven (325°) 45 minutes. Add mint and fluff with fork. Sprinkle toasted almonds over top. Bake uncovered 10 minutes more. Makes about 6 servings.

---

## TEST KITCHEN TIPS

### To reheat, refrigerate, or freeze rice

REHEAT: *For each cup of cooked rice, add 2 tablespoons liquid. Simmer in a covered saucepan 4 to 5 minutes.*
REFRIGERATE: *Tightly cover cooked rice and refrigerate up to one week.*
FREEZE: *Freeze cooled rice in a freezer tray. When frozen, remove rice and wrap in foil or freezer paper. Freeze up to 8 months. Reheat as indicated above.*

---

## RICE AND CHEESE BAKE

Combine 2½ cups water, 1 envelope *dry* chicken-rice soup mix, and 1 cup uncooked long-grain rice in saucepan. Bring to boiling. Cover tightly; simmer 20 minutes.

In a greased 2-quart casserole, combine rice mixture, one 10½-ounce can condensed cream of chicken soup, 4 ounces sharp process American cheese, cubed (1 cup), one 6-ounce can (⅔ cup) evaporated milk, and ¼ cup chopped canned pimiento. Mix lightly; sprinkle top with freshly ground pepper or paprika. Bake at 350° for 25 to 30 minutes. Serves 6.

## GREEN RICE BAKE

2 slightly beaten eggs
2 cups milk
¾ cup packaged precooked rice
⅓ cup finely chopped onion

1 10-ounce package frozen chopped spinach, cooked and drained

4 ounces sharp process American cheese, shredded (1 cup)
½ teaspoon garlic salt

Combine eggs and milk. Add uncooked rice, onion, cooked spinach, cheese, and garlic salt. Pour into 10x6x1½-inch baking dish. Bake in slow oven (325°) for 35 to 40 minutes or till firm. Makes 4 to 6 servings.

---

## TEST KITCHEN TIPS

### How much rice to cook and how to test for doneness

*One cup uncooked long-grain rice will yield 3 to 4 cups cooked rice. One cup precooked rice makes 2 cups cooked rice.*

*To test for doneness: Pinch grain of rice between thumb and forefinger. When no hard core remains, it's done.*

---

## POTATO PUFF SOUFFLE

2 teaspoons minced onion
¼ cup butter or margarine
¼ cup all-purpose flour
1 teaspoon salt

1 cup dairy sour cream
2 cups hot mashed potatoes
4 well-beaten egg yolks
4 stiffly beaten egg whites

In a saucepan cook onion in butter till tender. Blend in flour,

salt, and dash pepper. Heat till bubbly. Remove from heat.
Stir in sour cream and potatoes; beat till smooth. Add small
amount of hot mixture to egg yolks, stirring constantly. Return to remaining hot mixture, mixing well. Fold in egg
whites. Pour into 1½-quart souffle dish. Bake at 350° for 30
to 35 minutes or till knife inserted in center comes out clean.
Makes 6 servings.

## TEST KITCHEN TIPS

### How to prepare and cook potatoes

WHOLE: *Scrub potato skin thoroughly, or wash and pare.
Cook covered in boiling, salted water to cover for 25 to 40
minutes.*

CUT UP: *Cook tightly covered in small amount of boiling,
salted water. Cook quartered potatoes 20 to 25 minutes, or
cubed potatoes for 10 to 15 minutes.*

## SKILLET POTATO SALAD

Cook 6 medium potatoes in jackets till tender; peel and dice;
keep warm. In a skillet cook 8 slices bacon till crisp. Remove
bacon from skillet; drain and crumble. Pour off all but
about 4 tablespoons bacon drippings. Cook ½ cup chopped
onion in bacon drippings till tender but not brown. Blend in
one 10½-ounce can condensed cream of celery soup, ⅓ cup
milk, 2 tablespoons sweet pickle relish, 2 tablespoons vinegar,
and ½ teaspoon salt. Cook and stir till mixture boils.

Gently stir in the warm diced potatoes and all but 1 tablespoon bacon. Heat through. Sprinkle reserved bacon over top.
Garnish with parsley and wedges of hard-cooked egg, if desired. Makes 4 to 6 servings.

## BASIC SCALLOPED POTATOES

| | |
|---|---|
| 4 medium potatoes, pared and thinly sliced (about 4 cups) | 2 tablespoons all-purpose flour |
| 1½ teaspoons salt | 1 tablespoon chopped onion |
| ¼ teaspoon pepper | 1 tablespoon butter or margarine |
| | 1½ to 2 cups milk |

Rinse potatoes in cold water; drain. Place a *third* of the potatoes in greased 1½-quart casserole. Sprinkle with ¾ teaspoon salt, ⅛ teaspoon pepper, 1 tablespoon flour, and 1½ teaspoons onion. Dot with *half* the butter or margarine. Repeat layers ending with potatoes. Pour milk over potatoes to barely cover. Bake covered in moderate oven (350°) for 1 hour. Uncover and bake for an additional 30 minutes. Makes 6 servings.

## CHEESE SCALLOPED POTATOES

4 to 5 medium potatoes, pared (about 1½ pounds)
1 11-ounce can condensed Cheddar cheese soup
1 package sour cream sauce mix
½ cup milk

½ teaspoon salt
Dash pepper
1 tablespoon butter or margarine, melted
¼ cup fine dry bread crumbs

Cook potatoes in boiling salted water till tender; drain and thinly slice. Combine soup, sour cream sauce mix, milk, salt, and pepper. Place *half* the potatoes in 1½-quart casserole. Top with *half* the soup mixture. Repeat with remaining potatoes and soup mixture.

Combine melted butter or margarine and bread crumbs. Sprinkle over top. Cover and bake in moderate oven (375°) for 25 minutes. Uncover and bake for an additional 10 to 15 minutes. Makes 6 servings.

## HOT DILL POTATO SALAD

1 tablespoon butter or margarine
1 tablespoon all-purpose flour
¼ teaspoon dried dillweed
1 teaspoon salt
⅛ teaspoon pepper
1 cup milk

½ cup mayonnaise or salad dressing
2 tablespoons finely chopped onion
5 medium potatoes, cooked, peeled, and diced (4 cups)
Paprika

Melt butter or margarine over low heat. Stir in flour, dillweed, salt, and pepper. Add milk all at once. Cook and stir till mixture thickens and bubbles. Blend in mayonnaise and onion; fold in cooked potatoes. Spoon into serving dish; sprinkle with paprika. Garnish with parsley, if desired. Makes 4 to 6 servings.

## TEST KITCHEN TIPS

*Easy way to peel cooked potatoes for a hot salad*

Score raw potatoes around center with point of knife. Cook covered in boiling salted water till tender. Spear potatoes with fork tines in the score mark and peel.

## FIESTA POTATO BAKE

In a bowl combine 3 cups loose-pack frozen hash brown potatoes, one 10½-ounce can condensed cream of celery soup, ½ cup dairy sour cream, and 1 teaspoon snipped chives. Place *half* the potato mixture in 10x6x1½-inch baking dish. Top with ½ cup shredded sharp process American cheese. Cover with remaining potato mixture and an additional ½ cup shredded cheese. Bake covered at 350° for 1 hour or till done. Makes 5 or 6 servings.

## STUFFED ONIONS

Peel 6 medium onions. Cut thick slice from top of each; set aside. Scoop out center of each onion and set aside. Cook onion shells in boiling salted water 25 minutes, or till tender; drain. Brush each with salad oil and sprinkle generously with paprika.

Coarsely chop tops and centers of onions. In a saucepan cook chopped onion in ¼ cup butter or margarine till tender. Stir in ¼ cup light cream, ¼ cup chopped ripe olives, 2 tablespoons chopped pecans, and ¼ teaspoon salt. Spoon into cooked onion shells.

Combine ¼ cup dry bread crumbs and 1 tablespoon butter or margarine, melted; sprinkle over onions. Dash with paprika. Bake at 350° for 15 minutes. Makes 6 servings.

## BEAN POT LIMAS

1 pound (2½ cups) large dry
    lima beans
6 cups water
¼ pound salt pork
1 medium onion, sliced

2 teaspoons salt
½ teaspoon dry mustard
1 tablespoon vinegar
⅓ cup dark molasses
⅓ cup chili sauce

Rinse beans; soak in 6 cups water overnight. Do not drain. Cover; simmer over low heat until just tender, about 30 minutes (do not boil). Drain, reserving bean liquid.

Cut salt pork in half; grind or finely chop one piece, score the other piece. Combine lima beans, 2 cups hot bean liquid, ground pork, onion, salt, dry mustard, vinegar, molasses, and chili sauce. Pour into 2-quart bean pot or casserole. Top with salt pork slice.

Cover and bake in slow oven (300°) for 2½ hours, uncovering last 30 minutes. (If necessary, add more hot bean liquid or hot water during baking.) Makes 8 servings.

## VERMONT LIMA BAKE

1 pound (2½ cups) large dry
    lima beans
1 large onion, quartered
2 whole cloves
6 cups water
½ cup maple syrup
½ cup catsup

2 teaspoons Worcestershire
    sauce
1 teaspoon salt
¼ teaspoon pepper
1 bay leaf
¼ pound sliced salt pork, cut in
    1-inch pieces

Rinse beans; place in 3-quart saucepan. Stud onion quarters with whole cloves. Add water and onion to saucepan. Boil 5 minutes. Let stand 1 hour. Combine undrained lima bean mixture, maple syrup, catsup. Worcestershire sauce, salt, pepper, bay leaf, and pork.

Turn into 3-quart casserole. Cover and bake at 300° for 2½ hours. Uncover and bake 30 minutes, stirring once or twice. Remove bay leaf. Serves 6 to 8.

# BAKED BEANS

1 pound (2 cups) dry navy beans    ¼ cup molasses*
⅔ cup brown sugar*    ¼ pound salt pork
1 teaspoon dry mustard    1 medium onion, sliced

Rinse beans; add to 2 quarts cold water. Bring to boiling; simmer 2 minutes; remove from heat; cover, let stand 1 hour. (Or, add beans to water; let soak overnight.)

Add ½ teaspoon salt to beans and soaking water; cover; simmer till tender, 1 hour. Drain, reserving liquid. Measure 2 cups liquid, adding water if needed; mix with sugar, mustard, and molasses.

Cut salt pork in half; score one half. Grind or thinly slice remainder. In 2-quart bean pot or casserole, combine beans, onion, and ground salt pork. Pour sugar-bean liquid over. Top with scored salt pork.

Cover and bake at 300° for 5 to 7 hours. Add more liquid if needed. Makes 8 servings.

*For more traditional New England baked beans, decrease brown sugar to ⅓ cup and increase molasses to ½ cup.

# CALICO BEAN BAKE

1 cup chopped onion    1 to 2 tablespoons vinegar
1 clove garlic, minced    1 1-pound can pork and beans
½ cup catsup      in tomato sauce
2 tablespoons brown sugar    1 1-pound can kidney beans,
1 teaspoon dry mustard      drained
1 teaspoon salt    1 1-pound can baby limas, drained

Cook onion and garlic in 1 tablespoon shortening till tender. Add catsup and remaining ingredients. Turn into 1½-quart casserole. Bake at 350° for 1½ hours. Serves 6.

# SWISS CORN BAKE

3 cups fresh corn cut from cob*    Dash pepper
1 6-ounce can (⅔ cup)    4 ounces process Swiss cheese,
  evaporated milk      shredded (1 cup)
1 beaten egg    ½ cup soft bread crumbs
2 tablespoons finely chopped    1 tablespoon butter or margarine,
  onion      melted
½ teaspoon salt

Cook fresh corn in 1 cup boiling salted water for 2 to 3 minutes, or till just tender; drain well. Combine corn, evaporated milk, egg, onion, salt, pepper, and ¾ *cup* of the cheese.

Turn into 10x6x1½-inch baking dish. Toss bread crumbs with butter or margarine and the remaining ¼ cup cheese. Sprinkle over corn mixture. Bake in moderate oven (350°) for 25 to 30 minutes. Garnish with green pepper rings, if desired. Makes 4 to 6 servings.

*Or use two 9-ounce packages frozen corn, cooked according to package directions and drained, *or* two 1-pound cans whole kernel corn, drained.

## RED BEAN TOSS

1 1-pound can (2 cups) red or
    kidney beans, drained
1 cup thinly sliced celery
⅓ cup chopped sweet pickle
¼ cup finely chopped onion
4 ounces sharp process American
    cheese, diced (1 cup)
½ teaspoon salt

½ teaspoon chili powder
½ teaspoon Worcestershire sauce
    Few drops bottled hot pepper
    sauce
½ cup mayonnaise or salad
    dressing
1 cup coarsely crushed corn chips

Combine beans, celery, pickle, onion, and cheese. Blend seasonings with mayonnaise; add to bean mixture and toss lightly. Spoon into a 1-quart shallow baking dish; sprinkle with corn chips. Bake at 450° about 10 minutes. Garnish with green pepper rings, if desired. Makes 4 servings.

## SAVORY SUCCOTASH

1 1-pound can (2 cups) French-
    style green beans, drained
1 1-pound can (2 cups) whole
    kernel corn, drained

. . .

½ cup mayonnaise or salad
    dressing
½ cup chopped green pepper

2 ounces sharp process American
    cheese, shredded (½ cup)
½ cup chopped celery
2 tablespoons chopped onion

. . .

1 cup soft bread crumbs
2 tablespoons butter or
    margarine, melted

Combine French-style green beans, whole kernel corn, mayonnaise or salad dressing, shredded American cheese, chopped green pepper, celery, and onion. Turn mixture into a 10x6x1½-inch baking dish.

Combine soft bread crumbs and melted butter or margarine. Sprinkle crumb mixture atop casserole. Bake in moderate oven (350°) for 30 minutes or till crumbs are toasted and mixture is heated through. Serves 6.

# CHIVE 'N CORN SPOONBREAD

2 cups milk
¾ cup yellow cornmeal
2 tablespoons butter or margarine
1 teaspoon salt
. . .
4 egg yolks
1 8-ounce can (1 cup) whole
  kernel corn, drained
3 tablespoons snipped chives
4 stiffly beaten egg whites

Scald milk; stir in cornmeal. Cook and stir till thickened. Remove from heat; stir in the 2 tablespoons butter and the salt; set aside to cool slightly. Beat egg yolks, one at a time, into slightly cooled cornmeal mixture. Fold in corn, chives, and egg whites.

Turn into greased 10x6x1½-inch baking dish. Bake in a moderate oven (350°) for 35 to 40 minutes or till golden brown. Serve with butter. Makes 6 servings.

---

## TEST KITCHEN TIPS

### Time-saver—Casserole doubles as a bowl

*When you're making a mix-in-one-bowl main dish, combine it right in the casserole. Saves effort and dishwashing, too.*

---

# INDIAN CORN CASSEROLE

Combine 3 well-beaten eggs, ¼ cup flour, and 2 tablespoons sugar; beat well. Add 1½ cups shredded sharp process American cheese and two 1-pound cans whole kernel corn, drained. Cook 10 slices bacon; drain and crumble. Stir in ¾ *of the bacon.*

Turn mixture into a 10x6x1½-inch baking dish; sprinkle with remaining bacon. Bake at 350° for 30 minutes or till knife inserted in center comes out clean. Makes 8 servings.

## CORN CUSTARD CASSEROLE

1 10½-ounce can condensed
   cream of celery soup
2 tablespoons all-purpose flour
1 tablespoon prepared mustard
1 12-ounce can whole kernel corn
1 6-ounce can evaporated milk

2 tablespoons chopped green
   pepper
2 tablespoons chopped onion
2 tablespoons chopped pimiento
2 slightly beaten eggs
1 teaspoon Worcestershire sauce

Blend soup, flour, mustard, and dash salt; stir in remaining
ingredients. Turn into 10x6x1½-inch baking dish. Bake at
350° for 30 to 40 minutes or till knife inserted in center comes
out clean. Makes 6 servings.

## CORN CAULIFLOWER BAKE

1 10-ounce package frozen
   cauliflower, thawed
1 1-pound can whole kernel
   corn, drained
1 10½-ounce can condensed
   cream of celery soup

2 tablespoons chopped pimiento
4 ounces sharp process American
   cheese, shredded (1 cup)
½ cup cornflake crumbs
1 tablespoon butter, melted

Slice large pieces of cauliflower in half. Place in 10x6x1½-
inch baking dish. Combine next 3 ingredients; bring to boil.
Pour over cauliflower. Bake at 375° for 25 minutes. Top with
cheese and combined crumbs and butter. Bake 5 minutes
longer. Serves 6.

## GREEN BEANS SUPREME

½ teaspoon grated onion
2 tablespoons butter or margarine
2 tablespoons all-purpose flour
½ teaspoon sugar
½ teaspoon salt
   Dash pepper
½ cup milk
½ cup dairy sour cream

2 1-pound cans cut green beans,
   drained
4 ounces process Swiss cheese,
   shredded (1 cup)
   . . .
⅓ cup cornflake crumbs
1 tablespoon butter or margarine,
   melted

In skillet cook onion in butter slightly, about 1 minute. Blend
in flour, sugar, salt, and pepper. Add milk all at once and
cook till thick and bubbly. Remove from heat; stir in sour
cream. Add beans. Spread *one-third* of the bean mixture in

1-quart casserole. Sprinkle *one-half* the Swiss cheese over beans; repeat layers, ending with beans.

Combine cornflake crumbs and melted butter or margarine; toss until well mixed. Top beans with cornflake mixture. Bake in hot oven (400°) for 20 minutes. Makes 3 servings.

# FESTIVE CELERY CASSEROLE

4 cups celery cut in ¼-inch slices
2 tablespoons butter or margarine
1 10½-ounce can condensed cream of celery soup
2 tablespoons chopped canned pimiento

2 tablespoons milk
½ cup finely crushed cheese-flavored rich round cracker crumbs (12 crackers)
1 tablespoon butter or margarine, melted

In a saucepan cook celery, covered, in 2 tablespoons butter for 15 to 20 minutes or till tender. Stir in soup, milk, and pimiento. Pour into a 1-quart casserole. Combine the cracker crumbs and 1 tablespoon melted butter. Sprinkle crumbs over casserole. Bake at 350° for 30 minutes or till hot. Serves 4 to 6.

---

## TEST KITCHEN TIPS

### Oven-cooked vegetables—for easy meals

*Place a package of frozen beans, broccoli, or corn in a shallow baking dish. Add a little butter, salt, and pepper. Cover and bake vegetables along with the rest of the dinner. Allow about 45 minutes at 350° or 55 minutes at 325° for the vegetables to cook. Stir occasionally. Helps reduce last-minute fuss.*

---

## POTATO-TOMATO SCALLOP

In a skillet cook ½ cup chopped onion in 2 tablespons butter or margarine till tender but not brown. Blend in 2 tablespoons all-purpose flour, 1 teaspoon paprika, ½ teaspoon salt, and ⅛ teaspoon pepper. Add 1 cup water, one 8-ounce can (1 cup) tomatoes, and 2 chicken bouillon cubes.

Cook and stir over medium heat till bouillon cubes dissolve

and mixture thickens and bubbles. Layer 5 cups pared and thinly sliced raw potatoes in greased 2-quart casserole. Pour the tomato sauce over sliced potatoes.

Cover and bake in hot oven (400°) for 1 to 1¼ hours. Makes 6 to 8 servings.

## STUFFED TOMATOES

6 medium tomatoes
1 pint fresh mushrooms, chopped (about 1½ cups)
2 tablespoons butter or margarine
½ cup dairy sour cream
2 beaten egg yolks
¼ cup fine dry bread crumbs

1 teaspoon salt
Dash pepper
Dash dried thyme, crushed
1 tablespon butter, melted
3 tablespoons fine dry bread crumbs

Cut stem end from tomatoes; scoop out pulp. Drain shells. Chop pulp fine; measure 1 cup; set aside. Cook mushrooms in 2 tablespoons butter till just tender (about 5 minutes). Combine sour cream and egg yolks. Add to mushrooms with reserved tomato pulp; mix well. Stir in ¼ cup crumbs, salt, pepper, and thyme. Cook and stir till mixture thickens and bubbles. Place tomato shells in 10x6x1½-inch baking dish. Spoon mushroom mixture into tomatoes.

Combine 1 tablespoon melted butter and 3 tablespoons fine dry bread crumbs; sprinkle atop tomatoes. Bake in moderate oven (375°) for 25 minutes. Makes 6 servings.

## BAKED TOMATOES

4 medium whole tomatoes
¼ cup salad oil
1 tablespoon sugar
1½ teaspoons instant minced onion
¼ teaspoon salt

¼ teaspoon dry mustard
1½ tablespoons vinegar
¼ teaspoon Worcestershire sauce
⅓ cup medium cracker crumbs
1 tablespoon butter or margarine, melted

Cut thin slices from top of each tomato. Hollow out slightly. Combine salad oil, sugar, onion, salt, mustard, vinegar, and Worcestershire sauce. Spoon into center of each tomato. Combine cracker crumbs and butter. Sprinkle over top of tomatoes. Place in 9-inch pie plate or shallow baking dish. Bake in moderate oven (350°) 30 minutes. Makes 4 servings.

## MUSHROOM CASSEROLE

½ cup chopped onion
½ cup butter or margarine
2 6-ounce cans mushroom crowns, drained
¼ cup all-purpose flour
½ teaspoon dried marjoram, crushed
2 tablespoons dry sherry

1 10½-ounce can condensed beef broth
2 tablespoons snipped parsley
½ cup coarse cracker crumbs
2 tablespoons grated Parmesan cheese
1 tablespoon butter or margarine, melted

Cook onion in butter until almost tender. Add mushrooms; cook lightly. Blend in flour and marjoram. Add beef broth all at once. Cook and stir till mixture thickens and bubbles. Remove from heat; stir in wine and parsley. Pour into 1-quart casserole.

Combine cracker crumbs, Parmesan cheese, and melted butter; sprinkle over casserole. Bake in a moderate oven (375°) about 15 minutes or till hot and bubbly. Serves 6.

# CHEESE AND EGG SPECIALS

## CHEESE SOUFFLE

6 tablespoons butter or
  margarine
⅓ cup all-purpose flour
½ teaspoon salt
  Dash cayenne

1½ cups milk
¾ pound sharp natural Cheddar
  cheese, shredded or diced
6 egg yolks
6 stiffly beaten egg whites

Melt butter; blend in flour and seasonings. Add milk all at
once. Cook over medium heat, stirring till thick and bubbly.
Remove from heat. Add cheese; stir till cheese melts.

Beat egg yolks till thick and lemon-colored. Slowly add
cheese mixture, stirring constantly. Cool slightly. Gradually
pour over beaten egg whites, folding in thoroughly. Pour into
*ungreased* 2-quart souffle dish.

Attach a "collar" to the souffle dish for a high souffle:
Measure enough foil or waxed paper to go around casserole
plus a 2- to 3-inch overlap. Fold foil in thirds, lengthwise.
Lightly butter one side. Letting collar extend 2 inches above
top of casserole, fasten with pins around the dish (buttered
side in).

Bake in a slow oven (300°) about 1½ hours or till knife
inserted halfway between center and edge comes out clean.
Gently peel off collar and serve immediately. Serves 6 to 8.

## SPINACH SOUFFLE

1  10-ounce package frozen              ¼ cup grated Parmesan cheese
   chopped spinach
2  tablespoons butter or margarine      · · ·
2  tablespoons all-purpose flour        5  egg yolks
½  teaspoon salt                        5  stiffly beaten egg whites
½  cup milk                                Cheddar Cheese Sauce

Cook spinach following package directions. Drain *very thoroughly*. Add butter to spinach; cook and stir over high heat till butter is melted. Blend in flour and salt; add milk all at once. Cook and stir over medium heat till mixture thickens and bubbles. Remove from heat; stir in grated Parmesan cheese.

Beat egg yolks till thick and lemon-colored. Stir spinach into egg yolks. Pour spinach mixture over egg whites; fold together carefully. Pour into *ungreased* 1-quart souffle dish. Bake at 350° for 30 to 35 minutes or till knife inserted halfway between center and edge comes out clean. Makes 4 to 6 servings. Serve with *Cheddar Cheese Sauce:* Combine one 10½-ounce can condensed cream of mushroom soup and ⅓ cup milk; heat. Add 4 ounces sharp natural Cheddar cheese, shredded (1 cup); stir to melt.

---

## TEST KITCHEN TIPS

### These pointers assure a puffy souffle

*Yolks are not as likely to break if separated from the whites while still cold from refrigerator.*

*Let egg whites warm to room temperature before beating for greater volume.*

*Beat egg yolks till thick and lemon-colored. Egg whites are beaten till stiff but still glossy—never dry.*

*Stir the ready-and-waiting hot sauce slowly into the beaten egg yolks.*

*Fold sauce mixture into beaten whites; gently lift up-and-over in high strokes. Take your time.*

*To help the souffle "climb," use an ungreased dish.*

*Never keep a souffle waiting. Whisk it right from oven to*

*table. Treat this airy dish tenderly—break apart into servings with two forks.*

*For a souffle that's extra high, measure waxed paper or foil to go around top of dish and overlap 1 inch. Fold in thirds lengthwise. Butter one side. Letting collar extend 2 inches above casserole, fasten around dish (butter side in) with cellophane tape or pins.*

*For a top hat that puffs in the oven, use tip of spoon to trace circle in mixture 1 inch from edge and about 1 inch deep.*

## SOUR CREAM HAM OMELET

5 egg yolks
1 cup dairy sour cream
¼ teaspoon salt
5 stiffly beaten egg whites

1 cup finely diced cooked ham
2 tablespoons butter or margarine
Glazed Apples

Beat egg yolks till thick and lemon-colored, about 5 minutes. Beat in *half* of the dairy sour cream and ¼ teaspoon salt. Fold in stiffly beaten egg whites and ham.

Heat butter in 10-inch oven-going skillet. Pour in omelet mixture, leveling gently. Cook over low heat until lightly browned on bottom, about 10 minutes. Finish cooking in slow oven (325°) till top is golden brown, about 12 to 15 minutes. Loosen omelet; slide onto warm plate. Separate into wedges with two forks. Garnish with remaining sour cream and serve with Glazed Apples. Makes 4 servings.

## GLAZED APPLES

3 tablespoons butter or margarine
⅓ cup brown sugar
½ teaspoon ground cinnamon

Dash salt
3 unpared tart apples, thinly sliced

Melt butter in skillet. Stir in brown sugar, cinnamon, and salt. Add apples. Cook 10 to 15 minutes, stirring occasionally till apples are tender and glazed. Makes 4 servings.

## SAUCED BLUE CHEESE EGGS

Hard-cook 5 eggs; peel. Halve eggs lengthwise; remove yolks and mash. Add 3 tablespoons mayonnaise or salad dressing,

2 tablespoons crumbled blue cheese, and dash salt; mix well. Spoon into egg whites. Arrange egg halves in 8-inch round baking dish.

Prepare 1 envelope sour cream sauce mix according to package directions using 2 *tablespoons additional milk*. Stir in ½ teaspoon snipped chives. Pour over eggs. Combine ½ cup soft bread crumbs, 1 tablespoon butter, melted, and dash paprika. Sprinkle over eggs. Bake uncovered in moderate oven (350°) about 20 minutes. Makes 3 or 4 servings.

# Scrambled eggs

## BASIC SCRAMBLED EGGS

6 eggs
⅓ cup milk or light cream
¼ to ½ teaspoon salt

Dash pepper

· · ·

2 tablespoons butter, margarine,
    or bacon fat

Beat eggs, milk, salt, and pepper with fork. (Mix slightly for eggs with streaks of yellow and white; mix well for a uniform yellow.) Heat butter, margarine, or bacon fat in skillet till just hot enough to make a drop of water sizzle. Pour in egg mixture. Turn heat low. Don't disturb mixture till it starts to set on bottom and sides, then lift and fold over with wide spatula so uncooked part goes to bottom. Avoid breaking up eggs any more than necessary. Continue cooking (5 to 8 minutes) till eggs are cooked throughout, but still glossy and moist. Remove from heat immediately. Makes 3 or 4 servings.

*Herb Scrambled Eggs:* Prepare Basic Scrambled Eggs adding 1 tablespoon snipped parsley *or* chives and dash dried thyme, crushed, to the seasoned egg-milk mixture. Continue as directed in Basic Scrambled Eggs.

*Cheese Scrambled Eggs:* Prepare Basic Scrambled Eggs adding one 3-ounce package cream cheese with chives, cut into pieces, to the seasoned egg-milk mixture. Continue as directed in Basic Scrambled Eggs.

*Deviled Scrambled Egg:* In skillet cook 1 tablespoon chopped onion in 2 tablespoons butter, margarine, or bacon fat till tender. Prepare Basic Scrambled Eggs adding ¼ teaspoon monosodium glutamate, ½ teaspoon dry mustard, 1 tablespoon snipped parsley, ¼ teaspoon Worcestershire sauce, and one 2-ounce canned chopped mushrooms, drained, to the seasoned egg-milk mixture. Add to skillet; continue as in Basic Scrambled Eggs.

## MEXICAN SCRAMBLE

| | |
|---|---|
| ½ cup chopped onion | Dash pepper |
| ¼ cup chopped green pepper | 2 ounces sharp process American |
| 2 tablespoons butter or margarine | cheese, diced (½ cup) |
| 1 8-ounce can (1 cup) tomatoes | 4 beaten eggs |
| ½ teaspoon paprika | . . . |
| ¼ teaspoon salt | 4 slices buttered toast |

In skillet cook onion and green pepper in butter till tender. Add tomatoes and simmer 5 minutes. Add paprika, salt, pepper, and cheese; stir to melt cheese. Stir small amount of hot mixture into eggs; return to hot mixture. Cook till thick (like scrambled eggs), but moist, stirring frequently. Serve with hot buttered toast. Makes 4 servings.

## VIENNA SAUSAGE SCRAMBLE

| | |
|---|---|
| 1 4-ounce can Vienna sausages, sliced (1 cup) | 2 tablespoons butter or margarine |
| | 8 eggs |
| 2 tablespoons chopped green pepper | ½ cup milk |
| | ½ teaspoon salt |
| 2 tablespoons chopped green onion | Dash pepper |

In medium skillet cook sliced Vienna sausages, green pepper, and onion in hot butter till sausage is lightly browned; reduce heat. Beat eggs, milk, salt, and pepper with fork. (Mix slightly for eggs with streaks of yellow and white; mix well for a uniform yellow.) Pour into skillet. When mixture starts to set at bottom and sides, lift and turn over cooked portions with spatula or large spoon.

Continue cooking till the eggs are cooked throughout, but still glossy and moist. Serve immediately. Garnish with additional green onion tops, if desired. Makes 4 or 5 servings.

## CLASSIC CHEESE STRATA

| | |
|---|---|
| 8 slices day old bread | 2½ cups milk |
| 8 ounces sharp natural Cheddar cheese, sliced | 1 tablespoon minced onion |
| | 1½ teaspoons salt |
| 4 eggs | ½ teaspoon prepared mustard |

Trim crusts from 5 *slices* of the bread; cut in half diagonally. Use trimmings and remaining 3 slices *untrimmed* bread to cover bottom of 8- or 9-inch square baking dish. Top with cheese. Arrange the 10 trimmed "triangles" in 2 rows atop the cheese. (Points should overlap bases of the preceding "triangles.")

Beat eggs; blend in milk, onion, salt, dash pepper, and mustard. Pour over bread and cheese. Cover with waxed paper; let stand 1 hour at room temperature or several hours in refrigerator. Bake in slow oven (325°) for 1 hour or till knife inserted halfway between center and edge comes out clean. Let stand 5 minutes before serving. Makes 6 servings.

## CHEESE CORN STRATA

Prepare Classic Cheese Strata increasing onion to 2 tablespoons and decreasing salt to 1 teaspoon. Using a 9-inch square baking dish, spread one 1-pound can whole kernel corn over top of *untrimmed* bread and cheese layer. Arrange the 10 trimmed "triangles" in 2 rows atop corn. Continue as directed for Classic Cheese Strata. Makes 6 to 8 servings.

## MACARONI OMELET

| | |
|---|---|
| ¼ cup elbow macaroni | ¼ cup shredded sharp process American cheese |
| 4 egg yolks | |
| Dash salt | 2 tablespoons butter or margarine |
| 4 stiffly beaten egg whites | Creole Sauce |

Cook macaroni in boiling salted water till tender; drain. Beat

egg yolks with salt till thick and lemon-colored; stir in macaroni and cheese. Fold in egg whites. Melt butter in 10-inch
skillet; when hot, pour in omelet mixture. Cook over low heat
8 minutes or till lightly browned. Loosen with spatula. Make
shallow cut across center of omelet; fold in half. Remove to
hot platter; serve with Creole Sauce. Makes 4 to 6 servings.

*Creole Sauce:* Cook 3 tablespoons finely chopped onion
and 3 tablespoons finely chopped green pepper in 2 tablespoons butter or margarine till tender but not brown. Add
one 8-ounce can tomato sauce, one 3-ounce can broiled
chopped mushrooms with liquid, and dash pepper. Simmer
uncovered 10 minutes, stirring occasionally. Makes 1⅓ cups.

## TEST KITCHEN TIPS

### Some hints for cooking with cheese

*When cooking on top of the range, use low heat and a short
cooking time. Cook, stirring constantly, just till cheese melts.
High temperatures and prolonged cooking will toughen cheese.
For minimum melting time, use grated, shredded, or cubed
cheese.*

*If cheese is to be used as a topping on baked dishes,
sprinkle it on during the last 5 minutes of baking time.*

## EGGS A LA ASPARAGUS

3 tablespoons butter or margarine
3 tablespoons all-purpose flour
½ teaspoon salt
  Dash pepper
2 ounces sharp process American
  cheese, shredded (½ cup)

2 cups milk
4 hard-cooked eggs, sliced
1 10-ounce package frozen
  asparagus spears, cooked and
  drained
4 slices toast

In 2-quart saucepan, melt butter over low heat; blend in flour,
salt, and pepper. Add milk all at once; cook, stirring constantly, till mixture thickens and bubbles.

Add cheese; stir till melted. Fold in egg slices. Arrange hot asparagus spears on toast. Pour egg mixture over asparagus. Sprinkle with paprika, if desired. Makes 4 servings.

## CREOLE RAREBIT

4 slices bacon, diced
½ cup chopped onion
½ cup diced green pepper
1 1-pound can (2 cups) tomatoes
½ teaspoon salt
  Dash pepper
1 teaspoon Worcestershire sauce

2 tablespoons butter or margarine
3 tablespoons all-purpose flour
⅔ cup milk
2 ounces sharp process American cheese, shredded (½ cup)
4 to 6 slices buttered toast

Cook bacon till crisp; add onion and green pepper and cook till tender but not brown. Add tomatoes, salt, pepper, and Worcestershire sauce; simmer uncovered for 15 minutes.

In a saucepan melt butter; blend in flour. Add milk all at once. Cook, stirring constantly, till mixture thickens and bubbles. Add shredded process cheese; stir till cheese is melted. Remove from heat.

Slowly stir hot tomato mixture into cheese sauce. Serve tomato-cheese sauce over buttered toast. Makes 4 to 6 servings.

## SWISS CHEESE-EGG BAKE

6 hard-cooked eggs, sliced
6 ounces process Swiss cheese, shredded (1½ cups)
1 10½-ounce can condensed cream of chicken soup

¾ cup milk
½ teaspoon prepared mustard
6 slices buttered French bread, ½ inch thick

Reserve 6 egg slices for garnish. Place remaining egg slices in bottom of 10x6x1½-inch baking dish or 1½-quart casserole. Sprinkle eggs with shredded cheese. In a saucepan mix soup, milk, and mustard; heat, stirring till smooth. Pour sauce over eggs, being sure some sauce goes to bottom of dish.

Place buttered bread slices on top, overlapping slightly. Bake in moderate oven (350°) for 35 minutes or till heated through. Garnish with reserved egg slices. Sprinkle with paprika, if desired. Makes 6 servings.

# EGGS IN SPANISH SAUCE

½ cup chopped onion
3 tablespoons butter or margarine
3 tablespoons all-purpose flour
2 teaspoons sugar
¾ teaspoon salt
Dash pepper
1 1-pound 12-ounce can tomatoes
1 small bay leaf

6 hard-cooked eggs
¼ cup mayonnaise or salad dressing
1 teaspoon prepared mustard
⅛ teaspoon salt
Dash pepper
¾ cup fine dry bread crumbs
2 tablespoons butter, melted

In a skillet cook onion in butter till tender. Blend in flour, sugar, salt, and pepper. Add tomatoes and bay leaf. Cook till thick and bubbly, stirring constantly. Remove bay leaf. Pour into 10x6x1½-inch baking dish. Prepare deviled eggs: Halve eggs lengthwise. Remove yolks and mash. Mix with mayonnaise, mustard, salt, and pepper; refill egg whites. Put in dish. Combine crumbs and butter; sprinkle atop. Bake at 425° for 10 minutes or till hot. Serve over buttered noodles or toast. Serves 6.

# MACARONI CHEESE DELUXE

1 7-ounce package elbow macaroni
2 cups small curd cream-style cottage cheese
1 cup dairy sour cream
1 slightly beaten egg

¾ teaspoon salt
Dash pepper
8 ounces sharp process American cheese, shredded (2 cups)
Paprika

Cook macaroni according to package directions; drain well. Combine cottage cheese, sour cream, egg, salt, and pepper. Add shredded cheese, mixing well; stir in cooked macaroni. Turn into a greased 9x9x2-inch baking dish. Sprinkle with paprika. Bake in moderate oven (350°) for 45 minutes. Serves 6 to 8.

# BEST MACARONI AND CHEESE

1 7-ounce package macaroni
6 ounces sharp process American cheese, shredded (1½ cups)
3 beaten eggs
1½ cups milk
1 teaspoon salt

½ teaspoon monosodium glutamate
1 tablespoon Worcestershire sauce
Dash bottled hot pepper sauce

Cook macaroni according to package directions; drain. Turn
into 10x6x1½-inch baking dish. Thoroughly combine cheese,
eggs, milk, salt, monosodium glutamate, Worcestershire sauce,
and bottled hot pepper sauce. Pour mixture over macaroni.

Place baking dish in shallow pan; pour hot water into
pan to depth of 1 inch. Bake at 325° for 40 to 45 minutes.
Serves 6 to 8.

## MACARONI AND CHEESE PUFF

| | |
|---|---|
| ½ cup uncooked small elbow macaroni | 3 beaten egg yolks |
| 1½ cups milk | 1 cup soft bread crumbs |
| 6 ounces sharp process American cheese, shredded (1½ cups) | ¼ cup chopped canned pimiento |
| | 1 tablespoon snipped parsley |
| 3 tablespoons butter or margarine | 1 tablespoon grated onion |
| | 3 egg whites |
| | ¼ teaspoon cream of tartar |

Cook macaroni according to package directions; drain. Combine milk, cheese, and butter; cook and stir over low heat till
cheese is melted. Stir small amount of hot mixture into egg
yolks; return to remaining hot mixture in pan; blend thoroughly. Add cooked macaroni, crumbs, pimiento, parsley, and
onion.

Beat egg whites and cream of tartar till stiff but not dry.
Gently fold into macaroni mixture. Pour into *ungreased*
1½-quart soufflé dish. Bake in slow oven (325°) for 1 hour
or till set. Serve immediately. Serves 6.

---

## TEST KITCHEN TIPS

### Cheese—how to melt and measure

*When the casserole starts with cheese sauce, get it off to a
smooth start.*

Process cheese *melts easily and quickly. Slice it into a saucepan of milk, broth, or sauce—either hot or cold. Heat only
till cheese melts, stirring frequently.*

*To keep* natural cheese *smooth in cooking, place sauce
over hot water before adding the cheese. Crumble, shred
cheese, or cut julienne style; stir into hot mixture.*

*When buying cheese, allow 4 ounces for each 1 cup shredded or cubed cheese.*

# CANADIAN CHEESE SOUP

¼ cup finely chopped onion
2 tablespoons butter or margarine
¼ cup all-purpose flour
2 cups milk
2 cups chicken broth

¼ cup finely diced carrot
¼ cup finely diced celery
2 ounces sharp process American cheese, cubed (½ cup)
Snipped parsley

In a saucepan cook onion in butter till tender. Blend in flour. Add milk, chicken broth, carrots, celery, dash paprika, and dash salt. Cook, stirring constantly till mixture thickens and bubbles. Reduce heat; add cheese and stir till melted. Simmer for 15 minutes or until vegetables are tender. Garnish with snipped parsley. Makes 4 cups soup.

# NOODLES, SPAGHETTI, MACARONI

## CHEDDAR-MACARONI BAKE

Cook 4 ounces (1½ cups) corkscrew macaroni in large amount of boiling salted water; drain. Combine with 2 tablespoons all-purpose flour, ¼ teaspoon dry mustard, ¼ teaspoon salt, dash pepper, and ¼ cup sliced pimiento-stuffed green olives. Turn into a 1-quart casserole.

Combine 1¾ cups milk, 6 ounces sharp process American cheese, shredded (1½ cups), and ½ teaspoon Worcestershire sauce. Heat till cheese melts. Pour over macaroni mixture. Combine 1 cup soft bread crumbs and 2 tablespoons melted butter. Sprinkle atop casserole. Bake in moderate oven (350°) for 40 minutes, or until hot. Serves 4.

## CHICKEN-NOODLE BAKE

8 ounces lasagne noodles
⅓ cup chopped onion
⅓ cup chopped green pepper
2 tablespoons butter
1 10½-ounce can condensed cream of mushroom soup
1 cup milk
½ teaspoon poultry seasoning

2 3-ounce packages cream cheese, softened
1 cup cream-style cottage cheese
¼ cup sliced pimiento-stuffed green olives
¼ cup snipped parsley
3 cups diced cooked chicken
1 cup buttered soft bread crumbs

Cook noodles in large amount of boiling salted water till tender; drain; rinse in cold water. In saucepan cook onion and green pepper in butter till tender. Add soup, milk, and poultry seasoning; heat. Beat cheeses together; stir in green olives and parsley.

Place *half* the noodles in a 12x7½x2-inch baking dish; layer with *half* the cheese mixture, *half* the chicken, and *half* the soup mixture. Repeat layers. Top with crumbs.

Bake at 375° for 45 minutes or till heated through. Let stand 10 minutes. Serves 8.

## CHILI MOSTACCIOLI

1 pound ground beef
½ cup milk
1 cup soft bread crumbs
1 teaspoon salt
Dash pepper
2 tablespoons shortening
1 clove garlic, minced

¼ cup chopped onion
2 11-ounce cans condensed chili-beef soup
1 soup can water
7 ounces mostaccioli or tubular macaroni (3 cups)
Grated Parmesan cheese

Combine meat, milk, crumbs, salt, and pepper; shape into five oblong patties. In skillet brown patties in hot shortening. Remove. Cook garlic and onion in skillet till tender but not brown. Blend in soup and water. Return patties to skillet. Bring mixture to boil; simmer covered 15 minutes.

Cook mostaccioli according to package directions; drain; place on large heated platter. Arrange patties on noodles. Pour sauce over meat; sprinkle cheese atop. Serves 5.

## HOMEMADE NOODLES

Combine 1 beaten egg, 2 tablespoons milk, and ½ teaspoon salt. Add enough of 1 cup sifted all-purpose flour to make stiff dough. Roll *very thin* on floured surface. Let stand 20 minutes. Roll up loosely; slice ¼ inch wide. Unroll, spread out, and let dry 2 hours. To cook, drop noodles into boiling soup or boiling salted water. Cook uncovered about 10 minutes. Makes 3 cups cooked noodles.

*Note:* To store for later use, place uncooked noodles in plastic bag.

## TEST KITCHEN TIPS

### Do not overcook noodles and macaroni

Cook pasta "al dente." This means the noodle or macaroni is cooked till tender, yet firm. The thinner or finer the noodle the faster it cooks—be a pot watcher. Drain immediately when done.

## HUNGARIAN NOODLE BAKE

| | |
|---|---|
| 4 ounces fine egg noodles | 1 cup dairy sour cream |
| ¼ cup finely chopped onion | 1 teaspoon Worcestershire sauce |
| 1 clove garlic, minced | Dash bottled hot pepper sauce |
| 1 tablespoon butter or margarine | 2 teaspoons poppy seed |
| 1½ cups cream-style cottage | ½ teaspoon salt |
|    cheese | Dash pepper |

Cook noodles in large amount of boiling salted water till tender; drain. Meanwhile, cook onion and garlic in butter or margarine till tender but not brown. Combine noodles and onion mixture with cream-style cottage cheese, dairy sour cream, Worcestershire sauce, bottled hot pepper sauce, poppy seed, salt, and pepper. Turn into a greased 10x6x1½-inch baking dish. Bake in moderate oven (350°) for about 25 minutes or till heated through. Sprinkle with paprika, if desired. Serve with grated Parmesan cheese. Makes 6 servings.

*Note:* Add one 9¼-ounce can (1 cup) tuna, flaked, if desired. Makes 8 servings.

# NOODLES ROMANO

¼ cup butter or margarine,
   softened

2 tablespoons dried parsley flakes

1 teaspoon dried basil, crushed

1 8-ounce package cream cheese,
   softened

⅛ teaspoon pepper

⅔ cup boiling water

8 ounces fettucini, thin
   noodles, or spaghetti

1 clove garlic, minced

¼ cup butter or margarine

¾ cup shredded or grated Romano
   or Parmesan cheese

*Cream Cheese Sauce:* Combine the ¼ cup butter, parsley flakes, and basil; blend in cream cheese, and pepper; stir in ⅔ cup boiling water; blend mixture well. Keep warm over pan of hot water.

Cook noodles in large amount boiling salted water till just tender; drain. Cook garlic in the ¼ cup butter 1 to 2 minutes; pour over noodles; toss lightly and quickly to coat well.

Sprinkle with ½ *cup of the cheese;* toss again. Pile noodles on warm serving platter; spoon the warm Cream Cheese Sauce over; sprinkle with remaining ¼ cup cheese; garnish with additional parsley, if desired. Serves 6.

# SPAGHETTI TURNOVER

1 tablespoon salt

3 quarts boiling water

7 ounces spaghetti

. . .

½ cup chopped celery

¼ cup chopped onion

1 tablespoon poppy seed

½ teaspoon salt

¼ teaspoon pepper

½ cup light cream

8 ounces sharp natural Cheddar
   cheese, shredded (2 cups)

Snipped parsley (optional)

Add 1 tablespoon salt to rapidly boiling water. Gradually add spaghetti so that water continues to boil. Cook uncovered, stirring occasionally, until just tender. Drain. Combine spaghetti, celery, onion, poppy seed, ½ teaspoon salt, pepper and cream.

Lightly grease a large skillet; heat. Spoon *half* the spaghetti mixture into the skillet; top with 1½ *cups* of the Cheddar cheese. Top with remaining spaghetti mixture and sprinkle with remaining cheese. Cover and cook over medium heat 25 to 30 minutes, running spatula under mixture occasionally to prevent sticking. Unmold onto serving platter. Garnish with parsley, if desired. Serves 6.

## TEST KITCHEN TIPS

### An easy way to cook long spaghetti

*No need to break long spaghetti—hold a handful at one end, dip the other into the boiling water. As spaghetti softens, curl it around in pan till immersed.*

## TEST KITCHEN TIPS

### This is the way to cook pasta

*A large pan is important in cooking pasta—spaghetti, macaroni, fine noodles, or lasagne. Use lots of water—3 quarts is the minimum for cooking 8 ounces of pasta. Add 1 teaspoon salt for each quart water.*

*Don't cover; stir at the start of cooking to prevent sticking. The addition of a teaspoon of salad oil helps prevent sticking and water boiling over.*

*To keep spaghetti hot: Drain spaghetti in colander and place colander over pan containing small amount of boiling water. Coat spaghetti with 3 or 4 tablespoons butter or margarine (for 6 servings) to keep spaghetti strands from sticking together. Cover colander.*

*Or, for a short time, return drained spaghetti to the empty cooking pan, add butter, then cover to keep warm.*

*Yield of uncooked pasta: As a general rule, macaroni and spaghetti double in volume with cooking. Egg noodles give approximately the same volume before and after cooking.*

## MUSHROOM PASTA SAUCE

| | |
|---|---|
| 1 cup chopped onion | 2 8-ounce cans tomato sauce |
| 1 clove garlic, minced | 3 tablespoons snipped parsley |
| 2 tablespoons olive or salad oil | 1 tablespoon sugar |
| 1 6-ounce can broiled chopped mushrooms, undrained (1⅓ cups) | ½ teaspoon salt |
| | 1 teaspoon dried basil, crushed |

Cook onion and garlic in hot oil till tender but not brown. Add tomato sauce, mushrooms with liquid, parsley, sugar, salt, and basil; mix together thoroughly.

Simmer uncovered about 45 minutes or till of desired consistency. Serve over hot spaghetti or other pasta. Pass grated Parmesan cheese to sprinkle atop. Serves 4 to 6.

# An encore for leftovers

Turn lowly leftovers into winning casseroles. Our guide to leftovers suggests ways to use every last morsel of beef, chicken, turkey, ham, lamb, and veal. Use the suggestions below and those from the chart to add new interest to your leftover foods.

• Limit the number of leftover ingredients in a casserole.

• Combine foods that are compatible in flavor and color, but contrasting in texture.

• Keep food in identifiable pieces so the mixture won't be homogenized. Layer ingredients occasionally instead of combining them.

• Casseroles absorb some liquid during baking, so avoid too thick a sauce.

• Make the most of canned and frozen soups, dry soup and sauce mixes, canned gravies, and bottled gravy bases for quick sauces.

• Use herbs and spices imaginatively.

• Perk up casseroles with a dash of wine.

# SWISS TURKEY-HAM BAKE

*Leftovers made elegant with water chestnuts and wine—*

In a skillet cook ½ cup chopped onion in 2 tablespoons butter or margarine till onion is tender but not brown. Blend in 3 tablespoons all-purpose flour, ½ teaspoon salt, and ¼ teaspoon pepper. Add one 3-ounce can sliced mushrooms, undrained (⅔ cup), 1 cup light cream, and 2 tablespoons dry sherry; cook and stir mixture till thick and bubbly.

Add 2 cups cubed cooked turkey, 1 cup cubed cooked ham, and one 5-ounce can water chestnuts, drained and sliced (⅔ cup).

Pour into 1½-quart casserole; top with 2 ounces process Swiss cheese, shredded (½ cup). Mix 1½ cups soft bread crumbs and 3 tablespoons butter or margarine, melted; sprinkle around edge of casserole.

Bake in hot oven (400°) for 25 minutes, till lightly browned. Makes 6 servings.

# A GUIDE FOR LEFTOVERS

| MEAT | HERBS AND SPICES | FLAVOR ACCENTS | WINES | RECIPES |
|------|------------------|----------------|-------|---------|
| Beef | Allspice, Basil, Bay Leaves, Caraway Seed, Celery Seed, Chili Powder, Cumin, Ginger, Mace, Marjoram, Oregano, Rosemary, Savory, Tarragon, Thyme | Barbecue Sauce, Beets, Cheddar Cheese, Eggplant, Green Peppers, Tomato Sauce, Zucchini | Burgundy, Claret | Bavarian-style Stew Best Oven Hash Burgundy Beef Stew Chuck Wagon Stew Curried Beef Cubes Monday Meat Pie Pioneer Beef Stew Skillet Hash Sweet-sour Stew |
| Chicken and Turkey | Bay Leaves, Curry, Ginger, Marjoram, Oregano, Rosemary, Saffron, Sage, Tarragon, Thyme | Almonds, Lemon Juice, Olives, Pecans, Potato Chips, Soy Sauce, Spiced Peaches, Sweet Potatoes, Water Chestnuts | Rhine, Rosé, Sauterne, Sherry | Chicken a la King Bake Chicken-chip Bake Chicken Dinner Bake Chicken-pecan Waffles Chicken Strata Chicken with Noodles Chinese Chicken Easy Chicken Divan Fancy Chicken a la King Gourmet Delight Ham-turkey Casserole Jiffy Turkey Paella Quick Chicken a la King Quick Turkey Pie Sweet Potato Chicken Pie Swiss Turkey-ham Bake Turkey Cheese Puff Turkey Noodle Casserole Turkey Parisian |
| Ham | Allspice, Cloves, Ginger, Mustard | Asparagus, Green Pepper, Peaches, Pineapple, Sour Cream, Soy Sauce, Swiss Cheese, Water Chestnuts | Rosé | Cantonese Casserole Cauliflower-ham Bake Chinese Fried Rice Ham in Sour Cream Ham-potatoes au Gratin Ham Medley Ham 'n Cheese Delight Ham Puffs Ham Succotash Ham-turkey Casserole Hawaiian Sweet-sour Ham Sour Cream Ham Omelet Swiss Ham Pie Swiss Turkey-ham Bake |
| Lamb | Allspice, Basil, Caraway Seed, Curry, Dill, Garlic, Ginger, Marjoram, Mint, Oregano, Rosemary, Savory, Thyme | Coconut, Crab Apples, Currants, Green Onions, Kumquats, Mango Chutney, Mint Jelly, Peanuts, Raisins | Brandy, Madeira, Sauterne, Sherry | Curried Lamb Lamb Stew 'n Dumplings Shepherd's Pie Spring Lamb Stew |
| Veal | Bay Leaves, Ginger, Mace, Marjoram, Mint, Oregano, Rosemary, Savory, Thyme | Bacon, Mozzarella Cheese, Olives, Parmesan Cheese, Spinach, Tomato Sauce | Sauterne | Veal and Carrots Veal Noodle Bake Veal Olive Saute Veal Stew with Ravioli |

# Freezing one-dish meals

Make your dinner casserole a "double header." Freeze half and keep it as a main dish ready to heat and eat on a busy day.

Take advantage of peak-of-the-season vegetables and plentiful meats. Buy in quantity, then whip up a batch of a la king, stew, or a casserole. Freeze in family-size portions.

Before fixing food for the freezer, brush up on these do's and don'ts:

• Don't oversalt or overseason—it's better to add more later if needed. Some ingredients—garlic, pepper, and celery—intensify during freezing, so decrease amounts slightly.

• Don't overcook foods to be frozen.

• Undercook noodles, rice, macaroni, and spaghetti products. Reheating the casserole later will complete the cooking.

• Use as little fat in cooking as possible. It doesn't blend in well when reheated.

• Mashed potatoes, macaroni, rice, noodles, and biscuits tend to be pasty if frozen with sauce or a moist food.

• Add toppings—crushed potato chips, crumbs, and grated cheese—at reheating time rather than before freezing to prevent them from becoming tough and soggy.

• Cool quickly before packaging. The best way is to set the pan of cooked food in a bowl, pan, or sink containing cold water with ice. When cooled to room temperature, ladle immediately into freezer containers.

• Best to freeze casseroles *before* baking.

• Allow headspace when packing semiliquid foods to leave room for food to expand.

• To save freezer space and free dish for reuse, line casserole with heavy foil, leaving long ends. Fill. Fold ends of foil together over food to seal. Place container in freezer. When food is frozen, remove from container neatly packaged. (Be sure foil is tightly sealed.) Label and store in freezer. To heat, place in same casserole, foil and all.

• Use dishes which are not too deep so the products will not take so long to thaw.

• Wrap with moisture-vapor-proof materials or use freezer containers. Use only containers with wide top openings so the food doesn't have to be completely thawed before it is removed from the container.

• The best protective food wrappings include moisture-proof cellophane, polyester and polyethylene films, clear plastic wrap, freezer-weight aluminum foil, laminated wrap.

• To wrap for feeezer, use wrapping about 1½ times as long as needed to go around item. Put food in the center. Bring sides of wrapper together at top. Fold edges down in a series of locked folds. Press wrapper against food. Crease ends into points. Press wrap to remove pockets of air. The coated side of paper should be next to the food. Turn ends under. Secure with freezer tape. Label with contents and date. Freeze quickly for best end results.

• Store at zero degrees. Fluctuating temperatures above zero will damage food quality.

• Only oven-proof containers can safely be transferred from freezer to hot oven.

• It is better to reheat frozen cooked main dishes without thawing. If you prefer to thaw the food before heating, thaw in the refrigerator. Once thawed, use immediately.

• To remove frozen main dishes from glass canning-freezing jars, let cool water run on cap 2 to 3 minutes (just till surface of food touching glass thaws). Remove cap and invert jar. Let food slide into pan for reheating.

• Never attempt to refreeze foods.

# FREEZE-THAW-COOK GUIDE

| FOODS | PREPARATION FOR FREEZING | STORAGE | THAWING AND COOKING |
|---|---|---|---|
| Baked beans with tomato sauce | Chill mixture quickly. Package in moisture-, vapor-proof container. Cover tightly. | 6 months | Partially thaw in package. Heat in casserole or top of double boiler. |
| Casseroles: Chicken, turkey, fish, or meat with vegetable and/or cereal product | Season well. Cool mixture quickly. Turn into freezer container or casserole. Cover tightly. | 2 to 4 months | If frozen in oven-proof container, uncover. Bake at 400° for 1 hour for pints; 1¾ hours for quarts or till food is heated. Or, steam over hot water in top of double boiler. |
| Creamed dishes: Chicken, turkey, fish, or seafood | Cool quickly. Freeze any except those containing hard-cooked egg white. Don't overcook. Use fat sparingly when making sauce. This helps prevent separation of sauce when reheating. Cover tightly. | 2 to 4 months | Heat in top of double boiler from the frozen state, stirring occasionally. If sauce separates, beat with fork or spoon during reheating. About 30 minutes is needed for thawing and heating 1 pint of creamed mixture. |
| Meatballs with tomato sauce | Cook till done; cool quickly. Ladle into jars or freezer containers, allowing headspace. Freeze immediately. | 3 months | Heat over low heat, stirring frequently, or in top of double boiler, stirring occasionally. Or, defrost overnight in refrigerator. Heat thoroughly in saucepan. |
| Meat pies and scallops | Cook meat till tender. Cook vegetables till almost tender. Cool quickly. Put in baking dish. Top with pastry, or freeze pastry separately. Wrap tightly and freeze. | 2 to 3 months | Bake pies with pastry topper at 400° for 45 minutes for pints and 1 hour for quarts, or till hot and crust is lightly browned. |
| Roast beef, pork, other meats, poultry | Do not freeze fried meats or poultry. Prepare as for serving. Remove excess fat and bone. Cool quickly. Wrap tightly. Best to freeze small pieces or slices; cover with broth, gravy, or sauce. Wrap tightly, seal, and freeze. | 2 to 4 months | Thaw large pieces of meat in the refrigerator before heating. Heat meat in sauces in top of double boiler. |
| Spaghetti sauce | Cool sauce quickly; ladle into jars or freezer containers, allowing headspace. Freeze. | 2 to 3 months | Heat over low heat, stirring frequently, or in top of double boiler, stirring occasionally. |
| Spanish rice | Use converted rice. Cook till rice is tender, but not mushy. Cool quickly, package, freeze. | 3 months | Heat in top of double boiler about 50 minutes. Add small amount of water, if needed. |
| Stews and soups | Select vegetables that freeze well. Omit potatoes. Onions lose flavor. Green pepper and garlic become more intense in flavor. Omit salt and thickening if stew is to be kept longer than 2 months. Do not completely cook vegetables. Cool quickly, wrap tightly, freeze. | 2 to 4 months | Heat quickly from frozen state. Do not overcook. Separate with fork as it thaws. Do not stir enough to make the mixture mushy. |

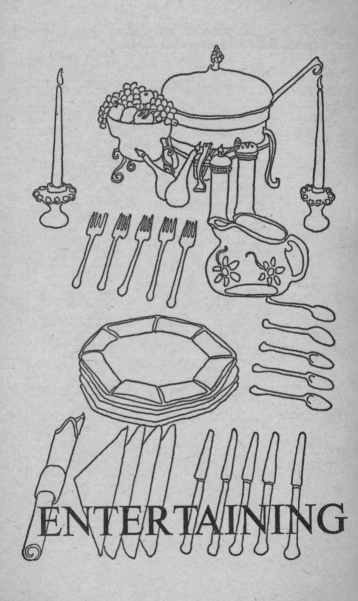

ENTERTAINING

Choose from this array of entertaining ideas to put extra appeal into your next special occasion.

For the ladies, plan a brunch that borrows the best from both morning and midday meals. When a party comes up suddenly, casseroles are made to order. Set the table buffet style and let guests help themselves.

To entertain in a way that is different, fun, and amazingly easy, try the novelty of cooking at the table. Choose from tangy stroganoffs, Swiss fondues or seafood Newburgs.

If a crowd is coming, you're sure to find the answers here to shopping and planning for large groups.

Discover the table-setting ideas that will set the stage for the perfect party, whether you want it to be casual or fancy, small or large.

# COMPANY LUNCHES AND BRUNCHES

## CLASSIC CHICKEN DIVAN

2 bunches fresh broccoli **or**
   2 10-ounce packages frozen
   broccoli spears
¼ cup butter or margarine
6 tablespoons all-purpose flour
½ teaspoon salt

2 cups chicken broth
½ cup whipping cream
3 tablespoons dry sherry
3 chicken breasts, cooked, boned,
   and cut in half
¼ cup grated Parmesan cheese

Cook broccoli in boiling, salted water; drain. Melt butter; blend in flour, salt, and dash pepper. Add chicken broth all at once; cook and stir till mixture thickens and bubbles. Stir in cream and wine.

Place broccoli crosswise in 12x7½x2-inch baking dish. Add *half* the sauce. Top with chicken pieces. To remaining sauce, add Parmesan cheese; pour over chicken; sprinkle with extra Parmesan cheese. Bake at 350° for 20 minutes or till heated. Then broil just till sauce is golden. Makes 6 to 8 servings.

SPAGHETTI
AND
MEATBALLS

SHRIMP CREOLE
PARSLEY RICE
RING

BEAN POT
LIMAS

CHEESE
SOUFFLE

DEVILED CORN
AND
CRAB

CHICKEN-PECAN
WAFFLES
BROILED PEACHES

BEEF FONDUE
TERIYAKI MEATBALLS
JAZZY BEEF BITES

SPEEDY
CHOP SUEY

# CHICKEN STRATA

Using 6 slices white bread, cube 2 slices and trim crusts from remaining 4 slices bread (cut up crusts). Place cubed bread and crusts in bottom of 8x8x2-inch baking dish (reserve bread slices for use later). Combine 2 cups diced cooked chicken, ½ cup chopped onion, ½ cup finely chopped celery, ¼ cup chopped green pepper, ½ cup mayonnaise, ¾ teaspoon salt, and dash pepper. Spoon over bread cubes. Arrange reserved bread slices atop turkey mixture.

Combine 2 beaten eggs and 1½ cups milk; pour over all. Cover and chill 1 hour or overnight. Stir one 10½-ounce can condensed cream of mushroom soup and spoon over top. Bake in slow oven (325°) about 1 hour or till set. Sprinkle ½ cup shredded sharp process American cheese over top last few minutes of baking. Makes 6 servings.

# RICE AND HAM STACK-UPS

1 cup uncooked long-grain rice
3 tablespoons butter or margarine
2 beaten eggs
¼ cup milk
¼ cup snipped parsley
6 slices (about 4 inches square) boiled ham

6 slices sharp process American cheese
6 very thin onion slices
6 tomato slices
6 pimiento-stuffed green olives, sliced

Cook rice according to package directions. Combine rice, butter or margarine, eggs, milk, and parsley. Mix well and spread in a greased 12x7½x2-inch baking dish. Bake in moderate oven (350°) 10 minutes.

Meanwhile, arrange remaining ingredients in 6 stacks, each containing 1 slice ham, 1 slice cheese, 1 slice onion, 1 slice tomato, and sliced stuffed green olives. Remove rice from oven and arrange the 6 ham stacks on rice. Bake 10 minutes more, or till cheese is melted. Serve in squares. Makes 6 servings.

# CHEDDAR SQUASH BAKE

Simmer 6 cups thinly sliced unpared zucchini squash till tender; drain. Sprinkle with salt. Combine 2 slightly beaten egg yolks, 1 cup dairy sour cream, and 2 tablespoons all-purpose flour. Fold in 2 stiffly beaten egg whites. Place *half* the squash in 12x7½x2-inch baking dish. Top with *half* the egg mixture, ¾ cup shredded sharp natural Cheddar cheese, and 6 slices crisp-cooked bacon, drained and crumbled.

Layer remaining squash, egg mixture, and ¾ cup shredded cheese. Melt 1 tablespoon butter; stir in ¼ cup fine dry bread crumbs; sprinkle over all. Bake at 350° for 20 to 25 minutes. Makes 8 to 10 servings.

## TURKEY CHEESE PUFF

1 10-ounce package frozen broccoli spears

2 cups sliced cooked turkey

1 10¾-ounce can chicken gravy Cheese Topper

Cook broccoli according to package directions; drain. Place in bottom of 10x6x1½-inch baking dish. Cover with turkey slices and gravy. Place in a 375° oven for 10 minutes, while preparing *Cheese Topper:* Beat 2 egg whites with ¼ teaspoon salt to stiff peaks; set aside. Beat 2 egg yolks till thick and lemon-colored; fold into whites with ¼ cup grated Parmesan cheese. Pour over hot turkey. Top with ¼ cup toasted sliced almonds. Bake at 375° for 15 to 20 minutes. Makes 6 servings.

## TUNA SOUFFLE RING

In mixing bowl combine two 6½- or 7-ounce cans tuna, drained and flaked, one 10½-ounce can condensed cream of mushroom soup, 3 slightly beaten egg yolks, 1 cup fine cracker crumbs (20 to 22 crackers), ¼ cup finely chopped onion, 2 tablespoons snipped parsley, 2 tablespoons chopped canned pimiento, 1 tablespoon lemon juice, and dash pepper; mix till well blended. Fold into 3 stiffly beaten egg whites. Turn into a *well-greased and lightly floured* 5-cup ring mold.

Bake in moderate oven (350°) 30 minutes. Loosen edges of ring and invert on serving plate. Cook two 10-ounce packages frozen peas with cream sauce according to package directions. Serve creamed peas with souffle ring. Pass lemon wedges. Makes 6 servings.

## CRAB-SHRIMP BAKE

1 cup cleaned cooked or canned shrimp

¼ cup chopped green pepper

2 tablespoons finely chopped onion

1 cup diced celery

1 7-ounce can crab meat, flaked (cartilage removed)

½ teaspoon salt
Dash pepper

1 teaspoon Worcestershire sauce

¾ cup mayonnaise or salad dressing

1 cup soft bread crumbs

1 tablespoon butter or margarine

Cut large shrimp in half lengthwise. Combine all ingredients, except crumbs and butter; place in 6 baking shells or 1-quart casserole. Combine crumbs with melted butter; sprinkle over mixture. Bake in moderate oven (350°) for 20 to 25 minutes for shells or 30 to 35 minutes for casserole. Makes 6 servings.

## SALMON ROLL-UPS

1 7¾-ounce can salmon, drained and flaked
1 beaten egg
1 teaspoon dried parsley flakes
1 teaspoon instant minced onion
½ teaspoon dried dillweed
1 8-ounce package refrigerated crescent rolls (8 rolls)
2 tablespoons butter or margarine

2 tablespons all-purpose flour
½ teaspoon salt
Dash pepper
1 cup milk
2 ounces sharp process American cheese, shredded (½ cup)
2 beaten egg yolks
1 tablespoon lemon juice

Combine salmon, egg, parsley, onion, and dillweed. Separate crescent rolls and spread each with about 1 tablespoon of the salmon mixture. Roll up, from wide end. Bake on baking sheet at 375° for 12 to 15 minutes.

Serve with *Cheese Sauce:* Melt butter; blend in flour, salt, and pepper. Add milk; cook and stir until thick and bubbly. Stir in cheese, egg yolks, and lemon juice; heat till cheese melts. Makes 4 servings.

## DEVILED HAM ELEGANTE

Spread tops of 4 crisp rusks with prepared mustard, then with one 4½-ounce can deviled ham. Heat in slow oven (325°) about 10 minutes. Chop 2 hard-cooked eggs and combine with one 10½-ounce can condensed cream of mushroom soup, ¼ cup milk, 2 tablespoons finely chopped onion, and dash Worcestershire sauce. Heat mixture till hot and spoon over rusks. Slice 2 hard-cooked eggs for garnish. Sprinkle with paprika. Makes 4 servings.

## DEVILED CORN AND CRAB

¼ cup butter or margarine
2 tablespoons all-purpose flour
1 teaspoon prepared mustard
½ teaspoon Worcestershire sauce
1 tablespoon lemon juice
½ teaspoon monosodium glutamate

1 7½-ounce can crab meat, flaked (cartilage removed)
2 hard-cooked eggs, chopped
1 1-pound can whole kernel corn, drained
1 1-pound can cream-style corn

½ teaspoon salt
  Dash pepper
½ cup milk

½ cup grated Parmesan cheese
½ cup medium cracker crumbs
  (about 14 crackers)
1 tablespoon butter, melted

In saucepan melt the ¼ cup butter; stir in flour, mustard, Worcestershire, lemon juice, monosodium glutamate, salt, and pepper. Add milk all at once; cook and stir till mixture thickens and bubbles. Remove from heat; carefully stir in crab meat, eggs, whole kernel corn, and cream-style corn.

Spoon into a 1½-quart casserole; sprinkle cheese over top. Combine cracker crumbs and the 1 tablespoon melted butter; sprinkle over cheese. Bake at 350° for 45 minutes or till heated through. Garnish with hard-cooked egg wedges and olive slices. Makes 6 servings.

## LOBSTER THERMIDOR BAKE

4 frozen lobster tails (about
  1 pound), cooked
⅓ cup chopped onion
1 clove garlic, minced
2 tablespoons butter or margarine

. . .

1 11-ounce can condensed
  Cheddar cheese soup

1 3-ounce can sliced mushrooms,
  drained (½ cup)
⅓ cup light cream
¼ cup dry sherry
2 tablespoons snipped parsley
1 10-ounce package frozen peas,
  cooked and drained
2 tablespoons buttered soft bread
  crumbs

With a sharp knife, cut through lobster shell lengthwise. Remove meat from shells; cut meat into large pieces. In medium skillet cook onion and garlic in butter or margarine till tender but not brown. Stir in soup and mushrooms; gradually blend in cream, wine, and parsley. Add lobster pieces and peas. Cook, stirring occasionally, till heated through. Spoon into four 1-cup casseroles; top each with a wreath of crumbs. Bake at 350° for 25 to 30 minutes. Makes 4 servings.

## PARSLEY CHEESE SOUFFLE

In a saucepan melt 3 tablespoons butter or margarine and blend in 3 tablespoons all-purpose flour. Add 1 cup milk; cook and stir till thick and bubbly. Remove from heat. Add 8 ounces sharp process American cheese, shredded (2 cups); stir to melt. Add 1 cup cooked rice and ¼ cup finely snipped parsley.

Beat 4 egg yolks till thick and lemon-colored; slowly stir in cheese mixture. Cool slightly; gradually pour over 4 stiffly beaten egg whites, folding together thoroughly. Pour into ungreased 12x7½x2-inch baking dish. Bake at 300° for 30 to 35 minutes, or till knife inserted off center comes out clean. Cut in squares and serve with Mushroom Sauce.

*Mushroom Sauce:* In a saucepan combine one 10½-ounce can condensed cream of mushroom soup, ⅓ cup milk, and one-half 10-ounce package (1 cup) frozen peas, cooked and drained; heat through. Serves 8.

## SWISS 'N CRAB SUPPER PIE

4 ounces natural Swiss cheese, shredded (1 cup)
1 unbaked 9-inch pastry shell
1 7½-ounce can crab meat, flaked and cartilage removed
2 green onions, sliced (with tops)
3 beaten eggs
1 cup light cream
½ teaspoon grated lemon peel
½ teaspoon salt
¼ teaspoon dry mustard
Dash ground mace
¼ cup sliced almonds

Arrange cheese evenly over bottom of pastry shell. Top with crab meat; sprinkle with green onions. Combine eggs, cream, lemon peel, salt, dry mustard, and mace. Pour evenly over crab. Top with almonds. Bake in slow oven (325°) for 45 minutes or till set. Let stand 10 minutes. Makes 6 servings.

## SHRIMP CURRIED EGGS

8 hard-cooked eggs
⅓ cup mayonnaise or salad dressing
½ teaspoon salt
¼ to ½ teaspoon curry powder
½ teaspoon paprika
¼ teaspoon dry mustard
Shrimp Sauce

Cut eggs in half lengthwise; remove yolks and mash; mix with mayonnaise and seasonings. Refill egg whites; arrange eggs in 10x6x1½-inch baking dish.

*Shrimp Sauce:* Melt 2 tablespoons butter; blend in 2 tablespoons all-purpose flour. Stir in one 10-ounce can frozen condensed cream of shrimp soup and 1 soup can milk; cook and stir till sauce thickens and bubbles. Add ½ cup shredded sharp process American cheese; stir till melted. Cover eggs with sauce. Sprinkle 1 cup soft buttered bread crumbs around edge of mixture. Bake at 350° for 15 to 20 minutes or till heated through. Serves 6 to 8.

## HAM PUFFS

1½ cups ground cooked or canned
    ham
4 ounces process American
    cheese, grated (1 cup)
¼ finely chopped onion

1¼ cups milk
2 beaten egg yolks
2 cups soft bread crumbs
2 stiffly beaten egg whites
    Mushroom Sauce

Combine ham, cheese, green pepper, and onion. Stir in milk,
egg yolks, and crumbs. Fold in egg whites. Fill six greased
6-ounce custard cups. Bake in a pan of hot water at 350° for
40 to 50 minutes or till set. Turn out on plates; top with Mushroom Sauce. Serve immediately. Makes 6 servings.

## MUSHROOM SAUCE

In a saucepan melt 3 tablespoons butter or margarine. Blend
in 3 tablespoons flour. Stir in 1 cup milk and one 3-ounce can
broiled sliced mushrooms with liquid. Cook, stirring constantly, till mixture thickens and bubbles. Add 1 tablespoon
grated onion and 1 tablespoon snipped parsley. Season with
¼ teaspoon salt and dash pepper. Spoon over Ham Puffs or
other main dish just before serving. Makes about 1½ cups
sauce.

## ASPARAGUS HAM BAKE

Cook 1 cup packaged precooked rice using package directions, omitting salt. In a bowl combine one 10½-ounce can
condensed cream of mushroom soup and ¾ cup milk. Add 2
cups cubed cooked or canned ham, 2 ounces sharp process
American cheese, shredded (½ cup), 3 tablespoons finely
chopped onion, and the cooked rice.

Spoon *half* of ham mixture into 10x6x1½-inch baking dish;
top with one 10-ounce package frozen asparagus cuts, cooked
and drained. Then add remaining ham mixture.

Combine ½ cup fine dry bread crumbs and 2 tablespoons
butter, melted; sprinkle over top. Bake at 375° for 45 to 50
minutes or till heated through and brown. Serves 6.

## CHICKEN-PECAN WAFFLES

Sauce:

| | |
|---|---|
| ¼ cup butter or margarine | 1 tablespoon lemon juice |
| 3 chicken bouillon cubes | 2 cups cubed cooked chicken |
| ⅓ cup all-purpose flour | ½ cup chopped celery |
| ¼ teaspoon poultry seasoning | ½ cup coarsely chopped pecans |
| 2½ cups milk | 2 tablespoons chopped pimiento |

In medium saucepan melt butter; add bouillon cubes and crush with back of spoon. Stir in flour and poultry seasoning. Add milk and lemon juice. Cook and stir over medium heat till mixture thickens and bubbles. Stir in chicken, celery, all but 2 tablespoons of the pecans, and the pimiento. Heat. Trim with reserved nuts. Serve over waffles. Serves 4.

Waffles:

| | |
|---|---|
| 1¾ cups sifted all-purpose flour | 1¾ cups milk |
| 3 teaspoons baking powder | ½ cup salad oil |
| ½ teaspoon salt | 2 stiffly beaten egg whites |
| 2 beaten egg yolks | |

Sift together dry ingredients. Combine egg yolks and milk; stir into dry ingredients. Blend in oil. Fold in egg whites, leaving a few fluffs—don't overmix. Bake in preheated waffle baker according to manufacturer's directions. Makes about 8 individual waffles.

## BROILED PEACHES

On broiler pan, arrange, cut side up, one 1-pound 13-ounce can peach halves, drained. Dot each with a small amount of butter. Sprinkle lightly with nutmeg. Broil 4 to 5 minutes or till browned. Serve with Chicken-pecan Waffles. Makes 5 to 7 peach halves.

# BUFFET-STYLE SUPPERS

## LASAGNE

1 pound Italian sausage
1 clove garlic, minced
1 tablespoon dried basil, crushed
1½ teaspoons salt
1 1-pound can (2 cups) tomatoes
2 6-ounce cans tomato paste
10 ounces lasagne **or** wide noodles
3 cups fresh ricotta **or** cream-style cottage cheese

½ cup grated Parmesan **or** Romano cheese
2 tablespoons dried parsley flakes
2 beaten eggs
1 teaspoon salt
½ teaspoon pepper
1 pound mozzarella cheese, thinly sliced

Brown meat slowly; spoon off excess fat. Add next 5 ingredients. Simmer uncovered 30 minutes, stirring occasionally.

Cook noodles in large amount boiling salted water till tender; drain and rinse. Combine remaining ingredients, except mozzarella.

Place *half* the noodles in 13x9x2-inch baking dish. Spread with *half* the cottage cheese filling; add *half* the mozzarella cheese and *half* the meat sauce. Repeat layers.

Bake in a moderate oven (375°) about 30 minutes. Let stand 10 minutes before cutting in squares—filling will set slightly. Makes 8 to 10 servings.

## CRAB-RICE SQUARES

Cook ¼ cup chopped onion in 1 tablespoon butter or margarine till tender. Stir in 2 cups milk, 3 slightly beaten eggs, 3 cups cooked rice, 4 ounces process American cheese, shredded (1 cup), one 7½-ounce can crab meat, flaked and cartilage removed, ¼ cup chopped canned pimiento, 1 teaspoon Worcestershire sauce, several dashes bottled hot pepper sauce, and 1 teaspoon snipped parsley.

Turn into a greased 12x7½x2-inch baking dish. Bake at 350° about 40 minutes, or till knife inserted off center comes out clean. Serve with shrimp sauce made by heating one 10½-ounce can frozen condensed cream of shrimp soup with ½ cup milk. Serves 8 to 10.

## FANCY CHICKEN A LA KING

| | |
|---|---|
| ¼ cup chopped green pepper | ½ teaspoon paprika |
| 1 cup fresh mushrooms | ¼ cup butter or margarine, softened |
| 2 tablespoons butter or margarine | |
| 2 tablespoons all-purpose flour | 2 tablespoons dry sherry |
| ¾ teaspoon salt | 1 tablespoon lemon juice |
| 2 cups light cream | 1 teaspoon onion juice |
| 3 cups cooked chicken cut in pieces | 2 tablespoons chopped canned pimiento |
| 3 egg yolks | |

Cook green pepper and thinly sliced mushrooms in 2 tablespoons butter till tender but not brown; push vegetables to one side and blend flour and salt into the butter. Stir in cream; cook and stir till thick and bubbly. Add chicken and heat; stir occasionally.

Meanwhile, in small bowl blend egg yolks, paprika, and ¼ cup softened butter; set aside. To chicken mixture add wine, lemon juice, and onion juice. Have chicken bubbling; then add yolk mixture all at once, stirring till blended. Immediately remove from heat. Stir in pimiento. Serve on toast. Serves 6 to 8.

# TURKEY PARISIAN

2 tablespoons chopped green
  pepper
¼ cup butter or margarine
¼ cup all-purpose flour
¾ teaspoon salt
1½ cups milk
1 cup light cream
2 cups cubed cooked turkey
1 3-ounce can sliced mushrooms,
  drained (½ cup)

1 5-ounce can lobster, broken
  into bite-size pieces
¼ cup grated Parmesan cheese
2 tablespoons chopped canned
  pimiento
2 tablespoons dry white wine
2 10-ounce packages frozen
  chopped broccoli, cooked
  and drained

Cook green pepper in butter till tender. Blend in flour, salt,
and dash pepper. Add milk and cream and stir constantly till
mixture thickens and bubbles. Stir in turkey, mushrooms,
lobster, cheese, pimiento, and wine. Place broccoli in a
12x7½x2-inch baking dish. Top with turkey mixture. Sprinkle
additional cheese atop, if desired. Bake at 350° for 30 to 35
minutes. Makes 8 servings.

# HAM-TURKEY CASSEROLE

¼ cup butter or margarine
¼ cup all-purpose flour
1 cup milk
1 cup light cream
1 3-ounce can sliced mushrooms,
  drained (½ cup)
2 teaspoons instant minced
  onion
2 teaspoons prepared mustard

1 cup dairy sour cream
4 ounces medium noodles,
  cooked and drained (about
  2 cups)
1½ cups cubed cooked ham
1½ cups cubed cooked turkey
2 tablespoons toasted slivered
  almonds

Melt butter; stir in flour and ½ teaspoon salt. Add milk and
cream. Cook and stir till thick and bubbly. Stir in remaining
ingredients, except nuts. Turn into 2-quart casserole. Top
with almonds. Bake at 325° for 25 minutes. Makes 6 to 8
servings.

# HAM MEDLEY

1 cup chopped celery
½ cup chopped green pepper
½ cup chopped onion
¼ cup butter or margarine,
  melted
¼ cup all-purpose flour
½ teaspoon salt
  Dash pepper
2½ cups milk

3 cups cream-style cottage
  cheese
4 cups cooked ham cut in
  ½-inch cubes
1 8-ounce package noodles,
  cooked and drained
2 tablespoons butter or margarine
½ cup fine dry bread crumbs

Cook vegetables in ¼ cup butter till tender. Blend in flour, salt, and pepper. Stir in milk and cottage cheese; cook and stir till mixture boils. Stir in ham and noodles; transfer to a 3-quart casserole. Combine remaining ingredients; sprinkle over top. Bake at 350° for 1 hour. Serves 10 to 12.

## SALMON TETRAZZINI

| | |
|---|---|
| 4 ounces uncooked spaghetti | 2 tablespoons dry sherry |
| 1 1-pound can (2 cups) salmon | 1 3-ounce can sliced mushrooms, |
| Milk | drained (½ cup) |
| 2 tablespoons butter or margarine | 2 tablespoons fine dry bread |
| 2 tablespoons all-purpose flour | crumbs |
| ¼ teaspoon salt | 2 tablespoons grated Parmesan |
| Dash ground nutmeg | cheese |

Cook spaghetti according to package directions; drain. Meanwhile, drain salmon, reserving liquid. Add milk to salmon liquid to make 2 cups. Break salmon into large pieces.

Melt butter; blend in flour, salt, dash pepper, and nutmeg. Add salmon liquid and milk all at once. Cook over medium heat, stirring constantly, till thick and bubbly. Add wine. Stir in spaghetti, mushrooms, and salmon. Turn into 1-quart casserole. Combine crumbs and Parmesan; sprinkle over top. Bake at 350° for 35 to 40 minutes. Serves 6.

## SAUCY CHICKEN 'N HAM

| | |
|---|---|
| 3 chicken breasts, boned and | ⅓ cup uncooked wild rice |
| halved lengthwise | 2 cups water |
| 2 tablespoons butter or margarine | 1 envelope dry mushroom soup |
| ½ cup chopped onion | mix |
| 1 envelope dry chicken-noodle | ⅓ cup dry white wine |
| soup mix | 1 3-ounce can sliced mushrooms, |
| ⅔ cup uncooked long-grain rice | drained (½ cup) |
| ½ teaspoon dried rosemary, | 6 thin slices boiled ham |
| crushed | |

In skillet brown chicken in butter; remove from skillet. Add onion to skillet; cook till tender. Add next 5 ingredients; bring to boiling. Pour into 9x9x2-inch baking dish; top with chicken. Bake covered at 350° for 50 minutes. Prepare mushroom soup according to package directions; add wine and mushrooms. Lift chicken; slide ham under. Pour soup mixture over. Bake uncovered 15 minutes longer. Makes 6 servings.

## JIFFY TURKEY PAELLA

1 1-pound 12-ounce can tomatoes
1 1-pint 2-ounce can ( 2¼ cups)
   tomato juice
¼ cup salad oil
¼ cup chopped onion
¼ cup chopped green pepper
1 teaspoon salt
1 teaspoon garlic salt

Dash cayenne
1 cup uncooked long-grain rice
2 9-ounce packages frozen
   artichoke hearts, thawed
3 cups diced cooked turkey
¼ cup sliced pimiento-stuffed
   green olives

In large saucepan combine first 8 ingredients. Stir in rice. Cover; bring to boiling. Add artichoke hearts, turkey, and olives. Turn into 3-quart casserole. Bake covered at 350° for 1 hour and 25 minutes or till rice is tender, stirring once or twice. Garnish with additional stuffed green olives. Makes 12 servings.

## VEAL PARMESAN WITH SPAGHETTI

6 thin veal cutlets
   (about 1½ pounds)
2 tablespoons olive or salad oil
½ cup chopped onion
¼ cup chopped green pepper
⅓ cup dry white wine
1 1-pound can (2 cups) tomatoes
2 8-ounce cans tomato sauce

1 6-ounce can tomato paste
1 clove garlic, minced
1 tablespoon snipped parsley
1 teaspoon dried oregano, crushed
½ pound long thin spaghetti
1 6-ounce package sliced
   mozzarella cheese

Brown meat in oil. Remove meat; add onion and green pepper; cook till tender. Stir in next 7 ingredients. Add meat; cover; simmer 30 minutes, stirring occasionally. Cook spaghetti according to package directions; drain. Remove *half* the sauce from meat; stir into spaghetti. Top cutlets with cheese; cover pan for 5 minutes. Arrange spaghetti and meat on platter; pass extra sauce and Parmesan cheese. Makes 6 servings.

## CREAMY CHICKEN AND RICE

½ cup uncooked wild rice
½ cup uncooked long-grain rice
½ cup chopped onion
½ cup butter or margarine
1 6-ounce can (1⅓ cups) broiled
   sliced mushrooms
   (undrained)
Chicken broth

¼ cup all-purpose flour
1½ cups light cream
3 cups diced cooked chicken
¼ cup chopped canned pimiento
¼ cup snipped parsley
1 teaspoon salt
Dash pepper
¼ cup toasted slivered almonds

Rinse wild rice in cold water. Add with ½ teaspoon salt to 2 cups boiling water. Cook 20 minutes. Add long-grain rice, 1 cup boiling water, and ½ teaspoon salt; cook 20 minutes longer. Meanwhile, cook onion in butter till tender. Remove from heat. Stir in flour.

Drain mushrooms reserving liquid. Add enough chicken broth to liquid to measure 1½ cups. Stir into flour mixture. Add cream. Cook and stir till thickened. Add rice, mushrooms, chicken, and next 4 ingredients. Turn into 2-quart casserole. Top with nuts. Bake at 350° for 25 to 30 minutes. Makes 8 servings.

## CHICKEN LIVERS AND RICE

1⅓ cups packaged precooked rice
½ pound chicken livers, cut up
1 10-ounce package frozen chopped spinach, thawed
2 tablespoons Burgundy

2 tablespoons butter or margarine
4 ounces sharp natural Cheddar cheese, shredded (1 cup)

Cook rice according to package directions. Brown livers in a small amount of butter. Combine rice, livers, spinach, butter, wine, ½ teaspoon salt, dash pepper, and cheese. Spoon into a 1½-quart casserole. Bake covered at 350° for 25 minutes. Garnish with additional shredded cheese, if desired. Serves 5 or 6.

## CHICKEN-RICE BAKE

1 cup uncooked long-grain rice
3 chicken breasts, boned and halved
½ cup chopped onion
1 clove garlic, minced
1 cup chopped celery
1 10½-ounce can condensed beef broth

½ cup water
½ teaspoon salt
½ teaspoon monosodium glutamate
¼ teaspoon dried oregano, crushed
¼ teaspoon dried rosemary, crushed
Cheese Sauce

Toast rice at 350° about 25 minutes or till golden; stir occasionally. Coat chicken with a mixture of flour, salt, and pepper; brown in ¼ cup hot fat. Remove chicken from skillet; add onion and garlic; cook till tender.

Stir in next 7 ingredients and rice; transfer to a 12x7½x2-inch baking dish. Top with chicken breasts. Cover tightly with foil; bake at 350° for 50 minutes, or till chicken is done and rice is tender. Sprinkle with snipped parsley and toasted sliced almonds. Serves 6.

Serve with *Cheese Sauce:* Over low heat, melt 2 tablespoons butter or margarine. Blend in 2 tablespoons all-purpose flour, ¼ teaspoon salt, and dash white pepper. Add 1¼ cups milk, all at once. Cook and stir till mixture thickens and bubbles. Stir in 4 ounces sharp process American cheese, shredded (1 cup); heat, stirring till cheese melts.

## CHILIES RELLENOS BAKE

| | |
|---|---|
| 1 pound ground beef | 1½ cups milk |
| ½ cup chopped onion | ¼ cup all-purpose flour |
| 2 4-ounce cans green chilies, cut in half crosswise and seeded | ½ teaspoon salt |
| | Dash pepper |
| | 4 beaten eggs |
| 6 ounces sharp natural Cheddar cheese, shredded (1½ cups) | Several dashes bottled hot pepper sauce |

Brown beef and onion; drain off fat. Sprinkle meat with ½ teaspoon salt and ¼ teaspoon pepper. Place *half* the chilies in 10x6x1½-inch baking dish; sprinkle with cheese; top with meat mixture. Arrange remaining chilies over meat. Combine remaining ingredients; beat till smooth. Pour over meat-chilie mixture. Bake at 350° for 45 to 50 minutes, or till knife inserted just off center comes out clean. Let cool 5 minutes. Serves 6.

## BURGUNDY BEEF STEW

| | |
|---|---|
| 1 10¾-ounce can condensed tomato soup | 1½ pounds beef chuck, cut in 1-inch cubes |
| 1 10½-ounce can condensed beef broth | 4 medium potatoes, pared and halved |
| ½ cup red Burgundy | 4 medium carrots, quartered |
| 3 tablespoons all-purpose flour | 1 large onion, sliced |
| ½ teaspoon dried basil, crushed | |

In a large saucepan, combine first 3 ingredients; blend in flour, 1 teaspoon salt, dash pepper, and basil. Add meat and vegetables; stir to distribute through gravy. Cover; simmer 1½ hours; stir occasionally. Serves 6.

# BEEF CASSEROLE SUPREME

In skillet, cook 1 pound ground beef and ¼ cup chopped onion until lightly browned. Drain off fat. Stir in one 8-ounce can stewed tomatoes, one 10¾-ounce can condensed tomato soup, 2 teaspoons salt, and 1 clove garlic, crushed. Simmer 5 to 10 minutes.

Blend in 1 cup dairy sour cream and one 3-ounce package cream cheese, softened. Stir in 5 ounces cooked and drained mafalde (thin lasagne noodles) or medium noodles.

Turn into a 2-quart casserole. Bake covered in a moderate oven (350°) 30 to 35 minutes or till heated through. Garnish with fresh tomatoes. Makes 4 to 6 servings.

# SWEDISH MEATBALLS

¾ pound lean ground beef
½ pound ground veal
¼ pound ground pork
1½ cups soft bread crumbs
1 cup light cream
. . .
½ cup chopped onion
1 tablespoon butter or margarine
1 egg

¼ cup finely snipped parsley
1¼ teaspoons salt
Dash pepper
Dash ground ginger
Dash ground nutmeg
2 tablespoons butter or margarine
Gravy

Have meats ground together twice. Soak bread in cream about 5 minutes. Cook onion in 1 tablespoon butter till tender but not brown. Mix meats, crumb mixture, onion, egg, parsley, and seasonings. Beat 5 minutes at medium speed on mixer, or mix by hand until well combined. Shape into 1½-inch balls. (Mixture will be soft—for easier shaping, wet hands or chill mixture first.)

Brown meatballs in 2 tablespoons butter. Remove from skillet. For *Gravy:* Melt 2 tablespoons butter in skillet with drippings. Stir in 2 tablespoons all-purpose flour. Add 1 beef bouillon cube dissolved in 1¼ cups boiling water and ½ teaspoon instant coffee powder. Cook and stir till gravy thickens.

Add meatballs. Cover; cook *slowly* about 30 minutes; baste occasionally. Makes 30 balls.

# Trims for the final touch

## PASTRY FOR 1-CRUST PIE

Sift together 1½ cups sifted all-purpose flour and ½ teaspoon salt. Cut in ½ cup shortening with pastry blender or blending fork till pieces are size of small peas. (For extra tender pastry, cut in *half* the shortening till mixture looks like cornmeal. Then cut in remaining till like small peas.) Sprinkle 1 tablespoon cold water over part of mixture. Gently toss with fork; push to side of bowl. Sprinkle 1 tablespoon water over dry part; mix lightly; push moistened part to side. Repeat till all is moistened, using a total of 4 to 5 tablespoons cold water. Form into ball. Continue as directed in recipe.

# PASTRY TOPPER

Prepare 1 stick pie crust mix according to package directions or prepare Pastry for 1-crust Pie. Roll out on lightly floured surface to an 8-inch circle, about ¼ inch thick. Using pastry wheel or sharp knife, cut in 6 pie-shaped wedges. Prick with fork. Bake on ungreased baking sheet in very hot oven (450°) for 12 to 15 minutes.

Or, prepare *Lattice Squares:* For 6 small "lattice rafts," prepare 2 sticks pie crust mix according to package directions. Divide dough in half; form each in ball and roll to ⅛ inch thick on lightly floured surface. Cut in strips ¾ inch wide, making 24 strips 3 inches long, and 18 strips 4 inches long. Weave in 6 lattice sections: For each, line up three 4-inch strips side by side, ¼ inch apart. Weave four 3-inch strips crosswise. Bake on ungreased baking sheet in a very hot oven (450°) for 8 to 10 minutes. Place pastry wedges or "lattice rafts" atop hot baked casserole or cooked stew just before serving.

# BREAD CRUMBS

Tear slices of fresh bread into quarters. Using small amounts at a time, add to blender. Turn blender on and off quickly till desired fineness. About 1 slice bread (depending on thickness) makes 1 cup soft bread crumbs.

For fine dry bread crumbs, dry bread in oven. Crush with rolling pin till fine, or break up in large pieces and add to blender container, a small amount at a time. Blend quickly till desired fineness. Four slices bread (depending on thickness) makes 1 cup crumbs.

# BUTTERY BREAD CRUMBS

Combine ½ cup fine dry bread crumbs with 2 tablespoons melted butter or margarine. Sprinkle top of casserole with mixture. Makes enough to trim a 1-quart casserole or four 8-ounce individual baking dishes.

# DECORATIVE BORDERS

Experiment with bread or cracker crumbs (plain, buttered,

or mixed with shredded cheese), potato chips—whole or crushed, canned shoestring potatoes, crushed corn chips, or chow mein noodles.

Or, transform the "border" into diagonal stripes, spokes, or a whirligig.

## TEST KITCHEN TIPS

### Toast bonnets

*Spread toast with butter or sharp cheese spread. For extra zest, sprinkle with seasoned or garlic salt. Cut in small cubes; place on hot casserole just before serving.*

*Or, cut toast with doughnut cutter, spread with butter, and top with shredded or grated cheese. Broil to melt cheese. Place on baked casserole.*

### Thimble Biscuits

*Prepare biscuit mix according to package directions. Roll to ½ inch; cut in 1½-inch rounds. Place biscuits atop hot casserole 15 minutes before it's done. (Or, heat mixture, pour in baking dish, add biscuits.) Increase oven temperature to 450°. Bake 15 minutes or till biscuits are done.*

## Cheese in fancy shapes

*Cut squares of process cheese slices in half diagonally making triangles. Make a whirligig or fancy shape atop hot casserole or overlap alongside of baking dish.*

*Last 5 minutes of baking, sprinkle shredded or grated process cheese on top of the casserole; dash with paprika for appetizing color.*

# MEAT DOES DOUBLE DUTY

Meat may double as ingredient and garnish. In recipes containing shrimp, crumble crisp-cooked bacon, luncheon meat, or ham strips, reserve some for trim.

Parade sausages or franks in rows or whirls atop casserole. Cut Canadian-style bacon slices in half; arrange the half rounds in scallops.

Roll thin salami slices in cornucopias; fasten with wooden picks. Tuck parsley sprigs into ends; arrange salami rolls spoke-style on casserole.

## TEST KITCHEN TIPS

### Vegetable toppers

*Use pinwheel of hot cooked asparagus (on ham or chicken bakes), overlapped green pepper and onion rings, or mushroom slices (with meat), or tomato slices alternated with cheese or luncheon meat triangles.*

*Try canned or frozen French-fried onions on top of casserole. Bake long enough to heat through.*

## LEMON AND SEAFOOD

Lemon wedges—whirl in a star or line up. To add more color, dip edges in paprika or snipped parsley.

Lemon slices—overlap in a row and poke tiny parsley fluff into each.

## PINEAPPLE WITH HAM

Pineapple—brush rings or sticks with melted butter; broil. Arrange rings with cherries. Form a daisy of pineapple sticks; center with parsley.

## TEST KITCHEN TIPS

### Sliced olive or pickle

For wreath effect, sprinkle circle of snipped parsley atop casserole. Slice pimiento-stuffed olives and arrange in a trio as shown. Or, tumble olive slices in center of casserole or in dizzy rows. Turn olive halves, cut side down, in daisy effect. Add parsley.

Pickle fans—slice pickles lengthwise almost to stem end, making thin slices. Spread each fan and press uncut end so fan will hold shape. Swirl several fans from center of casserole.

# Many ways with pizza

## SPECIAL SAUSAGE PIZZA

1 pound Italian sausage
2 fresh tomatoes, peeled and cut
   in thin slices
2 12-inch pizza-dough circles
1 6-ounce package mozzarella
   cheese, thinly sliced, and cut
   in pieces

1 6-ounce can tomato paste
2 cloves garlic, minced
2 tablespoons dried oregano,
   crushed
1 tablespoon dried parsley flakes
2 tablespoons olive oil
¼ cup grated Romano cheese

Break up sausage in skillet; brown slowly till lightly browned, about 10 minutes, stirring occasionally. Drain off excess fat.

Place layer of tomato slices on pizza-dough circles; cover with *half* the mozzarella. Mix tomato paste and garlic; spread over cheese. Sprinkle with oregano and parsley; dash with salt and freshly ground pepper. Drizzle with some of the oil. Top with sausage and remaining mozzarella. Sprinkle with Romano cheeese; drizzle with remaining olive oil. Dash with salt and pepper. Bake as directed for crust. Makes two 12-inch pizzas.

# SAUSAGE PIZZA

½ pound Italian **or** bulk pork
    sausage
1 clove garlic, crushed
1 teaspoon dried oregano, crushed
1 teaspoon dried basil, crushed
1 package cheese pizza mix
    (for 1 pizza)

1 3-ounce can sliced mushrooms,
    drained (½ cup)
1 6-ounce package mozzarella
    cheese, thinly sliced and cut
    in pieces
6 salami slices
6 pimiento-stuffed green olives

In a skillet break sausage in small bits. Brown slowly. Drain.
Add garlic, oregano, and basil.

Prepare pizza crust according to package directions. Roll
or pat out to fit 12-inch pizza pan. Crimp edges. Shake on
*half* the grated cheese from mix package; cover with pizza
sauce (from mix package), sausage mixture, remaining grated
cheese, mushrooms, then mozzarella cheese. Bake in hot oven
(425°) for 15 to 20 minutes till crust is done.

Roll salami slices in cone shape. Arrange in center of pizza.
Garnish with olives and sprigs of parsley in center of salami
"wheel." Makes one 12-inch pizza.

# PEPPERONI PIZZA

Biscuit Pizza Crust
2 8-ounce cans tomato sauce
½ cup chopped onion
2 to 3 teaspoons dried oregano,
    crushed
½ teaspoon salt
Dash pepper

1 teaspoon anise seed
2 cloves garlic, minced
8 ounces pepperoni, thinly sliced
2 6-ounce packages mozzarella
    cheese, thinly sliced and cut
    in pieces

Prepare crust. Mix tomato sauce, onion, oregano, anise, salt,
pepper, and garlic; spread over the two 12-inch dough circles.
Scatter pepperoni slices over crusts, reserving some pepperoni
for trim. Add cheese. Top with reserved pepperoni. Bake
according to directions for crust. Makes two 12-inch pizzas.

# BISCUIT PIZZA CRUST

1 package active dry yeast
¾ cup warm water

2½ cups packaged biscuit mix
    Olive or salad oil

Soften yeast in *warm* water (110°). Add biscuit mix; beat
vigorously by hand for 2 minutes. Dust surface with biscuit

mix; knead till smooth, 25 strokes. Divide in half.

Roll each half to a 12-inch circle; place on greased pizza pans or baking sheets; crimp edge. Brush dough with oil. Fill crusts. Bake at 425° for 15 minutes or till crusts are done. Makes two 12-inch pizza crusts.

## MUSHROOM PIZZA

2 12-inch pizza dough circles
4 ounces mozzarella cheese, shredded (1 cup)
1 6-ounce can chopped mushrooms, drained
½ cup finely chopped onion

2 10-ounce cans (2½ cups) pizza sauce
¼ cup chopped green pepper
Dash salt and pepper
4 ounces mozzarella cheese, shredded (1 cup)

Prepare pizza dough circles and sprinkle with 4 ounces cheese. Top with mushrooms.

In saucepan combine pizza sauce, onion, green pepper, salt, and pepper. Boil 15 minutes. Spread on pizza. Top with remaining cheese. Bake as directed for crust. Makes two 12-inch pizzas.

## HOMEMADE PIZZA CRUST

Soften 1 package active dry yeast in 1 cup *warm* water (110°). Beat in 1½ cups sifted all-purpose flour; mix in 1 tablespoon salad oil and 1 teaspoon salt. Stir in 2 cups flour. Knead till smooth and elastic, about 12 minutes (will be firm). Place in lightly greased bowl; turn greased side up. Cover. Let rise in warm place till more than double, 1½ to 2 hours. Punch down, cover, chill.

Cut dough in half. On lightly floured surface, roll each into 12-inch circle, about ⅛ inch thick. Place in two greased 12-inch pizza pans, forming edges. With knuckles, dent dough. Brush each circle with 1 tablespoon salad oil. Fill. Bake at 425° for 20 to 25 minutes. Makes two 12-inch crusts.

## JIFFY PIZZA CRUST

Prepare one 13¾-ounce package hot roll mix according to package directions, but using *1 cup warm water* (110°) and *no egg. Do not let rise.* Cut in half. With oiled hands, pat each into 12-inch circle on greased baking sheet. Clip edge at 1-inch intervals; press so it stands up. Brush with salad oil. Fill. Bake at 450° for 15 to 20 minutes or till crusts are done. Makes two 12-inch pizza crusts.

## PIZZA SUPPER PIE

| | |
|---|---|
| 1 stick pie crust mix | 4 eggs |
| 1 pound bulk pork sausage | ½ cup milk |
| ¾ cup chopped onion | 4 ounces sharp process American |
| ½ teaspon dried oregano, crushed | cheese, shredded (1 cup) |
| ¼ teaspoon pepper | ⅔ cup canned pizza sauce |

Prepare one 9-inch pastry shell from pie crust mix according to package directions. Bake in very hot oven (450°) *only 7 minutes* or just till lightly browned; remove from oven. Reduce oven temperature to 325°.

Slowly brown sausage and onion, breaking up sausage; drain. Add oregano and pepper. Beat eggs and milk together; stir in sausage and cheese. Pour into pastry shell.

Bake in slow oven (325°) 20 to 25 minutes or till knife inserted in center comes out clean. Spread top with sauce; garnish with additional sharp process American cheese slices, if desired. Bake 10 minutes longer, Serve immediately. Makes 6 to 8 servings.

# HOSTESS NOTE:

## ENTERTAINING BUFFET-STYLE

A successful buffet always looks delightfully easy to the guests —but, as every hostess knows, it does require special planning. The most logical place to set up the table service is out of the general flow of traffic, yet within easy reach. If space allows, set the buffet table out into the middle of the room so guests can circulate around it. Or, you may choose to place the table just far enough away from the wall for the hostess to work comfortably behind it. Use a cart or small table nearby for beverages.

There is no hard-and-fast rule for setting a buffet, but it is important that guests can serve themselves in a logical sequence. At one end of the buffet table place the dinner plates and main dish. Place other foods, such as salad, vegetable, buttered rolls, and relishes near the edge of the table within easy reach. Leave enough room near each serving dish for guests to put down their dinner plates. Include a serving fork or spoon alongside each serving dish.

Set the table attractively. If the table is crowded, serve the beverage from a nearby cart or small table. Arrange silver and napkins so they can be picked up last from the table. Carefully go over every item on the menu to see that everything is in order. After seconds have been served, clear the buffet table and arrange the dessert course.

If a sit-down buffet is possible, set small tables in another room with silver, napkins, and water glasses. Provide beverage cups, cream, and sugar at the tables, then serve the beverage, if you wish.

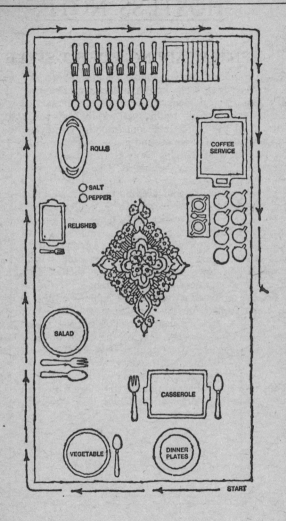

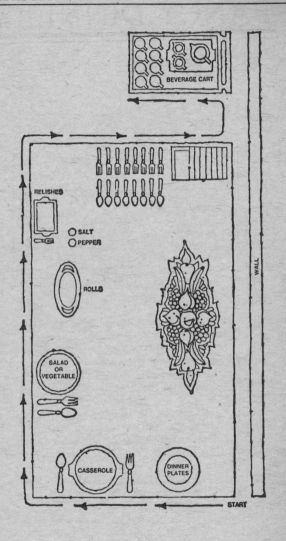

## MOUSSAKA

2 medium eggplants
1 pound ground beef
1 cup chopped onion
¼ cup red Burgundy
¼ cup water
2 tablespoons snipped parsley
1 tablespoon tomato paste
1 teaspoon salt
1 slice bread, torn in crumbs
2 beaten eggs
¼ cup shredded sharp process American cheese

Dash ground cinnamon
3 tablespoons butter or margarine
3 tablespoons all-purpose flour
1½ cups milk
½ teaspoon salt
Dash pepper
Dash ground nutmeg
1 beaten egg
¼ cup shredded sharp process American cheese

Pare eggplants; cut into slices ½ inch thick. Sprinkle with a little salt and set aside.

In skillet brown meat with onion; drain off any excess fat. Add wine, water, parsley, tomato paste, 1 teaspoon salt, and dash pepper. Simmer till liquid is nearly absorbed. Cool; stir in *half* the bread crumbs, the 2 beaten eggs, ¼ cup cheese, and cinnamon.

In saucepan melt butter; stir in flour. Add milk; cook and stir till thick and bubbly. Add ½ teaspoon salt, dash pepper, and nutmeg. Add a small amount of hot sauce to the beaten egg; return to hot mixture. Cook over low heat 2 minutes, stirring constantly.

Brown eggplant slices on both sides in a little hot oil. Sprinkle bottom of 12x7½x2-inch baking dish with remaining bread crumbs. Cover with a layer of eggplant slices (reserve remainder). Spoon on all of meat mixture. Arrange remaining eggplant over meat mixture. Pour milk-egg sauce over all. Top with ¼ cup shredded cheese. Bake in moderate oven (350°) for about 45 minutes. Serve hot. Makes 6 to 8 servings.

## PARTY VEAL BAKE

Combine 2 tablespoons all-purpose flour, ½ teaspoon salt, ½ teaspoon paprika, ¼ teaspoon dried rosemary, crushed, ¼ teaspoon curry powder (optional), and dash pepper.

Coat 4 veal cutlets with flour mixture. Brown in 2 tablespoons hot shortening. Dissolve 1 chicken bouillon cube in 1 cup boiling water. Reserving ½ cup, pour remainder over meat in skillet. Simmer covered 20 minutes, or till the meat is tender.

Remove meat to bed of hot buttered noodles. Keep hot. Stir ½ cup dairy sour cream into pan drippings. Stir in enough of remaining chicken bouillon to make gravy desired consistency. Heat through, but do not boil. Pour over meat. Makes 4 servings.

## CURRIED LAMB

2 pounds lean lamb, cut in 1-inch cubes
2 tablespoons butter or margarine
1 cup chopped onion
1 clove garlic, minced
1 to 1½ tablespoons curry powder
1 teaspoon grated fresh gingerroot or ½ teaspoon ground ginger
2 tomatoes, peeled and chopped
3 tablespoons all-purpose flour

Brown meat in butter; remove from skillet. Add onion and garlic to skillet. Cook till onion is tender but not brown. Return meat to skillet. Add curry powder, 1½ teaspoons salt, gingerroot, tomatoes, and ¼ cup water. Cover; simmer 45 to 60 minutes, stirring occasionally, till lamb is tender. Stir in flour. Cook and stir till thickened. Serve with cooked rice tossed with raw grated carrot. Pass curry condiments. Makes 6 to 8 servings.

## CHICKEN ALMOND

2 cups finely sliced raw chicken breasts
¼ cup shortening or salad oil
2 5-ounce cans bamboo shoots, drained and diced
2 cups diced celery
1 cup diced bok choy (Chinese chard) or romaine
3 cups chicken broth
2 5-ounce cans water chestnuts, drained and sliced
2 tablespoons soy sauce
2 teaspoons monosodium glutamate
⅓ cup cornstarch
½ cup toasted halved almonds
Hot cooked rice

In large heavy skillet quickly cook chicken in hot shortening*. Add next 7 ingredients; mix thoroughly. Bring to boiling; cover, cook 5 minutes over low heat, or till crisp-tender.

Blend cornstarch and ½ cup cold water; add to chicken. Cook, stirring constantly, till mixture thickens and bubbles. Salt to taste. Garnish with almonds. Serve immediately over hot rice. Makes 6 to 8 servings.

* High heat and quick stirring are essential. The secret is to avoid overcooking.

## GOURMET CHICKEN

⅓ cup chopped onion
1 tablespoon butter or margarine
4 ounces linguini or fine noodles
2¾ cups chicken broth
½ teaspoon monosodium glutamate
¼ teaspoon grated lemon peel

2 tablespoons dry sherry
1 cup dairy sour cream
2 cups diced cooked or canned chicken
Toasted slivered almonds
Snipped parsley

Cook onion in butter till tender. Add uncooked noodles, broth, monosodium glutamate, ½ teaspoon salt, and lemon peel; bring to boiling. Cover; cook over *low* heat 25 minutes or till noodles are done.

Stir in wine, sour cream, and chicken; heat through. Turn into serving dish. Sprinkle with almonds and parsley. Makes 4 servings.

## CHICKEN CURRY IN PINEAPPLE SHELLS

4 tiny or 1 large ripe pineapple
¼ cup sugar
1½ teaspoons curry powder
1 tablespoon butter or margarine
⅓ cup minced onion
⅓ cup diced celery
1 3-ounce can sliced mushrooms, drained (½ cup)

½ cup light cream
½ cup milk
¼ cup chicken broth
1 tablespoon cornstarch
1 cup cubed cooked chicken
½ teaspoon monosodium glutamate

Cut slice off top of each pineapple. Scoop out fruit, leaving shells ½ inch thick. Dice ½ cup pineapple (discard core). In a saucepan combine diced pineapple, sugar, and ½ cup water; cook, covered, about 8 minutes. Drain and set aside. Heat pineapple shells on baking sheet at 450° about 10 minutes.

Meanwhile heat curry powder in butter or margarine. Add onion and celery; mix well. Stir in mushrooms, cream, milk, and broth; bring to boiling. Combine cornstarch and 1 table-spoon cold water; stir into hot mixture. Cook and stir till sauce thickens and bubbles. Add chicken, cooked pineapple, mono-sodium glutamate, and ¼ teaspoon salt; heat through. Serve in hot pineapple shells. Serve with hot rice. Serves 4.

## TURKEY STRATA

Trim crusts from 4 slices white bread; cube crusts. Cube 2 slices white bread; place with cubed crusts in bottom of 8x8x2-inch baking dish. Combine 2 cups diced cooked turkey, ½ cup chopped onion, ½ cup finely chopped celery, ¼ cup chopped green pepper, ½ cup mayonnaise, ¾ teaspoon salt, and dash pepper. Spoon over bread cubes.

Arrange trimmed bread slices atop turkey mixture. Com-bine 2 beaten eggs and 1½ cups milk; pour over all. Cover; chill 1 hour or overnight. Stir one 10½-ounce can condensed cream of mushroom soup; spoon atop. Bake at 325° about 1 hour or till set. Sprinkle ½ cup shredded sharp process American cheese atop last few minutes. Serves 6.

## BOMBAY CHICKEN

| | |
|---|---|
| 1 2½- to 3-pound ready-to-cook broiler-fryer chicken, cut up | 3½ cups boiling water |
| ⅓ cup all-purpose flour | 1 cup uncooked long-grain rice |
| 1 teaspoon paprika | ½ cup light raisins |
| ¼ cup butter or margarine | ½ cup flaked coconut |
| 1 medium onion, thinly sliced | ¼ cup coarsely chopped peanuts |
| 4 chicken bouillon cubes | 1 teaspoon curry powder |

Coat chicken with mixture of flour, 1 teaspoon salt, dash pepper, and paprika. In skillet brown chicken in butter; re-move. In skillet cook onion in remaining butter till tender but not brown. Dissolve bouillon cubes in boiling water; add to onions. Stir in remaining ingredients. Turn rice mixture into 12x7½x2-inch baking dish. Top with chicken. Bake covered at 350° about 1¼ hours or till rice is cooked and chicken is tender. Serves 4.

# COMPANY CHICKEN

2 chicken bouillon cubes
1 2½- to 3-pound ready-to-cook
    broiler-fryer chicken, cut up
¼ cup all-purpose flour
1 teaspoon paprika
2 tablespoons butter or margarine

⅓ cup chopped onion
1 clove garlic, minced
4 small potatoes (about ¾
    pound), pared and halved
2 tablespoons all-purpose flour
3 tablespoons dry sherry

Dissolve bouillon cubes in 1¼ cups boiling water; cool. Coat
chicken with mixture of ¼ cup flour, ½ teaspoon salt, and
paprika. In skillet brown chicken in butter, 10 to 15 minutes.
Add chicken bouillon, onion, garlic, and lightly salted potatoes. Cover and cook 25 to 30 minutes or till tender. Remove
chicken and potatoes to serving platter. Blend 2 tablespoons
flour with ¼ cup cold water. Stir into pan juices; cook and
stir till mixture bubbles. Add wine and dash pepper. Cook 1
minute longer. Pass gravy. Serves 4.

# HOSTESS NOTE:

## FORMAL TABLE SETTING

Allow 20 to 30 inches width for each cover. All appointments are placed about one inch from the edge of the table, forks to the left in order of their use. Place the bread-and-butter plate above the forks with the butter knife straight across the top. The dinner salad may be placed on the bread-and-butter plate. Salad bowls are considered optional.

Water goblets are lined up above the tip of the knife. If wine is served, place the glass to the right of the forks. The napkin is placed in the center of the cover when both salad and butter plates are on the table.

When the main dishes are served at the table, stack dinner plates in front of the host. The serving utensils are placed next to his silver. Place food within easy reach.

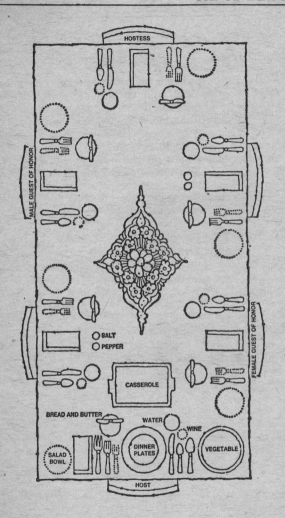

## CHICKEN LIVER STROGANOFF

| | |
|---|---|
| 1 cup chopped onion | 1 tablespoon paprika |
| 2 tablespoons butter or margarine | ½ teaspoon salt |
| | Dash pepper |
| · · · | 1 cup dairy sour cream |
| ½ pound chicken livers, halved | |
| 1 3-ounce can broiled sliced | · · · |
| mushrooms, undrained | 2 cups hot cooked rice |
| (⅔ cup) | Snipped parsley |

Cook onion in butter till tender but not brown. Add halved chicken livers and mushrooms with liquid. Stir in paprika, salt, and pepper. Cover, cook over low heat 8 to 10 minutes or till livers are tender.

Stir in sour cream; heat through (do not boil). Serve over hot cooked rice. Trim with parsley. Makes 4 servings.

## CAULIFLOWER-HAM BAKE

| | |
|---|---|
| 2 cups cubed cooked ham | 1 cup milk |
| 1 medium head cauliflower | 4 ounces sharp process American |
| 1 3-ounce can sliced mushrooms, | cheese, cubed (1 cup) |
| drained (½ cup) | ½ cup dairy sour cream |
| · · · | · · · |
| 2 tablespoons butter or margarine | 1 tablespoon fine dry bread |
| 2 tablespoons all-purpose flour | crumbs |

Break cauliflower into flowerets (about 4 cups); cook in salted water till tender; drain. Combine with ham and mushrooms.

In medium saucepan, melt butter or margarine. Stir in flour. Add milk all at once and stir constantly till mixture thickens and bubbles. Add cheese and sour cream to sauce; stir till cheese is melted. Combine with vegetables and ham. Turn into a 1½-quart casserole. Top with bread crumbs. Bake uncovered in a moderate oven (350°) for 40 minutes or till hot. Makes 6 servings.

## CRAB-CABBAGE SKILLET

| | |
|---|---|
| 2 tablespoons salad oil | ¼ teaspoon ground ginger |
| 4 medium green onions, sliced | 1 cup chicken broth |
| (¼ cup) | 1½ tablespoons cornstarch |
| 1 tablespoon dry sherry | 1 7½-ounce can crab meat, |
| ½ teaspoon sugar | flaked and cartilage removed |
| 1 head Chinese cabbage, cut in | Chow mein noodles |
| 1-inch pieces ( 6 cups) | |

Heat oil in skillet. Add next 4 ingredients, ½ teaspoon salt, and dash pepper. Cook and stir 1 minute. Add cabbage and broth. Cover and simmer 5 minutes or till tender-crisp. Blend cornstarch with 2 tablespoons cold water. Add to cabbage. Cook and stir till thick and bubbly. Add crab; heat. Serve over heated chow mein noodles. Serves 4.

## CRAB-MUSHROOM MORNAY

2 6-ounce cans mushroom
   crowns, drained* (2 cups)
1 7½-ounce can crab meat,
   flaked and cartilage removed
2 teaspoons lemon juice
3 tablespoons butter or
   margarine

3 tablespoons all-purpose flour
1½ cups milk
2 slightly beaten egg yolks
6 ounces sharp process
   American cheese, shredded
   (1½ cups)
2 tablespoons dry sherry

Arrange mushrooms, hollow side up, in 8¼x1¾-inch round ovenware baking dish. Cover with crab meat; sprinkle with lemon juice.

Melt butter in saucepan; blend in flour. Add milk all at once; cook and stir till mixture thickens and bubbles. Add small amount of hot mixture to egg yolks; return to sauce and cook 1 minute. Remove from heat. Stir in 1¼ *cups of the cheese* and the wine. Pour sauce over crab. Sprinkle with remaining cheese. Bake at 350° for 20 minutes. Serve over rice or toast points. Serves 6.

*Or use 2 pints fresh mushrooms. Wash; remove stems; use crowns and stems.

## SHRIMP NEW ORLEANS

½ cup chopped onion
¼ cup chopped green pepper
2 tablespoons butter or margarine

. . .

3 cups cleaned cooked or canned
   shrimp
2 cups cooked rice
¾ cup light cream

1 10¾-ounce can condensed
   tomato soup
¼ cup dry sherry
1 tablespoon lemon juice
¼ teaspoon salt
   Dash ground nutmeg
2 tablespoons toasted slivered
   almonds

In medium saucepan cook onion and green pepper in butter or margarine till tender but not brown. Stir in shrimp, rice, soup, cream, wine, lemon juice, salt, and nutmeg. Turn into a 2-quart casserole. Bake in a moderate oven (350°) for 40 minutes or till bubbly. Top with nuts. Serves 6.

# HADDOCK POLYNESIAN

3 pounds frozen haddock fillets, thawed
Butter or margarine

. . .

1 10½-ounce can frozen condensed cream of shrimp soup, thawed

1 cup dairy sour cream
3 tablespoons lemon juice
½ teaspoon salt
¼ teaspoon pepper

. . .

3 or 4 thinly sliced scallions or green onions

Place fish fillets in greased 9x9x2-inch baking dish. Dot with butter or margarine. Bake in moderate oven (375°) for 25 minutes.

Combine shrimp soup, sour cream, lemon juice, salt, and pepper. Spoon soup mixture over fish fillets. Bake an additional 5 minutes. Sprinkle with scallions or green onions just before serving. Makes 8 servings.

# CLAM-STUFFED SHRIMP

1 pound large raw shrimp in shells (about 16 shrimp)

. . .

¾ cup rich round cracker crumbs (about 18 crackers)
3 tablespoons butter or margarine, melted

. . .

1 7- or 7½-ounce can minced clams, drained
2 tablespoons snipped parsley
⅛ teaspoon garlic powder
⅛ teaspoon salt
Dash pepper
⅓ cup dry sherry

Shell and devein the raw shrimp. Slit each along vein side about halfway through.

Combine cracker crumbs and melted butter or margarine. Stir in clams, parsley, garlic powder, salt, and pepper. Stuff each shrimp with clam mixture. Arrange in 12x7½x2-inch baking dish. Bake in moderate oven (350°) for 18 to 20 minutes, basting occasionally with the wine. Makes 4 servings.

# SCALLOPS TETRAZZINI

Thaw one 12-ounce package frozen scallops; cut in halves. In saucepan, combine scallops, ½ teaspoon instant minced onion,

¼ teaspoon salt, and dash pepper. Add 1 cup water. Cover; simmer 10 minutes. Drain; reserve ½ cup cooking liquid. Melt 2 tablespoons butter. Blend in 2 tablespoons all-purpose flour, ¼ teaspoon paprika, 1 drop bottled hot pepper sauce, dash dried oregano, crushed, and dash salt. Add the ½ cup cooking liquid and ½ cup milk. Cook and stir till thickened. Stir a little hot sauce into 1 slightly beaten egg. Return to sauce; mix well.

Add one 3-ounce can broiled sliced mushrooms with liquid (⅔ cup) and scallops to sauce. Mix well. Spoon 4 ounces spaghetti, cooked and drained, into a 10x6x1½-inch baking dish. Top with scallop mixture; sprinkle with 2 tablespoons grated Parmesan cheese. Broil about 5 minutes. Serves 4.

## CLAM PUFF

2 7-ounce cans minced clams
1 cup fine cracker crumbs
2 tablespoons instant minced onion

4 well-beaten eggs
2 tablespoons snipped parsley
Dash bottled hot pepper sauce

Drain clams, reserving liquor; add milk to liquor to make 1 cup. Combine liquid with crumbs (24 crackers) and onion. Let stand 15 minutes. Fold in clams, ½ teaspoon salt, and last 3 ingredients. Pour into *ungreased* 1½-quart souffle dish. Bake at 325° for 60 to 65 minutes or till done. Serves 6.

## LOBSTER EN COQUILLE

1 9-ounce package frozen lobster
      tails
½ cup finely chopped celery
1 tablespoon butter or margarine
1 10-ounce can frozen condensed
      cream of shrimp soup, thawed
1 3-ounce can sliced mushrooms,
      drained (½ cup)

¼ cup milk
½ cup soft bread crumbs
1 tablespoon dry sherry

. . .

¼ cup soft bread crumbs
¼ cup shredded sharp process
      American cheese

Cook lobster tails according to package directions. Cool; remove meat from shells and cut in bite-size pieces.

In saucepan cook celery in butter or margarine till tender but not brown. Stir in thawed soup, milk, mushrooms, ½ cup bread crumbs, wine, and lobster. Bring mixture to boiling, stirring constantly. Spoon into 4 baking shells or individual casseroles.

Combine ¼ cup bread crumbs and shredded cheese; sprinkle over lobster mixture in shells. Bake in moderate oven (350°) for 20 minutes. Trim with parsley and serve with lemon wedges, if desired. Makes 4 servings.

## OYSTER PUDDING

6 slices white bread
Butter or margarine, softened
6 slices (6 ounces) sharp process
American cheese
· · ·

1 pint shucked fresh oysters
Milk
2 beaten eggs
1 teaspoon salt
¼ teaspoon pepper

Spread bread slices lightly on one side with softened butter. Cut in cubes. Place *half* the cubes in bottom of 12x7½x2-inch baking dish; top with cheese slices.

Drain oysters, reserving the liquor. Add enough milk to liquor to make 2½ cups. Arrange oysters on cheese. Top with remaining bread cubes. Combine liquid, eggs, salt, and pepper; pour over all in baking dish.

Bake in slow oven (325°) for 1 to 1¼ hours or till knife inserted just off center comes out clean. Makes 4 to 6 servings.

## SCALLOPED OYSTERS

1 pint shucked fresh oysters
2 cups medium-coarse cracker
crumbs (46 crackers)
½ cup butter or margarine, melted

· · ·

¾ cup light cream
½ teaspoon salt
¼ teaspoon Worcestershire sauce

Drain oysters, reserving ¼ cup liquor. Combine crumbs and butter. Spread a *third* of the crumbs in 8¼x1¾-inch round ovenware baking dish. Cover with *half* the oysters. Sprinkle with pepper. Using another third of the crumbs, spread a second layer; cover with remaining oysters. Sprinkle with pepper.

Combine cream, reserved oyster liquor, salt, and Worcestershire sauce. Pour over the oysters. Top with remaining cracker crumbs. Bake in moderate oven (350°) about 40 minutes. Makes 4 servings.

# SALMON FLORENTINE

2 10-ounce packages frozen
   chopped spinach
1 10½-ounce can condensed
   cream of chicken soup
¼ cup shredded sharp process
   American cheese
2 tablespoons mayonnaise or
   salad dressing

¼ cup dry sherry
1 teaspoon lemon juice
½ teaspoon Worcestershire sauce
1 1-pound can salmon, drained
1 cup soft bread crumbs
2 tablespoons butter or margarine,
   melted

Cook spinach according to package directions using unsalted water; drain.

In saucepan combine soup, cheese, wine, mayonnaise, lemon juice, and Worcestershire; bring to boiling. Blend ½ *cup* of the sauce with spinach. Divide mixture into 6 baking shells or individual casseroles. Break salmon in chunks, discarding bones and skin; layer over spinach. Spoon remaining sauce over top. Combine bread crumbs and butter; sprinkle over each casserole. Bake at 350° for 25 minutes, or till bubbly. Serves 6.

# COOKING AT THE TABLE

## CHINESE HOT POT

¾ pound large raw shrimp,
    shelled (about 12 shrimp)
2 uncooked chicken breasts,
    skinned and boned, sliced
    very thin across grain
½ pound uncooked beef sirloin,
    sliced **very** thin across grain
½ head Chinese cabbage **or** 1 head
    lettuce heart, coarsely
    cubed
1 cup cubed eggplant **or** 1
    5-ounce can water chest-
    nuts, drained and sliced thin
1½ cups halved fresh mushrooms
4 cups small spinach leaves,

    with stems removed

    • • •

6 13¾-ounce cans (10½ cups)
    or 2 46-ounce cans chicken
    broth (not condensed)
2 tablespoons monosodium
    glutamate
1 tablespoon grated gingerroot
    **or** 1 teaspoon ground ginger

    • • •

Chinese Mustard
Ginger Soy
Peanut Sauce
Red Sauce
Hot cooked rice

Shortly before cooking time, arrange raw meats and vegetables on large tray or platter and fill bowl with spinach.

Provide chopsticks, bamboo tongs, long-handled forks, or wire ladles as cooking tools for guests.

In an electric skillet, chafing dish, or Mongolian cooker, heat chicken broth, monosodium glutamate, and ginger to a gentle boil for cooking.

Set out little bowls of the dunking sauces. Each guest picks up desired food with chopsticks or tongs and drops it into the bubbling broth. When tidbits are cooked, he lifts them out and dips into sauces on plate. (Add more broth if needed.) Serve individual bowls of hot rice and Chinese tea. Makes 6 servings.

Dinner is dramatic, and definitely "company," when Chinese specialties are cooked and served at the table. The surprise: There's a minimum of last-minute fuss. Almost all Oriental dishes require a certain amount of chopping and slicing ahead of time—but the results are worth it. Small pieces get done presto, flavor is exotic, and guests can cook their own right at the table.

Chinese Hot Pot is a meal in itself, perfect to serve six people after the show or for a leisurely evening of dinner and conversation. Slice the food and make sauces early. When guests are hungry, just heat the broth and set out sauces and artistically arranged tidbits.

Everything on the tray is raw, of course—chunks of eggplant, crosscut strips of sirloin, halved fresh mushrooms, thin slices of chicken breasts, squares of Chinese cabbage, shelled shrimp. Fresh spinach to simmer along with the other foods is ready in a large salad bowl. The cooking liquid is chicken broth that boasts a faint overtone of ginger. Pick out a few choice tidbits at a time—with chopsticks, bamboo tongs, long-handled forks, or wire ladles—and drop them in the lazily bubbling broth. In a few minutes, fish them out, dip into the zesty sauces, and eat with fluffy rice, garnished with parsley.

Traditionalists poach eggs in the chicken broth at the very last, when it's subtly flavored from all the foods simmered in it. As a finale to this delicious dinner, dash dry sherry into the broth and pass it in dainty no-handle teacups.

Skip dessert, or serve fruit or fruit sherbet along with hot tea and fortune cookies.

For an outdoor party, the Mongolian cooker is the center of interest at the table. To use the Mongolian cooker: Fill the chimney with charcoal; add charcoal starter. Cover cooker, then light charcoal. Fill the cooking container with boiling chicken broth. When the broth returns to a simmer, seat the guests.

## CHINESE MUSTARD

¼ cup boiling water  
¼ cup dry mustard  
½ teaspoon salt  
1 tablespoon salad oil

Stir boiling water into dry mustard. Add salt and salad oil. For a more yellow color, add a little turmeric. Makes about ⅓ cup.

## GINGER SOY

½ cup soy sauce  
1½ teaspoons ground ginger

In a saucepan combine soy sauce and ginger. Bring to boiling; serve hot or cold. Serve with Chinese Hot Pot. Makes ½ cup sauce.

## PEANUT SAUCE

¼ cup chunk-style peanut butter  
2 teaspoons soy sauce  
1½ teaspoons water  
¼ teaspoon sugar  
1 drop bottled hot pepper sauce  
½ clove garlic, minced  
. . .  
¼ cup water

In a bowl thoroughly combine chunk-style peanut butter, soy sauce, 1½ teaspoons water, sugar, hot pepper sauce, and garlic; slowly stir in the ¼ cup water, mixing till smooth. Makes about ½ cup sauce.

## RED SAUCE

3 tablespoons catsup  
1½ tablespoons prepared horseradish  
3 tablespoons chili sauce  
1 teaspoon lemon juice  
Dash bottled hot pepper sauce

Mix all ingredients well. Serve with Chinese Hot Pot. Makes about ½ cup sauce.

## TEST KITCHEN TIPS
### Try chopsticks—they're fun to use

*Hold the top chopstick like a pencil, a little above the middle of the stick, small end down. Grip loosely between the index and middle finger; anchor gently with the thumb—whole hand must be relaxed. Practice moving stick to get the feeling.*

*Slip lower stick into position so that it rests lightly on V formed by thumb and index finger and on first joint of ring finger. Lower stick may touch middle finger. Lower stick never moves. Use sticks like tweezers.*

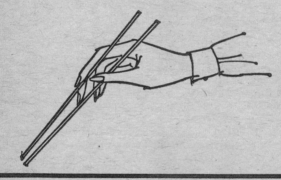

## ORIENTAL CHI CHOW

1 pound sirloin steak, 1 inch thick
1 pint fresh mushrooms, sliced
1 5-ounce can bamboo shoots, drained (⅔ cup)
1 5-ounce can water chestnuts, drained and sliced (⅔ cup)
1 medium onion, cut in wedges

½ cup sliced green onion
½ cup condensed beef broth
1 tablespoon sugar
¼ cup soy sauce
2 teaspoons cornstarch
1 1-pound can (2 cups) sliced peaches, drained

Partially freeze meat, then slice in thin strips. Brown meat, *half* at a time, in 2 tablespoons hot oil in skillet. Add next 7 ingredients. Cover; simmer 5 minutes. Blend soy, 1 tablespoon cold water, and cornstarch. Stir into meat mixture. Cook and stir till thick and bubbly. Add peaches; cover and heat through. Serve with *Ginger Rice:* Mix 2 cups hot cooked rice with ½ teaspoon ground ginger. Makes 4 or 5 servings.

## CHINESE FRIED RICE

½ cup finely diced cooked ham
  or cooked pork
2 tablespoons salad oil
¼ cup finely diced fresh
  mushrooms

4 cups cold cooked rice
1 teaspoon finely chopped green
  onion
2 tablespoons soy sauce
1 well-beaten egg

Brown diced cooked ham or pork lightly in hot oil. Add fresh mushrooms, cold cooked rice, chopped green onion, and soy sauce.

Cook over low heat 10 minutes, stirring occasionally. Add egg; cook and stir 2 to 3 minutes more. Serve immediately. Pass soy sauce. Serve as a main dish or as an accompaniment. Makes 4 to 6 servings.

## CLASSIC CHEESE FONDUE

1 clove garlic, halved
2 cups sauterne
½ pound gruyere cheese,
  shredded (2 cups)
1½ pounds **natural** Swiss cheese,
  shredded (6 cups)

1 teaspoon cornstarch
¼ cup Kirsch or dry sherry
¼ teaspoon ground nutmeg
French bread, cut in bite-size
  pieces each with a crust

Rub inside of heavy saucepan with cut surface of garlic. Pour in sauterne and warm till air bubbles rise and cover surface. (Don't cover or boil.) Remember to stir vigorously all the time from now on. Add a handful of combined cheeses (keep heat high but do not boil). When melted, toss in another handful. Stir cornstarch into Kirsch till well dissolved. After all cheese is blended and is bubbling gently and while stirring vigorously, add nutmeg, dash pepper, and Kirsch mixture. Quickly transfer to earthenware fondue pot; keep warm. (If fondue becomes thick, add a little warm sauterne.)

Fold bread cube on fork so crust is on outside. Dip a piece of bread into the cheese and swirl to coat. The swirling is important to keep fondue in motion. Serves 10.

## SHRIMP-CHEESE FONDUE

1 10-ounce can frozen condensed
  cream of shrimp soup, thawed
½ cup milk
2 teaspoons instant minced onion
¼ teaspoon dry mustard

1 pound process Swiss cheese,
  shredded (4 cups)
2 tablespoons dry sherry
French bread or hard rolls, cut
  in bite-size pieces each with
  a crust

In a saucepan heat soup and milk till blended. Stir in onion, mustard, and Swiss cheese. Heat and stir till cheese melts. Stir in wine. Serve immediately in earthenware fondue pot or chafing dish. Spear bread cube on long-handled fork and dip into cheese mixture, swirling to coat. Serves 6 to 8.

## TEST KITCHEN TIPS

### Keep natural cheese smooth in sauce

*Place sauce over hot water before adding the cheese. (Use water bath with chafing dish or a double boiler.) Crumble, cube, or shred cheese, or cut julienne style; add to hot mixture and stir till melted.*

## BEEF FONDUE

Pour salad oil in saucepan or beef fondue cooker to no more than ½ capacity or to depth of about 2 inches. Heat to 425° on range (do not let oil smoke). Transfer to cooker; place over alcohol burner or canned heat.

Have 1½ pounds trimmed beef tenderloin, cut in ¾-inch cubes, at room temperature in serving bowl. Set out small bowls of several or all of the special butters and sauces. Each guest spears a beef cube with fondue fork, then holds it in the hot oil until cooked to desired doneness—it doesn't take long to learn the length of time. Then transfer the meat to a dinner fork and dip it in a sauce on plate. Makes 4 servings.

*Butter-browned Mushrooms:* Melt 2 tablespoons butter in skillet. Add one 6-ounce can sliced mushrooms, drained (about 1 cup), *or* 1 pint fresh mushrooms, sliced. Cook over moderate heat, stirring occasionally, until evenly browned. Season with salt and pepper.

*Caper Butter:* Place ½ cup softened butter or margarine and 3 tablespoons capers with liquid in small mixing bowl. Beat till light and fluffy. Makes about ½ cup butter.

*Garlic Butter:* Whip ½ cup softened butter or margarine till fluffy. Stir in 1 clove garlic, crushed. Makes about ½ cup.

*Mustard Sauce:* Use regular bottled hot mustard, Dijon-style.

*Sour Cream-blue Cheese Sauce:* Combine 1 cup dairy sour cream, ¼ cup crumbled blue cheese, and dash of Worcestershire sauce. Chill. Makes about 1⅓ cups sauce.

*Red Sauce: Combine* ¾ cup catsup, 2 tablespoons vinegar, and ½ teaspoon prepared horseradish. Chill. Makes about ¾ cup sauce.

*Bordelaise Sauce:* In saucepan cook ½ cup fresh mushrooms, chopped, in 1 tablespoon butter till tender, about 4 minutes. Combine 3 tablespoons cornstarch and 2 cups beef broth; blend into mushrooms. Cook and stir till mixture boils. Add 3 tablespoons red wine, 2 tablespoons lemon juice, 2 teaspoons dried tarragon, crushed, and dash pepper. Simmer 5 to 10 minutes. Makes 2¼ cups.

# TERIYAKI MEATBALLS

1 tablespoon soy sauce
1 tablespoon water
2 teaspoons sugar
¼ teaspoon instant minced onion
Dash garlic salt
Dash monosodium glutamate
Dash ground ginger
½ pound lean ground beef
½ cup fine soft bread crumbs
Salad oil

Combine soy sauce, water, sugar, onion, garlic salt, monosodium glutamate, and ginger; let stand 10 minutes. Combine ground beef and bread crumbs; stir in soy mixture. Shape into ¾-inch meatballs.

Spear meatballs on bamboo skewers; cook in deep hot fat (375°) in a fondue pot about 1½ minutes. Makes about 2½ dozen balls.

## JAZZY BEEF BITES

1 tablespoon catsup
1 teaspoon prepared horseradish         ½ pound lean ground beef
1 teaspoon prepared mustard             ¼ cup fine soft bread crumbs
½ teaspoon instant minced onion            Sharp natural Cheddar cheese,
½ teaspoon salt                                cut in ¼-inch cubes
   Dash pepper                          Salad oil

Combine catsup, horseradish, mustard, onion, salt, and pepper; let stand 10 minutes. Combine ground beef and bread crumbs; stir in catsup mixture. Shape meat around cheese cubes into ¾-inch meatballs.

Spear meatballs on bamboo skewers; cook in deep hot fat (375°) in a fondue pot about 1½ minutes. Makes about 2½ dozen balls.

# Chafing dish cooking

Here are glamour foods for the chafing dish—or electric skillet —that you can cook with a flourish and serve with pride. (Any of these tasty main dishes can be prepared in an on-the-range skillet, too, if you wish.)

First step toward cooking for an audience; Know your chafing dish—each one has a personality of its own which affects length of cooking time.

*Chafing dishes* come in many handsome styles, from tiny ones for single servings to jumbo sizes for more than 20. And they come with different kinds of heating devices.

For actual cooking at the table, most cooks prefer heat you can adjust, whether alcohol (denatured), canned heat, or an electric unit.

Some chafing dishes are actually double boilers with water pan (*bain-marie*) and a cooking pan (*blazer*). The cooking pan is generally used directly over the flame. But when cooking sauces with several egg yolks, or cheese rarebits, you cook over hot water. When cooking in blazer pan, add water bath when cooking is done to keep food warm.

*Other chafing dishes* are the deep skillet type with just one pan—use like blazer pan.

There are special chafing dishes for fondues. The Continental choice for cheese fondue is an earthenware casserole on a heating unit, but any chafing dish can double nicely. Meat fondue calls for a deep one-pan chafing dish to hold hot oil.

*Food warmers* keep cooked foods at serving temperature on

the buffet. They might be pottery casseroles or meat pans with heat-proof glass liners. Candles, alcohol burners, or electric units furnish heat. A chafing dish with a *bain-marie* can serve as warmer, too.

*Choose speedy recipes.* If the sauce takes more than a few minutes to prepare, you'll probably want to fix it ahead of time. Pour the sauce in the chafing dish. Add last few ingredients at the table. It's speedier to brown meat on the range. Then transfer it to the chafing dish for final assembly at the table. Cooking at the table should be the spectacular ending of careful preparation.

Have everything ready for the main dish before guests arrive. Plan the rest of the meal so it takes minimum preserving preparation. Assemble cooking tools and ingredients on a tray for use at table. Now you're ready to go. Happy hostessing!

## SPEEDY STROGANOFF

1 pound beef sirloin, cut in
   ¼-inch strips
1 tablespoon shortening or oil
1 medium onion, sliced
1 clove garlic, crushed
1 10½-ounce can condensed cream
   of mushroom soup
1 cup dairy sour cream

1 3-ounce can broiled sliced
   mushrooms, undrained (⅔ cup)
2 tablespoons catsup
2 teaspoons Worcestershire sauce
4 ounces medium noodles, cooked
1 tablespoon butter or margarine
1 teaspoon poppy seed

In skillet or blazer pan of chafing dish brown meat strips in hot shortening. Add onion and garlic; cook till onion is crisptender. Blend soup, sour cream, mushrooms, catsup, and Worcestershire sauce. Pour over meat. Cook and stir over low heat till hot. Keep warm over hot water. Drain noodles; toss with butter and poppy seed. Serve sauce over noodles. Makes 4 servings.

## BEEF AND BEAN SKILLET

Cook one 10-ounce package frozen lima beans according to package directions; drain. In skillet or blazer pan of chafing dish brown 1 pound ground beef. Combine ½ clove garlic, minced, 1 tablespoon cornstarch, 1 tablespoon sugar, 2 tablespoons soy sauce, 1 teaspoon horseradish, ½ cup water, and few drops bottled hot pepper sauce. Add to meat. Cook until thickened. Add limas; cook and stir till heated through. Makes 6 servings.

## HAM IN SOUR CREAM

In skillet or blazer pan of chafing dish cook ¼ cup chopped onion and 2 cups cooked ham, cut in julienne strips, in 2 tablespoons butter till onion is tender. Sprinkle with 2 teaspoons all-purpose flour. Stir in 1 cup dairy sour cream and ½ cup milk. Add one 3-ounce can sliced mushrooms, drained. Cook and stir over low heat, just till mixture thickens and bubbles. Keep warm over hot water. Serve over toast points. Makes 4 servings.

## CLASSIC BEEF STROGANOFF

1 tablespoon all-purpose flour
½ teaspoon salt
1 pound beef sirloin, cut in ¼-inch strips
2 tablespoons butter or margarine
1 3-ounce can sliced mushrooms, drained (½ cup)
½ cup chopped onion
1 clove garlic, minced

2 tablespoons butter or margarine
3 tablespoons all-purpose flour
1 tablespoon tomato paste
1¼ cups beef stock or 1 10½-ounce can condensed beef broth
1 cup dairy sour cream
2 tablespoons dry sherry
6 ounces noodles, cooked

. . .

Combine 1 tablespoon flour and salt; coat meat with mixture. Heat blazer pan of chafing dish or skillet, then add 2 tablespoons butter or margarine. When melted, add sirloin strips and brown quickly on both sides. Add mushroom slices, onion, and garlic; cook 3 or 4 minutes or till onion is crisp-tender. Remove meat and mushrooms from pan.

Add 2 tablespoons butter or margarine to pan drippings; blend in 3 tablespoons all-purpose flour. Add tomato paste. Stir in cold meat stock. Cook and stir over medium-high heat till thickened and bubbly.

Return browned meat and mushrooms to blazer pan or skillet. Stir in sour cream and wine; cook slowly till heated through. Do not boil. Keep warm over hot water. Serve over hot buttered noodles. Serves 4 to 5.

*Making Classic Beef Stroganoff*

## CREAMED MUSHROOMS

Melt 6 tablespoons butter or margarine in medium skillet. Add ½ pound fresh mushrooms, sliced (3 cups); cook gently till tender and lightly browned. Push mushrooms to one side of pan; blend in 3 tablespoons all-purpose flour. Add 2 cups milk all at once. Cook and stir till mushroom mixture thickens and bubbles.

Add 1 tablespoon soy sauce, ¼ teaspoon salt, and dash pepper. Transfer to chafing dish and keep warm over hot water. Serve in crisp toast cups. Makes 4 or 5 servings.

---

## *TEST KITCHEN TIPS*

*Ways to use the versatile chafing dish*

- *Heat canned foods like a la kings, rabbits (rarebits), soups, and chowders.*
- *Prepare fruit sauces for desserts.*
- *Keep foods hot for buffet service.*
- *Serve hot spiced punch or tea.*

---

## CURRIED-EGG BISCUITS

| | |
|---|---|
| 1 8-ounce package refrigerated biscuits (10 biscuits) | 1 teaspoon curry powder |
| ¼ cup shortening | ½ teaspoon sugar |
| 1 tablespoon finely chopped onion | 2½ cups milk |
| 3 tablespoons all-purpose flour | 1 8-ounce can (1 cup) peas, drained |
| 1 teaspoon salt | 6 hard-cooked eggs, sliced |

Bake biscuits according to package directions. Meanwhile, melt shortening in blazer pan of chafing dish or saucepan. Add onion and cook till tender but not brown. Blend in flour, salt, curry powder, and sugar, stirring till smooth. Add milk all at once. Cook, stirring constantly, till mixture thickens and bubbles. Add drained peas and egg slices. Heat till mixture is hot through.

Split hot biscuits. Spoon curried mixture over biscuits. Makes 5 servings.

## EASY SHRIMP SAUTE

6 tablespoons butter or
    margarine
1 clove garlic, minced
1½ pounds (3 cups) shelled raw
    shrimp

¼ cup dry sherry
2 tablespoons snipped parsley
Hot cooked yellow or white
    rice

Melt butter in blazer pan of chafing dish or skillet; add garlic
and cook slightly. Add shrimp; cook, stirring frequently, till
shrimp are tender and turn pink, about 5 minutes. Stir in wine
and parsley. Heat to boiling. Serve with rice. Serves 4 to 6.

## STEAK DIANE

2 top loin or strip steaks, cut ½
    inch thick (about 7 ounces
    each)
Salt
Pepper

½ teaspoon dry mustard
2 tablespoons butter or margarine
1 tablespoon lemon juice
1 teaspoon snipped chives
½ teaspoon Worcestershire sauce

Sprinkle one side of each steak with salt, pepper, and ⅛ *teaspoon* of the dry mustard; pound into meat with meat mallet.
Repeat with other side of meat, pounding each piece to
about ⅓-inch thickness.

Melt butter in blazer pan of chafing dish or skillet. Add
meat and cook 2 minutes on each side. Transfer meat to
hot serving plate. In same skillet add lemon juice, chives, and
Worcestershire; bring to boiling. Pour over meat. Makes 2
servings.

## LOBSTER NEWBURG

6 tablespoons butter or
    margarine
2 tablespoons all-purpose flour
1½ cups light cream
3 beaten egg yolks
3 tablespoons dry sherry

1 5-ounce can lobster, drained
    and broken in large pieces
    (1 cup)
2 teaspoons lemon juice
¼ teaspoon salt
Paprika
Patty shells or Toast Cups

Melt butter in skillet or blazer pan of chafing dish; blend in
flour. Add cream all at once. Cook, stirring constantly, till
sauce thickens and bubbles. Place hot water bath under blazer
pan if using chafing dish.

Stir small amount of hot mixture into egg yolks, return to

hot mixture; cook, stirring constantly, till mixture thickens.
Add lobster; heat. Add wine, lemon juice, and salt. Sprinkle
with paprika. Serve in patty shells or in Toast Cups. Makes 5
servings.

## LOBSTER SUPREME

| | |
|---|---|
| 1 10-ounce package frozen artichoke hearts | ½ cup light cream |
| | 2 tablespoons dry sherry |
| 1 bay leaf | 2 ounces sharp process American |
| 1 tablespoon chopped onion | cheese, shredded (½ cup) |
| 1 teaspoon butter or margarine | 1 5-ounce can lobster, drained and broken in large pieces |
| . . . | (1 cup) |
| 1 10-ounce can condensed cream of mushroom soup | Hot cooked rice |

Cook artichoke hearts with bay leaf as directed on package
in *unsalted* water. Drain; remove bay leaf. Cut artichoke hearts
in half. In skillet or blazer pan of chafing dish cook onion in
butter till tender but not brown. Add soup, cream, and wine,
stirring till smooth. Add cheese; heat and stir till melted.

Add artichoke hearts and lobster; heat through. Keep warm
in skillet or over hot water. Serve over fluffy hot rice. Serves 4.

## SHRIMP NEWBURG

| | |
|---|---|
| 6 tablespoons butter or margarine | 1 pound shelled cooked shrimp |
| 2 tablespoons all-purpose flour | (2 cups) |
| ½ teaspoon salt | ¼ cup dry sherry |
| 1 cup light cream | 2 teaspoons lemon juice |
| 1 cup milk | Patty shells or Toast Cups |
| 4 slightly beaten egg yolks | |

In a skillet or blazer pan of chafing dish melt butter. Blend
in flour and salt; stir in cream and milk. Cook, stirring constantly, till sauce thickens and bubbles. Reduce heat of skillet
or place hot water bath under blazer pan of chafing dish.

Stir small amount sauce into egg yolks; return to skillet or
chafing dish and cook till blended, stirring constantly, about
1 minute. Add shrimp, wine, and lemon juice; heat thoroughly. Sprinkle with paprika. Serve in patty shells or Toast
Cups. Serves 5 or 6.

## BLACK MAGIC LUNCHEON

| | |
|---|---|
| 3 cups diced cooked ham | 2 cups dairy sour cream |
| ½ cup chopped onion | ½ cup sliced ripe olives |
| 2 tablespoons butter or margarine | ¼ cup toasted slivered almonds |
| 2 tablespoons all-purpose flour | 8 patty shells |
| ⅔ cup milk | |

In blazer pan of chafing dish or skillet, cook ham and onion in butter till onion is tender. Remove from heat. Blend flour and milk; stir into sour cream; add to skillet with sliced olives. Heat through, stirring constantly; *do not boil*. Stir in almonds. Serve in patty shells. Makes 8 servings.

## TOAST CUPS

Trim crusts from 4 slices white bread. Spread bread with ¼ cup softened butter or margarine. Carefully press into ungreased medium muffin cups. Toast at 350° for about 15 minutes. Makes 4 toast cups.

## JAPANESE TEMPURA

Turn vegetables into fare that is "suteki" (really great)—tempting enough to set before an Emperor. Since the tempura must be served piping hot, it's best done for small groups (not more than six to eight people).

Tempura is simple. Batter-dipped pieces of vegetables or sea food are deep-fat fried till light brown, with an almost "sheer" crust, and not a trace of greasiness. Your guests enjoy watching—and munching—as you fry the vegetables and seafood and transfer them to a draining rack at the side.

Provide your guests with individual paper napkin-lined plates or little baskets and chopsticks which they use to dunk the drained tempura-fried vegetables in a special tempura sauce. The sauce is rich in soy, indispensable to Oriental cooking. For condiments, offer grated radish combined with grated turnip, grated fresh gingerroot, and mustard sauce.

A variety of vegetables can be used—asparagus spears, parsley, sweet potatoes, spinach, mushrooms, and green beans. Try these or experiment on your own.

Wash and dry vegetables well. Cut into slices or strips where necessary.

Keep sauce and condiments covered and chilled if prepared ahead.

Mix batter, not too much at one time, just before using. Don't overstir—a few lumps help make a crisp, light crust.

Keep the batter well-chilled while using—a couple of ice cubes in the batter do the trick without diluting the batter.

Use one set of tongs to dip vegetables into batter, another set for the oil.

Use a fresh, bland cooking oil for frying. A deep electric skillet with a good thermostat control will keep the hot oil at an even temperature of 360° to 365°. Don't cook too much food at one time; skim off tiny drops of batter that form on surface of fat.

Drain the tempura-fried foods on rack set on a tray. Serve piping hot.

## TEMPURA BATTER

| | |
|---|---|
| 1 cup sifted all-purpose flour | 1 slightly beaten egg |
| ½ teaspoon sugar | 1 cup ice water |
| ½ teaspoon salt | 2 tablespoons salad oil |

Combine ingredients, beating together till dry ingredients are just moistened—a few flour lumps should remain. Prepare batter just before use; add one or two ice cubes.

## TEMPURA CONDIMENTS

1. Grated fresh gingerroot.
2. Equal parts grated turnip and radish, combined.
3. Blend 1½ tablespoons soy sauce and ¼ cup prepared mustard.

## SUKIYAKI

| | |
|---|---|
| 2 tablespoons salad oil | 1 cup thinly sliced fresh mushrooms |
| 1 pound beef tenderloin, sliced paper-thin across the grain | 1 5-ounce can water chestnuts, drained and thinly sliced |
| 2 tablespoons sugar | 1 5-ounce can bamboo shoots, drained |
| 1 teaspoon monosodium glutamate | |
| ½ cup beef stock or canned condensed beef broth | 5 cups small spinach leaves |
| ⅓ cup soy sauce | 1 1-pound can bean sprouts, drained |
| 2 cups 2-inch length bias-cut green onions | 12 to 16 ounces bean curd, cubed* (optional) |
| 1 cup 1-inch bias-cut celery slices | |

Preheat large skillet or Oriental saucepan; add oil. Add beef and cook quickly, turning it over and over, 1 or 2 minutes or just till browned. Sprinkle meat with sugar and monosodium glutamate. Combine beef stock and soy sauce; pour over. Push meat to one side. Let the soy sauce mixture bubble.

Keeping in separate groups, add onion and celery. Continue cooking and toss-stirring *each group* over high heat about 1 minute; push to one side. Again keeping in separate groups, add mushrooms, chestnuts, bamboo shoots, spinach, bean sprouts, and bean curd. Cook and stir each food just till heated through. Let guests help themselves to some of everything. Serve with rice. Pass soy sauce. Makes 4 servings.

*Bean curd (tofu) may be found at Japanese food shops, or obtained from mail-order houses that specialize in Oriental foods.

## TEST KITCHEN TIPS

### Cook sukiyaki indoors or out

*If the party is outside, cook in a real wok pan. These basin-shaped saucepans are found in some Oriental shops. To cook, place the wok on its base over a hibachi or other grill. Indoors use a skillet.*

# CASSEROLES FOR A CROWD

There's no trick to cooking for 25 or 50 people—if you plan ahead, and pick foods that are easy to fix with equipment on hand.

Begin by evaluating the number of helpers available for advance preparation and serving. An important factor when choosing the main dish is the cooking equipment available—size and number of cooking dishes or pans, ovens, and mixing dishes.

The easiest main dish is a casserole. It combines meat and vegetables for a tasty treat everyone will enjoy. It can be fixed ahead and heated at mealtime, and it's simple to serve.

Most of the recipes call for two 13x9x2-inch baking dishes or metal baking pans. You can substitute one 18x12x2½-inch baking pan, but allow for two inches of space around the pan when in the oven. This provides even heat circulation.

Keep the entire menu simple. Just add a salad, maybe a bread, dessert, and beverage. Before you order groceries, check Shopping Guide for a Crowd (see Index).

When you're the only chef, plan a make-ahead salad and dessert; put casseroles together early and refrigerate. Allow an extra 15 to 20 minutes in the oven when a casserole goes in cold. Slip bread into the oven to warm alongside the casserole. At serving time, put main course on buffet table; let guests serve themselves. Dessert and beverage can go on a side table for pick-up later.

When there's plenty of help, go fancy with the dessert that's served. If using a large coffee maker, know how long it takes; start the coffee in plenty of time.

For a large crowd, plan two buffet lines—speediest with hostesses serving. Put dessert at places ahead of time or serve it along with coffee, so guests needn't juggle.

These recipes make about 25 servings. If you're serving a group of 50 or 100, ask several helpers to each make one recipe.

# HAMBURGER PIE

5 pounds ground beef
4 medium onions, chopped (2 cups)
5 1-pound cans green beans, drained

4 10¾-ounce cans condensed tomato soup
Potato Fluff Topper

In 2 large skillets brown meat and onions (or oven brown in two 13x9x2-inch baking dishes at 350° for 40 minutes; stir occasionally). Spoon off fat. Turn into two 13x9x2-inch baking dishes. Lightly season *each* with ½ teaspoon salt and dash pepper. Add *half* the beans and soup to each pan; mix.

*Potato Fluff Topper:* Cook 3 pounds potatoes*. Mash while hot; add 1 cup milk and 2 eggs. Add ¼ cup butter or margarine and 1 teaspoon salt. Drop in mounds over meat mixture. If desired, sprinkle with 8 ounces process American cheese, shredded (2 cups). Bake in moderate oven (350°) for 30 minutes or till hot through. Makes 24 servings.

*For speed, use packaged instant mashed potatoes. Prepare enough for 16 servings, according to package directions, *but* reserve the milk. Add 2 eggs to potatoes. Season. Add butter to taste. Slowly add enough reserve milk to make potatoes hold shape.

# HAMBURGER-CORN BAKE

Lightly brown 4 pounds ground beef. Add 3 large onions, chopped (3 cups); cook till tender. Add two 1-pound cans whole kernel corn, drained, three 10½-ounce cans condensed cream of mushroom soup, three 10½-ounce cans condensed cream of chicken soup, 3 cups dairy sour cream, ¾ cup chopped canned pimiento, 1½ teaspoons monosodium glutamate, and ½ teaspoon pepper; mix well.

Divide 1 pound medium noodles, cooked and drained, between two 13x9x2-inch metal baking pans. Pour *half* the meat mixture over each; stir lightly. Combine 3 cups soft bread crumbs and 6 tablespoons butter, melted; sprinkle atop. Bake at 375° about 45 minutes, or till hot through. Serves 25.

## CHURCH-SUPPER TUNA BAKE

¾ cup diced green pepper
3 cups sliced celery
2 medium onions, chopped (1 cup)
¼ cup butter or margarine
3 10½-ounce cans condensed cream of mushroom soup
12 ounces process American cheese, cubed (3 cups)

2 cups milk
24 ounces medium noodles
1½ cups mayonnaise or salad dressing
1 4-ounce can chopped pimiento
3 9½-ounce cans tuna, drained and flaked
1 cup toasted slivered almonds

Cook green pepper, celery, and onion in butter for 10 minutes. In Dutch oven or kettle blend soup and milk together; add onion mixture and heat through. Add cheese; heat and stir till cheese melts. Cook noodles in large amount of boiling salted water till just tender; drain. Combine drained noodles and 2 *cups* of the soup mixture. Toss to coat noodles.

Turn noodles into 18x12x2½-inch pan or two 13x9x2-inch metal baking pans. Combine remaining soup mixture, mayonnaise, pimiento, and tuna. Pour over noodles. Mix lightly. Sprinkle almonds over top. Bake at 375° for 35 to 40 minutes. If chilled, allow an additional 15 minutes. Makes 25 (about 1 cup) servings.

## ROASTER BAKED BEANS

8 1-pound 15-ounce cans pork and beans in tomato sauce
2 14-ounce bottles catsup
1 large onion, chopped (1 cup)

½ pound brown sugar (1¼ cups)
2 tablespoons dry mustard
1 pound bacon, cut in pieces

Empty cans of beans into inset pan of electric roaster,* preheated to 300°. Stir next 4 ingredients into beans. Sprinkle bacon pieces over. Cook, covered, 300° for 2 hours. Uncover and continue cooking 2 hours, stirring occasionally. Makes 25 servings.

*Or, use roasting pan in oven. Bake, uncovered, in a moderate oven (350°) for 3½ to 4 hours; stir frequently.

## CHILI CON CARNE

4 pounds ground beef
1 tablespoon salt
4 large onions, chopped (4 cups)
4 medium green peppers,
    chopped (2 cups)
4 1-pound cans kidney beans,
    drained

2 1-pound 13-ounce cans
    tomatoes
2 15-ounce cans (3¾ cups)
    tomato sauce
1½ to 2 tablespoons chili powder
½ teaspoon paprika
3 bay leaves, finely crushed

Season ground beef with salt. Brown the meat in a 10-quart Dutch oven or kettle. Add onion and green pepper; cook till tender but not brown. Add remaining ingredients. Cover and simmer 2 hours, stirring occasionally. Add water, if needed for desired consistency. Makes 25 (about 1 cup) servings.

## SALMON AND POTATO
## CHIP CASSEROLE

½ cup butter or margarine
1 large onion, chopped (1 cup)
¼ cup all-purpose flour
5 10½-ounce cans condensed
    cream of mushroom soup
1 quart milk

1¼ pounds potato chips, coarsely
    crushed (12 cups)
5 1-pound cans salmon, drained
    and flaked
2 10-ounce packages frozen peas,
    cooked and drained

In 3-quart saucepan melt butter; add onion and cook till tender but not brown. Blend in flour, stirring till bubbly. Stir in soup. Gradually add milk till mixture is smooth. Set aside about 2 cups crushed potato chips. In two 13x9x2-inch metal baking pans, layer remaining potato chips, salmon, peas, and soup mixture alternately. Sprinkle reserved chips over top. Bake at 350° for 40 to 45 minutes or till heated through. Serves 25.

## BAKED FRANKS AND LIMAS

3 10-ounce packages frozen limas
1 cup chopped onion
2 cups chopped celery
¼ cup shortening or salad oil
2 1-pound 12-ounce cans
    tomatoes, undrained and
    broken up

2 10½-ounce cans condensed
    cream of mushroom soup
½ cup all-purpose flour
2 pounds frankfurters
1 cup fine dry bread crumbs
2 tablespoons butter, melted

Cook limas according to package directions in *unsalted* water; drain. In Dutch oven cook onion and celery in shortening till tender but not brown. Blend in soup. Reserving 1 cup tomato liquid, add remaining tomatoes with liquid to soup mixture. Blend flour with the 1 cup reserved tomato liquid; add to mixture. Cook and stir till mixture thickens and bubbles. Thinly slice franks. Divide franks and lima beans evenly between two 13x9x2-inch baking dishes. Pour *half* the tomato mixture over each; mix. Combine bread crumbs and butter; sprinkle atop each. Bake at 350° for 30 minutes or till hot. Let stand 10 minutes. Makes 25 (about 1 cup) servings.

## BEEF NOODLE CASSEROLE

Cook 1 pound medium noodles in large amount boiling salted water; drain. In Dutch oven combine 4 pounds ground beef, 1 cup chopped onion, 1 cup chopped green pepper, 1 cup chopped celery, and 2 cloves garlic, minced; cook till meat is lightly browned.

Stir in two 1-pound 12-ounce cans tomatoes, undrained, two 15-ounce cans tomato sauce, one 6-ounce can chopped mushrooms, drained, 8 ounces sharp process American cheese, shredded (2 cups), 1 teaspoon dried thyme, crushed, 1 teaspoon dried basil, crushed, ½ teaspoon salt, and ¼ teaspoon pepper. Heat and stir till cheese melts.

Spread noodles in two 13x9x2-inch baking dishes. Pour tomato mixture over; stir into noodles. Cover loosely with foil; bake 45 minutes. Uncover, stir lightly; bake 25 minutes. Sprinkle with 8 ounces sharp process American cheese, shredded (2 cups). Bake 5 minutes. Makes 25 (about 1 cup) servings.

## CHEVRON RICE BAKE

Cut two 12-ounce cans luncheon meat into 24 slices; reserve for top. Cube two 12-ounce cans luncheon meat. Combine cubed meat, 8 cups cooked rice, two 10-ounce packages frozen peas, thawed, *or* two 1-pound cans peas, drained, 4 slightly beaten eggs, two 10½-ounce cans condensed cream of chicken soup, 1 cup milk, ½ cup snipped parsley, 1 medium onion, chopped (½ cup), 2 teaspoons curry powder, and ⅛ teaspoon pepper.

Spread in two 13x9x2-inch metal baking pans. Drain three 1-pound 13-ounce cans peach halves *or* two 1-pound 13-ounce cans peach slices. Stud peaches with a few whole cloves. Arrange peaches and meat slices atop rice-meat mixture. Bake uncovered at 375° for 1 hour or till heated through. Makes 24 (¾ cup) servings.

## HAMBURGER CHEESE BAKE

16 ounces medium noodles
2 pounds ground beef
2 15-ounce cans tomato sauce
1 tablespoon sugar
2 teaspoons salt
½ teaspoon garlic salt
½ teaspoon pepper

. . .

2 cups cream-style cottage cheese

2 8-ounce packages cream cheese, softened
1 cup dairy sour cream
2 bunches green onions with tops (14 onions), sliced (1 cup)
1 medium green pepper, chopped (¾ cup)
½ cup shredded Parmesan cheese

Cook beef till brown. Stir in tomato sauce, sugar, salt, garlic salt, and pepper. Remove from heat.

Combine cottage cheese, cream cheese, sour cream, green onion, and green pepper. Spread *half* the noodles in two 13x9x2-inch baking dishes. Moisten noodles with some of the meat sauce. Cover with cheese mixture; top with remaining noodles, then meat sauce. Sprinkle with Parmesan. Bake covered at 375° for 45 minutes. Serves 24.

## SCALLOPED POTATOES

8 pounds potatoes, pared and thinly sliced (24 cups)
2 medium onions, finely chopped (1 cup)
4 cups milk

4 10½-ounce cans condensed cream of mushroom soup
2 10½-ounce cans condensed cream of celery soup
2 teaspoons salt

In two 13x9x2-inch baking dishes, spread 6 *cups* of the sliced potatoes in bottom of each dish. Combine onion, soups, milk, and salt. Pour *one-fourth* of the mixture over potatoes in *each* dish. Repeat layers. Cover with foil; bake at 375° for 1 hour. Uncover and bake 30 to 45 minutes longer. Makes 24 servings.

# SHOPPING GUIDE FOR A CROWD

When you shop for food for a large group use this table as a guide. We have indicated the size of one serving for each item listed—no seconds. For the hearty eater, plan more.

| FOODS | SERVINGS | SERVING UNIT | AMOUNT |
|---|---|---|---|
| **BEVERAGES** | | | |
| Coffee, ground | 40 to 50 | ¾ cup | 1 pound (5 cups) |
| Coffee, instant | 30 | ¾ cup | 2-ounce jar (1 cup) |
| Cream for coffee | 25 | 1 tablespoon | 1 pint |
| Milk | 24 | 1 cup | 1½ gallons |
| Tea leaves | 50 | ¾ cup | 1 cup |
| **BREADS AND CEREALS** | | | |
| Rice, long-grain | 24 | ½ cup, cooked | 1½ pounds uncooked |
| Rolls and biscuits | 24 | 1 roll | 2 dozen |
| Spaghetti | 25 | ¾ cup, cooked | 2¼ pounds uncooked |
| **DESSERTS** | | | |
| Cake | 24 | 1/12 of cake | 2 9-inch layer cakes |
| | 24 | 2½-inch squares | 1 15½x10½x1-inch sheet cake |
| Ice cream | 24 | ½ cup or 1 slice | 3 quarts |
| Pie | 30 | ⅙ of pie | 5 9-inch pies |
| **FRUIT** | | | |
| Canned | 24 | ½ cup | 1 6½- to 7¼-pound can |
| **RELISHES (combine several)** | | | |
| Carrot strips | 25 | 2 to 3 strips | 1 pound |
| Cauliflowerets | 25 | 2 ounces sliced, raw | 7 pounds |
| Celery | 25 | 1 2- to 3-inch pieces | 1 pound |
| Green pepper | 25 | 1 ounce strips, raw | 2 pounds |
| Olives | 25 | 3 to 4 olives | 1 quart |
| Pickles | 25 | 1 ounce | 1 quart |
| **SOUP** | 25 | 1 cup (main course) | 1½ gallons *or* 10 10½- to 11-ounce cans condensed *or* 2 50-ounce cans condensed |
| **SALADS** | | | |
| Fruit | 24 | ⅓ cup | 2 quarts |
| Potato | 24 | ½ cup | 3 quarts |
| Tossed vegetable | 25 | ¾ cup | 5 quarts |
| **VEGETABLES** | | | |
| Canned | 24 | ½ cup | 6 1-pound cans |
| | 28 | ½ cup | 4 1-pound 11-ounce to 1-pound 13-ounce cans |
| | 25 | ½ cup | 1 6½- to 7¼-pound can |
| Fresh: | | | |
| Onions | 25 | ⅓ cup, small whole or pieces | 6¼ pounds |
| Potatoes | 25 | ½ cup, mashed | 6¾ pounds |
| Potatoes | 25 | 1 medium, baked | 8½ pounds |
| Frozen: | | | |
| Beans, green or wax | 25 | ⅓ cup | 5¼ pounds |
| Carrots | 25 | ⅓ cup, sliced | 5 pounds |
| Corn, whole kernel | 25 | ⅓ cup | 5 pounds |
| Peas | 25 | ⅓ cup | 5 pounds |
| Potatoes, fried | 25 | 10 pieces | 3¼ pounds |
| Squash, summer | 25 | ⅓ cup, sliced | 5½ pounds |
| **MISCELLANEOUS** | | | |
| Butter | 32 | 1 pat | ½ pound |
| Jam or preserves | 25 | 2 tablespoons | 1½ pounds |
| Juice | 23 | ½ cup | 2 46-ounce cans |
| Potato chips | 25 | ¾ to 1 ounce | 1 to 1½ pounds |

## SWEET AND SOUR PORK

| | |
|---|---|
| 5 pounds pork, cut in 1-inch cubes | 4 green peppers, cut in strips |
| 4 teaspoons salt | 1 cup cornstarch |
| ½ teaspoon pepper | 3 cups sugar |
| 1 cup shortening | 8 cups chicken bouillon |
| 2 1-pound 4½-ounce cans pineapple chunks, drained (reserve 1 cup syrup) | 3 cups vinegar |
| | ½ cup soy sauce |
| | Hot cooked rice |

Season pork with salt and pepper. Place *half* of the shortening and *half* the pork in two 13x9x2-inch metal baking pans. Bake in a hot oven (400°) for 1 hour to brown meat, stirring often. Spoon off fat.

Add *half* of the pineapple chunks and *half* of the green pepper strips to each pan. In Dutch oven combine cornstarch and sugar; stir in bouillon, vinegar, soy sauce, and reserved pineapple syrup; cook and stir till mixture thickens and bubbles. Pour *half* the mixture into each pan; combine. Continue baking at 400° for 45 minutes. Stir mixture occasionally during baking. Serve over hot cooked rice. Makes 24 (about 1 cup) servings.

---

## TEST KITCHEN TIPS

### Food should be served at the right temperature

*Keep food hot by serving from casseroles over candle warmers, electrically heated glass trays, or from chafing dishes. Serve cold food from the refrigerator in serving dishes surrounded by cracked ice.*

---

## SPANISH RICE

| | |
|---|---|
| 1 pound sliced bacon | 1 cup chili sauce |
| 2 cups chopped onion | 1 tablespoon salt |
| 2 cups chopped green pepper | ¼ teaspoon pepper |
| 2 1-pound 12-ounce cans tomatoes | 1 tablespoon brown sugar |
| 5 cups water | 2 teaspoons Worcestershire sauce |
| 1 pound (5 cups) uncooked packaged precooked rice | 8 ounces sharp process American cheese, shredded (2 cups) |

Cook bacon till crisp; drain. Pour off all but ½ cup bacon fat. In remaining fat, cook onion and green pepper till tender. Add remaining ingredients except cheese. Pour mixture into two 13x9x2-inch baking dishes. Cover; bake at 350° about 25 to 30 minutes, or till rice is done. Crumble bacon; sprinkle each dish with *half* the bacon, then cheese. Return to oven to melt cheese. Serves 25.

## PORK CHOP SUEY BAKE

6 pounds pork, cubed
2 tablespoons salad oil
3 1-pound 4-ounce cans mixed Chinese vegetables, drained
2 cups chopped onion
2 cups chopped green pepper

2 cups uncooked long-grain rice
4 cups milk
½ cup soy sauce
4 10½-ounce cans condensed cream of mushroom soup
2 3-ounce cans chow mein noodles

In a kettle or Dutch oven brown meat in hot oil; sprinkle with 2 teaspoons salt. Drain off excess fat. Divide meat evenly between two 13x9x2-inch metal baking pans. Combine vegetables, onion, green pepper, and rice; add *half* the mixture to each pan. Gradually add milk and soy sauce to soup, stirring till smooth. Add *half* the soup mixture to each pan; mix well. Cover; bake at 350° about 2 hours, stirring occasionally, or till rice is done. Uncover; sprinkle one can noodles atop each pan. Bake 5 minutes. Serves 25.

---

## TEST KITCHEN TIPS

### Final touches make the difference

*As in all areas of cooking, the difference between a good and a great casserole is attention to one or two seemingly small details. Here are some points to help you.*

• *The "presentation": Give it a touch of showmanship. Make the most of the attractive casseroles, convenient warmers, and trivets available.*

• *The topping: It gives a finished look and adds to the eating enjoyment. Try crisp crackers, corn chips, puffs of biscuits, a piping of fluffy mashed potato, a sprinkle of shredded cheese, or toasted almonds. The variety is endless.*

• *Suitable go-alongs: Since casseroles frequently lack form, serve accompaniments that have a definite shape, like spiced fruits, molded salads, crisp relishes.*

## BAKED SPAGHETTI

| | |
|---|---|
| 1 pound spaghetti | 2 10½-ounce cans condensed |
| 4 pounds ground beef |    cream of mushroom soup |
| 2 large onions, chopped (2 cups) | 4 10½-ounce cans condensed |
| 1 large green pepper, chopped |    tomato soup |
|    (1 cup) | 1 quart milk |
| 2 teaspoons salt | 1 pound sharp process American |
|    . . . |    cheese, shredded (4 cups) |

Break spaghetti into 3-inch lengths; cook in large amount boiling salted water; drain. In Dutch oven or kettle cook meat, onion, and green pepper until meat is browned. Sprinkle with salt. Gradually stir in soups, milk, and 2 *cups* of the cheese. Divide cooked spaghetti evenly between two 13x9x2-inch baking dishes. Into each pan stir *half* the soup-meat mixture. Sprinkle remaining 2 cups cheese atop each. Bake uncovered in a moderate oven (350°) about 1 hour, or till hot through. Makes 20 servings.

## MACARONI AND CHEESE

| | |
|---|---|
| 1¼ pounds (6 cups) elbow | 10 cups milk |
|    macaroni | 1 cup chopped onion (optional) |
| ¾ cup butter or margarine | 1½ pounds sharp process American |
| ½ cup all-purpose flour |    cheese, cubed (6 cups) |
| 2 teaspoons salt | 4 tomatoes, sliced |
| ¼ teaspoon pepper | |

In two large kettles cook macaroni in large amount boiling salted water till tender; drain. In large kettle melt butter; blend in flour, salt, and pepper. Add milk; cook and stir till thick and bubbly. Add onion and cheese; stir till cheese is melted. Spread macaroni in two 13x9x2-inch metal baking pans. Add *half* the sauce to each pan; mix with macaroni.

Sprinkle tomato slices with salt; arrange on top, pushing edge of each slice into macaroni. Bake in moderate oven (350°) about 45 minutes, or till bubbly and hot in center. Makes 24 (about ¾ cup) servings.

# ITALIAN MEAT SAUCE

4 pounds ground beef
4 large onions, chopped (4 cups)
8 cloves garlic, minced
6 1-pound 14-ounce cans tomatoes, undrained and broken up
4 6-ounce cans tomato paste
8 cups water
1 cup snipped parsley
¼ cup brown sugar
2 tablespons ground oregano
1 tablespoon salt
2 teaspoons monosodium glutamate
1 teaspoon dried thyme, crushed
4 bay leaves
3 to 4 pounds spaghetti, cooked

In two large kettles or Dutch ovens, combine meat, onion, and garlic; brown lightly. Drain off excess fat. Divide remaining ingredients evenly between the two kettles. Simmer, uncovered, about 3 hours or till sauce is thickened; stir occasionally. Remove bay leaves. Serve over spaghetti. Pass shredded Parmesan cheese. Makes 25 (¾ cup) servings.

# TURKEY-DRESSING BAKE

3 7- or 8-ounce packages herb-seasoned stuffing mix
6 cups chicken broth
6 well-beaten eggs
3 10½-ounce cans condensed cream of mushroom soup
6 cups diced cooked turkey or chicken
1½ cups milk
2 tablespoons chopped canned pimiento
2 tablespoons snipped parsley

• • •

Toss stuffing mix with chicken broth, beaten eggs, and *half* of the mushroom soup. Spread mixture in two 13x9x2-inch metal baking pans. Top with cooked chicken or turkey.

Combine remaining soup with milk, pimiento, and parsley; pour over all. Cover with foil. Bake in a moderate oven (350°) for 55 to 60 minutes, or till set. Makes 24 servings.

# CHICKEN BAKE

1 pound medium noodles
1 cup butter or margarine
7 cups milk
½ cup all-purpose flour
¼ teaspoon white pepper
4 10¾-ounce cans chicken gravy (5 cups)
8 cups diced cooked chicken
¼ cup chopped canned pimiento
Bread Crumb Topper

• • •

Cook noodles in large amount of boiling salted water until tender; drain. Add ¼ *cup* of the butter and 1 *cup* of the milk.

In kettle melt remaining ¾ cup butter. Blend in flour, 1 teaspoon salt, and white pepper. Add remaining 6 cups milk all at once. Cook quickly, stirring constantly, till mixture thickens and bubbles. Add chicken gravy, diced chicken, pimiento, and noodles; mix. Spread mixture into two 13x9x2-inch baking dishes. Cover and bake at 350° for 25 minutes. *Bread Crumb Topper:* Combine 1 cup fine dry bread crumbs with 3 tablespoons melted butter; blend in 4 ounces process American cheese, shredded (1 cup). Sprinkle atop. Bake 10 minutes. Serves 24.

## CHICKEN-RICE SQUARES

10 cups diced cooked chicken **or** turkey (3 pounds)
5 cups chicken broth
4 cups cooked rice
11 beaten eggs
2 medium onions, chopped (1 cup)
1 large green pepper, chopped (1 cup)

1 1-ounce can (½ cup) chopped pimiento
1 tablespoon salt
½ teaspoon pepper
4 cups soft bread crumbs
4 cups milk
3 10½-ounce cans condensed cream of mushroom soup

Combine first 9 ingredients in large kettle. Combine the bread crumbs and 3 *cups* of the milk. Add to chicken mixture and stir only until ingredients are well blended. Turn into 2 greased 13x9x2-inch metal baking pans. Bake at 325° for 1¼ hours. Combine soup with remaining 1 cup milk for Mushroom Sauce; heat. Pass sauce. Makes 24 servings.

## HOT TURKEY-BEAN SALAD

11 cups diced cooked turkey
5 cups thinly sliced celery
3 15-ounce cans kidney beans, drained
10 ounces sharp process American cheese, shredded (2½ cups)
4 cups mayonnaise or salad dressing

⅓ cup pickle relish
¼ cup lemon juice
1 teaspoon salt
¼ teaspoon pepper
8 hard-cooked eggs, coarsely chopped
6 ounces potato chips, crushed (3 cups)

Combine turkey, celery, beans, and cheese. Blend together mayonnaise, pickle relish, lemon juice, salt, and pepper. Add to turkey mixture; add eggs. Blend lightly. Turn into two 13x9x2-inch metal baking pans. Top with crushed potato chips. Bake in moderate oven (350°) for 35 to 40 minutes, or till heated through. Makes 25 (1 cup) servings.

## HAM SUCCOTASH

4 9-ounce packages frozen cut green beans
4 1-pound cans (8 cups) whole kernel corn, drained
4 1-pound cans cream-style corn
4 cups soft bread crumbs (about 6 slices bread)
4 beaten eggs
2 tablespoons instant minced onion
4 teaspoons dry mustard
4 teaspoons dried basil, crushed
2 teaspoons salt
⅛ teaspoon pepper
3 pounds boneless cooked ham, sliced ½ inch thick
2 6-ounce cans sliced mushrooms, drained (2 cups)

Add frozen beans to boiling salted water; return just to boiling and drain. Set beans aside. Combine next 9 ingredients. Cube 1 *pound* of the ham; stir into corn mixture. Stir in green beans and musrooms. Turn into two 3-quart casseroles. Bake uncovered at 350° for 1 hour. Cut remaining ham into 24 serving-size pieces. Arrange 12 atop *each* casserole. Bake 30 minutes more. Serves 24.

## HAM MEDLEY

2 cups chopped celery
1 cup chopped green pepper
2 medium onions, chopped (1 cup)
½ cup butter or margarine
½ cup all-purpose flour
5 cups milk
6 cups cream-style cottage cheese
4 pounds cooked ham, cubed (8 cups)
16 ounces medium noodles, cooked and drained
¼ cup butter, melted
1 cup fine dry bread crumbs

Cook vegetables in ½ cup butter till tender; blend in flour, 1 teaspoon salt, and ⅛ teaspoon pepper. Stir in milk and cottage cheese; cook and stir till boiling. Stir in ham and noodles; turn into two 3-quart casseroles. Combine butter and crumbs; sprinkle over top of each. Bake in moderate oven (350°) for 1 hour. Makes 24 servings.

## EGG COFFEE

2 slightly beaten eggs (reserve shells)
2¼ to 2½ cups regular-grind coffee
10 quarts cold water

In a large kettle combine eggs, crumbled shells, and coffee. Pour in water. Bring to boiling. Stir when foam starts to appear and continue until foam disappears.

Remove from heat; let settle. If necessary, add 1 cup cold water to aid settling. Strain with fine mesh strainer or cloth before serving. (See Shopping Guide for a Crowd for drip or percolator method.) Makes 50 (¾ cup) servings.

## INSTANT COFFEE

1 2-ounce jar instant coffee powder     5 quarts cold water
   (1 cup)

Add instant coffee to a 6-quart container. Blend in part of water; then add remaining water. Bring *just* to boiling; do not boil. Or, stir boiling water into the coffee, cover and steep a few minutes. Makes 25 servings.

## TEA

Tie 1 cup tea leaves loosely in cheesecloth bag. Place tea leaves or 40 individual tea bags in large kettle. Bring 9 quarts cold water to a boil; immediately pour over tea. Cover; steep tea 3 to 5 minutes. Remove tea and serve. Makes 50 (about ¾ cup) servings.

# HOSTESS NOTE:

## BUFFET FOR A CROWD

The buffet service is a natural when guests outnumber the places at your dining table. Set the table away from the wall so that guests can circulate around it. A separate table can be set up for beverages.

When the group is quite large, make twin arrangements on each side of the table—of plates, food, silverware, and napkins. Guests form two lines helping themselves to the main dish, vegetable or salad, buttered rolls, relishes, and finally silver and napkins.

If a sit-down buffet is possible, arrange small tables in another room with silver, napkins, and water glasses. Provide beverage cups, cream, and sugar at the tables and serve the beverage, if desired.

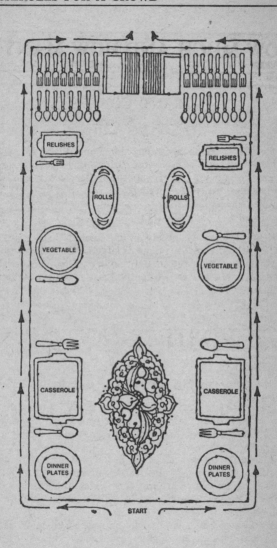

RELISHES

RELISHES

ROLLS

ROLLS

VEGETABLE

VEGETABLE

CASSEROLE

CASSEROLE

DINNER PLATES

DINNER PLATES

START

# HOW MUCH AND HOW MANY

| FOOD | AMOUNT |
|---|---|
| **CHEESE** | |
| Cheese, shredded or cubed ........ | 1 pound = 4 cups |
| **CRUMBS** | |
| Bread, soft crumbs ............... | 1½ slices = about 1 cup |
| fine dry crumbs ................. | 1 slice bread = about ¼ cup |
| Saltine cracker crumbs, | |
| finely crushed ................. | 28 crackers = about 1 cup |
| coarsely crushed ............... | 22 crackers = about 1 cup |
| Potato chips, | |
| coarsely crushed ............... | 4 oz. = about 2 cups |
| **PASTA** | |
| Macaroni ......................... | 4 oz. (1-1¼ cups) uncooked = 2¼ cups cooked |
| Noodles .......................... | 4 oz. (1½-2 cups) uncooked = 2 cups cooked |
| Rice, long-grain ................. | 6½-7 oz. (1 cup) uncooked = 3 to 4 cups cooked |
| packaged precooked .......... | 1 cup uncooked = 2 cups cooked |
| Spaghetti ........................ | 7 oz. uncooked = 4 cups cooked |
| **POULTRY** | |
| Chicken, cooked, diced or sliced | |
| Broiler-fryer ................... | about ¾ cup diced per pound |
| Stewing chicken .............. | about 1 cup diced per pound |
| Two chicken breasts, 10 oz. each | 1½ to 2 cups diced or 12 thin slices |
| Turkey Roll ...................... | 3 pounds = about 9 to 10 cups diced |
| **VEGETABLES** | |
| Celery, diced or chopped ......... | 1 bunch = about 1¾ pounds<br>8 stalks = 2¾ cups |
| Green onions, sliced with tops .... | 7 onions (1 bunch) = about ½ cup |
| Green pepper, diced ............... | 1 large (6 oz.) = 1 cup |
| Green olives, stuffed, sliced ....... | 4 oz. (about 48 small) = 1 cup |
| Onion, chopped ................... | 1 pound = 4 medium<br>1 medium = ½ cup |
| Potatoes ......................... | 1 pound = 3 or 4 medium<br>4 medium = 1 quart pared and thinly sliced<br>4 medium = 1 quart cooked and cubed |
| Radishes, sliced .................. | 1 bunch = about 1 cup |

# MEASUREMENTS AND EQUIVALENTS

4 quarts equals 1 gallon
4 cups equals 1 quart
2 cups equals 1 pint
1 cup equals 8 fluid ounces
1 pound equals 16 ounces
16 tablespoons equals 1 cup

12 tablespoons equals ¾ cup
10⅔ tablespoons equals ⅔ cup
8 tablespoons equals ½ cup
5⅓ tablespoons equals ⅓ cup
4 tablespoons equals ¼ cup
3 teaspoons equals 1 tablespoon

| CONTAINER | APPROXIMATE NET WEIGHT OR FLUID MEASURE | | APPROXIMATE CUPS |
|---|---|---|---|
| 8 oz. ........ | ................. 8 ounces ................. | | ...... 1 |
| Picnic ...... | ............ 10½ to 12 ounces ............ | | ........ 1¼ |
| 12 oz. (vac.) | ............ 12 ounces ............ | | .......... 1½ |
| No. 300 .... | ....... 14 to 16 ounces ....... | | .......... 1¾ |
| | (14 ounces to 1 pound) | | |
| No. 303 .... | .......16 to 17 ounces ....... | | ............ 2 |
| | ( 1 pound to 1 pound 1 ounce) | | |
| No. 2 ...... | 20 ounces | ........... 18 fluid ounces | .......... 2½ |
| | (1 pound 4 ounces) | (1 pint 2 fluid ounces) | |
| No. 2½ ... | ............ 27 to 29 ounces ............ | | .......... 3½ |
| | (1 pound 11 ounces to 1 pound 13 ounces) | | |
| No. 3 cyl. ... | 51 ounces ............ | ........ 46 fluid ounces | ........ 5¾ |
| or | (3 pounds 3 ounces) ..... | (1 quart 14 fluid ounces) | |
| 46 fl. oz. .... | | | |
| No. 10 ..... | ............ 6½ pounds to 7¼ pounds ............ | | ........12-13 |

## SUBSTITUTIONS FOR INSTITUTIONAL-SIZE CANS

1 6½-pound to 7¼-pound can equals.  . . .  ............7 16- to 17-ounce cans
1 6½-pound to 7¼-pound can equals.............................5 20-ounce cans
1 6½-pound to 7¼-pound can equals.........................4 27- to 29-ounce cans
1 6½-pound to 7¼-pound can equals.....................2 51-ounce to 46-fluid ounce cans

# TOSSED GREEN SALAD

3 heads (1½ to 2 pounds each)
    iceberg lettuce
1 bunch (½ pound) romaine
2 bunches radishes, sliced
2 large (1 pound) cucumbers,
    thinly sliced (4 cups)

2 large green peppers, chopped
    (2 cups)
1 large onion, chopped
    (1 cup) **optional**
1 pint French dressing
⅔ cup sweet pickle relish
⅓ cup vinegar

Tear iceberg lettuce and romaine in bite-size pieces. In several large salad bowls make layers of greens, radishes, cucumbers, green pepper, and onion. Chill. Combine remaining ingredients for dressing. Pour over salad *just before serving*. Toss lightly. Makes 25 (about 1 cup) servings.

# CABBAGE SLAW

2¼ pounds cabbage, shredded
    (15 cups)
¾ pound carrots, shredded
    (3 cups)
3 cups salad dressing or
    mayonnaise

¾ cup diced green pepper
⅓ cup sugar
⅓ cup vinegar
1 tablespoon prepared mustard
2 teaspoons salt
3 teaspoons celery seed

Combine chilled vegetables. Blend salad dressing, sugar, vinegar, mustard, salt, and celery seed for dressing. Just before serving, combine vegetables and dressing; toss lightly.

Serve in leafy cabbage bowl, if desired: Select a large cabbage head with curling leaves. Loosen leaves and spread out, petal fashion. With sharp knife, hollow center to within 1 inch of sides and bottom. Fill center with slaw. Makes 25 (½ cup) servings.

SPEEDY
SUPPERS

Use this selection of quick-preparing recipes when you've no time to spare at the end of a busy day. Most of the recipes require little preparation time; most take no extra steps during cooking so you'll be free for other things.

In this chapter you'll find perfect recipes for easy—and pleasant—meals. Included are dishes you can start with convenience foods—packaged and canned—straight from the shelf, and dishes that your kitchen appliances can make all the speedier.

There's also a section of recipes for best use of a pressure pan—a piece of equipment which can help shorten cooking time.

And if you're looking for a hurry-up version of an old favorite—such as spaghetti sauce or New England Dinner—this is where you'll find it.

# SKILLETS AND CASSEROLES

## MEATBALL PIE

½ cup chopped onion
1 tablespoon butter or margarine
2 12-ounce cans meatballs and gravy
1 1-pound can sliced carrots, drained (2 cups)
2 tablespoons snipped parsley

2 teaspoons Worcestershire sauce
¼ cup crisp rice cereal, crushed
½ teaspoon sesame seed
⅛ teaspoon salt
1 package refrigerated biscuits (10 biscuits)
Milk

Cook onion in butter till tender but not brown. Add meatballs and gravy, carrots, parsley, and Worcestershire. Heat till bubbling. Pour into 2-quart casserole.

Mix cereal, sesame seed, and salt. Brush tops of biscuits with milk; then dip in cereal mixture. Arrange biscuits atop *hot* meat. Bake in hot oven (425°) 10 to 12 minutes or till biscuits are done. Makes 6 servings.

## BIG MEAL COMBO

1 10½-ounce can condensed cream of chicken soup
4 ounces sharp process American cheese, shredded (1 cup)
2 1-pound cans (4 cups) tiny whole potatoes, drained
2 1-pound cans (3½ cups) small whole onions, drained
½ cup diced green pepper

1 3-ounce can sliced mushrooms, drained (½ cup)
1 12-ounce can corned beef, chilled
1 cup soft bread crumbs (about 2 slices)
1 tablespoon butter or margarine, melted

Combine soup and cheese; add vegetables. Turn into greased 9x9x2-inch baking dish. Cut corned beef into 6 slices; arrange atop vegetable mixture. Toss crumbs with butter. Sprinkle over mixture. Bake in moderate oven (350°) about 45 minutes. Serves 6.

## JAZZY HASH

1 15-ounce can corned beef hash | ½ cup dairy sour cream
2 tablespoons chopped onion | ¼ cup red Burgundy
1 small clove garlic, minced | 1 cup soft bread crumbs
2 beaten eggs | 1 tablespoon butter, melted

Combine first 6 ingredients and dash pepper; mix well. Spoon into 4 individual casseroles or one 8-inch pie plate. Combine crumbs, butter, and dash paprika; sprinkle over hash. Bake at 350° for 25 to 30 minutes. Serves 4.

## CORNED BEEF BAKE

1 12-ounce can corned beef, finely chopped | 3 slices sharp process American cheese
½ cup finely chopped green pepper | 1 10½-ounce can condensed cream of celery soup
½ cup finely chopped onion | 1 8¼-ounce can mixed vegetables, drained
½ cup mayonnaise or salad dressing | ⅓ cup milk
1 beaten egg | 3 large English muffins, halved and toasted
½ cup fine dry bread crumbs |
2 tablespoons shortening |

Combine corned beef, green pepper, onion, mayonnaise, and dash pepper. Shape into 6 patties. Blend egg and 1 tablespoon water; dip patties into egg, then crumbs. Brown lightly in hot shortening. Place patties in 10x6x1½-inch baking dish. Quarter cheese slices diagonally; overlap 2 triangles atop each. Combine soup, vegetables, and milk; heat. Pour around patties. Bake at 350° for 12 minutes or till hot. Serve on muffins. Serves 6.

## HAMBURGER STROGANOFF

1 pound ground beef | 1 10½-ounce can condensed cream of mushroom soup
3 slices bacon, diced | 1 cup dairy sour cream
½ cup chopped onion | Hot buttered poppy seed noodles
¾ teaspoon salt |
¼ teaspoon paprika |
Dash pepper |

In skillet brown ground beef with bacon. Add onion; cook until tender but not brown. Drain off the excess fat. Add seasonings to meat mixture. Stir in soup. Cook slowly, uncovered, 20 minutes, stirring frequently.

Stir in sour cream and heat through—do not boil. Serve over hot poppy seed noodles. Makes 4 to 6 servings.

# SHORTCUT LASAGNE

Brown 1 pound ground beef; spoon off excess fat. Add one 1-pound 13-ounce can tomatoes, one 8-ounce can tomato sauce, 1 envelope spaghetti sauce mix, and ¼ teaspoon garlic salt. Bring mixture to boiling; simmer uncovered about 10 minutes.

Cook 8 ounces lasagne or wide noodles in large amount of boiling salted water till tender; drain. Rinse in cold water. Place *half* the noodles in a 12x7½x2-inch baking dish. Cover with *one-third* of the sauce. Add *half* of a 6-ounce package sliced mozzarella cheese, then ½ cup cream-style cottage cheese. Repeat layers with noodles, one-third of the sauce, mozzarella, ½ cup cottage cheese, and end with sauce. Top with ½ cup grated Parmesan cheese. Bake in a moderate oven (350°) for 45 minutes. Let stand 10 minutes. Cut in squares. Serves 6 to 8.

# CHILI-BURGER SUPPER

1 cup elbow macaroni or spaghetti
1 pound ground beef
1 11-ounce can condensed chili-beef soup
1 10¾-ounce can condensed tomato soup
3 slices sharp process American cheese

Cook macaroni or spaghetti according to package directions; drain thoroughly.

Brown ground beef in skillet. Add the chili-beef soup, tomato soup, and cooked macaroni. Heat, stirring occasionally, for 5 to 7 minutes, or until the mixture is bubbly. Halve the cheese slices diagonally and overlap cheese triangles atop hot mixture. Cover for a few minutes to melt cheese slightly. Serve at once. Makes 6 servings.

# COTTAGE ENCHILADAS

Drain one 4-ounce can green chilies; remove seeds, if desired. Cut chilies in 12 strips. Cook 12 frozen tortillas in water according to package directions. Cut ½ pound sharp process American cheese into 12 strips.

Combine 1 cup dairy sour cream, one 12-ounce carton (1½ cups) cream-style cottage cheese, ½ teaspoon salt, and dash pepper. Reserve ½ cup of the mixture; spoon remaining mixture onto tortillas. Top each with a strip of green chili and a strip of cheese. Roll up each tortilla. Place the filled tortillas seam side down in a 12x7½x2-inch baking dish.

Combine reserved sour cream mixture and one 15-ounce can enchilada sauce. Pour over tortillas. Bake in a moderate oven (350°) for 25 to 30 minutes, or till hot. Serves 6.

## TEST KITCHEN TIPS

### Quick and easy meal endings

*Into sweetened whipped cream, fold applesauce. Spoon into parfait glasses.*

*Cube angel cake. Fold into chocolate pudding. Serve in sherbet glasses.*

*Sauce canned pears with mint-flavored chocolate syrup.*

## HURRY SUPPER BAKE

1  12-ounce can roast beef
⅓  cup cold water
¼  cup all-purpose flour
1  10¾-ounce can beef gravy
1  1-pound can cut green beans, drained

1  teaspoon instant minced onion
   Packaged instant mashed potatoes (enough for 4 servings)
2  ounces process American cheese, shredded (½ cup)

Place pieces of meat in a 1½-quart casserole. Blend water and flour; stir into gravy and cook and stir till thick and bubbly. Stir in beans and onion. Pour over meat. Top with mounds of mashed potatoes. Bake at 350° for 25 minutes. Sprinkle cheese on potatoes and bake 5 minutes. Serves 4.

## DANDY DIXIE BAKE

1  1-pound can (2 cups) applesauce
1  12-ounce can luncheon meat, cut in 8 slices
   Whole cloves
½  cup apricot preserves

1  1-pound can vacuum-packed sweet potatoes
1  tablespoon water
½  teaspoon dry mustard
¼  teaspoon salt

Spread applesauce in 9x9x2-inch baking dish. Lightly score meat slices and stud with cloves. Arrange potatoes and meat on applesauce. Combine remaining ingredients; spread over meat and potatoes. Bake in a moderate oven (375°) 35 minutes or till heated. Serves 4.

# BURGER CHILI AND CHIPS

1 pound ground beef
½ cup chopped onion
½ cup diced celery
¼ teaspoon salt
⅛ teaspoon pepper

. . .

1 15-ounce can chili with beans
1 8-ounce can tomato sauce

. . .

4 ounces process American
    cheese, shredded (1 cup)
1 cup slightly crushed corn chips

In skillet combine meat, onion, celery, salt, and pepper; cook till vegetables are just tender. Add chili and tomato sauce; mix.

Stir in cheese and *half* of the corn chips. Turn into 1½-quart casserole. Top with remaining ½ cup chips.

Bake in moderate oven (350°) 25 to 30 minutes or till heated through. Makes 6 servings.

# DEVILED HAM BEAN BAKE

½ cup chopped onion
1 4½-ounce can deviled ham
1 tablespoon molasses
1 teaspoon prepared mustard
    Dash salt

1 1-pound can pork and beans
    in tomato sauce
1 8-ounce can tomatoes, well
    drained (½ cup)

Combine all ingredients in a 1-quart casserole and bake uncovered in a moderate oven (350°) for 1½ hours. Makes 6 servings.

# MEXICALI CASSEROLE

1 1-pound 4-ounce can yellow
    hominy, drained
1 1-pound can tamales, cut in
    thirds
1 4- or 5-ounce can Vienna
    sausages, cut in thirds

1 10½-ounce can condensed
    cream of chicken soup
1 ounce sharp natural Cheddar
    cheese, shredded (¼ cup)

Combine hominy, tamales, sausages, and soup; mix. Turn into 1½-quart casserole. Bake uncovered at 350° for 35 to 40 minutes. If desired, garnish top with additional tamales. Sprinkle cheese atop. Return to oven to melt cheese and heat tamale garnish. Serves 6.

# GINGER PEACHY BEANS

2 1-pound cans pork and beans in tomato sauce

2 tablespoons brown sugar

1 teaspoon instant minced onion

½ teaspoon ground ginger

Dash dry mustard

1 12-ounce can luncheon meat, cut in 1-inch cubes (about 2 cups)

1 1-pound can peach halves, drained

Orange marmalade

Combine beans, brown sugar, onion, ginger, and mustard. Stir in meat; spoon into a 10x6x1½-inch baking dish. Bake at 325° for 1 hour. Top with peach halves, cut side up; put 1 teaspoon orange marmalade in each peach cavity. Bake 30 minutes longer. Serves 6.

# EGGS AU GRATIN

In skillet melt 2 tablespoons butter or margarine. Add 2 cups crisp rice cereal and mix gently. Spoon *half* the cereal mixture into bottoms of four 10-ounce casseroles.

In saucepan combine one 11-ounce can condensed Cheddar cheese soup, ¼ cup milk, and ¼ cup sliced ripe olives; heat through. Slice 6 hard-cooked eggs (reserve 8 slices for garnish). Fold eggs into soup mixture. Spoon into the 4 casseroles. Top each with 2 egg slices; wreathe with remaining cereal. Bake at 400° about 15 minutes. Makes 4 servings.

# DEVIL DECKER PIE

Prepare 1 stick pie crust mix according to package directions. Line a 9-inch pie plate with pastry; flute edges.

Combine one 4½-ounce can deviled ham and 1 tablespoon fine dry bread crumbs. Spread over bottom and sides of pastry.

Combine 1 cup dairy sour cream and one 10½-ounce can condensed cream of mushroom soup; blend in 4 slightly beaten eggs, 2 tablespoons snipped chives, and dash pepper. Pour into pie shell. Bake in hot oven (400°) about 30 minutes or till knife inserted halfway between center and edge comes out clean. Garnish with chives. Serves 6 to 8.

## LUNCHEON MEAT BARBECUE

1 1-pound can sliced peaches
1 8-ounce can tomato sauce
¼ cup brown sugar
1 teaspoon dry mustard
1 teaspoon instant minced onion

1 teaspoon chili powder
½ teaspoon Worcestershire sauce
2 tablespoons vinegar
1 12-ounce can luncheon meat, cut
   in strips

Drain peaches, reserving ½ cup syrup. In medium skillet combine the reserved peach syrup, tomato sauce, brown sugar, mustard, onion, chili powder, ½ teaspoon salt, Worcestershire, and vinegar; bring to boiling. Reduce heat and simmer 5 minutes. Add the luncheon meat and peaches. Cover; simmer 20 minutes longer. Serve over rice. Makes 4 or 5 servings.

## SAUSAGE-KRAUT SKILLET

Brown 1 pound bulk pork sausage; drain. Drain one 13½-ounce can pineapple tidbits; reserve ¼ cup syrup. Add pineapple and one 14-ounce can sauerkraut to meat. Cover; cook over low heat 20 minutes. Add 2 medium unpared apples, sliced; cook 10 minutes.

Combine reserved syrup and 1 tablespoon cornstarch; stir into sausage mixture. Cook just till thick and bubbly. Serves 4 to 6.

## SAVORY SAUSAGE STEW

1 12-ounce package smoked
   sausage links or 1 pound pork
   sausage links
1 10½-ounce can condensed
   onion soup
1 1-pound can (2 cups) tomatoes

1 10-ounce package frozen peas
   and onions
2 medium potatoes, pared and
   cubed (about 2 cups)
½ teaspoon Worcestershire sauce
¼ cup all-purpose flour

Cut each sausage link into 4 or 5 pieces; brown in large saucepan. Drain off excess fat. Add next 5 ingredients.

Simmer over low heat 15 to 20 minutees, till potatoes are tender. Combine flour and ½ cup water; stir into stew. Cook and stir till thick and bubbly. Makes 6 servings.

## HOT DOG BARBECUE

½ cup chopped onion
 1 tablespoon shortening
 1 12-ounce bottle (1¼ cups)
   extra-hot catsup
 2 tablespoons pickle relish

 1 tablespoon sugar
 ¼ teaspoon salt
 1 pound (8 to 10) frankfurters
   Hot cooked rice

Cook onion in hot shortening till tender but not brown. Stir
in catsup, ½ cup water, pickle relish, sugar, and salt. Score
franks; add to sauce. Simmer covered until frankfurters are
thoroughly heated, about 10 minutes. Serve over rice. Makes
4 or 5 servings.

## FRANK 'N CABBAGE SUPPER

1 medium head cabbage, cut in
   wedges
 1 pound (8 to 10) frankfurters
 1 envelope cheese sauce mix

 2 tablespoons prepared mustard
   Few drops bottled hot pepper
   sauce

Cook cabbage, covered, in small amount of boiling water
for 10 minutes; add franks and cook till cabbage is tender,
3 to 4 minutes longer. Meanwhile, prepare cheese sauce according to package directions; stir in mustard and hot pepper
sauce. Serve over cabbage wedges and franks. Makes 4 or 5
servings.

## WIENER BEAN POT

 2 1-pound cans (4 cups) pork and
   beans in tomato sauce
 ½ envelope (¼ cup) dry onion
   soup mix
 ⅓ cup catsup

 2 tablespoons brown sugar
 1 tablespoon prepared mustard
 1 pound (8 to 10) frankfurters,
   cut in ½-inch slices

Combine all ingredients and ¼ cup water in 2-quart casserole
or bean pot. Bake uncovered in moderate oven (350°) for 1
hour, stirring once or twice. Makes 6 to 8 servings.

## SAUCY FRANKS

5 slices bacon, diced
½ cup chopped onion
¼ cup chopped green pepper

   • • •

1 cup pineapple juice

 ¾ cup catsup
 ¼ cup water
 ⅛ teaspoon chili powder
 1 pound (8 to 10) frankfurters

Cook bacon, onion, and green pepper till tender but not brown. Stir in pineapple juice, catsup, water, and chili powder. Score franks diagonally every 1 inch; add to sauce. Cover; bring to boil; simmer 8 to 10 minutes. Serve with hot cooked rice. Makes 4 or 5 servings.

## CHILI CON WIENE

1 pound ground beef
½ cup chopped onion

1 15-ounce can (2 cups) chili with beans
½ pound (4 to 5) frankfurters, cut diagonally in ¼- to ½-inch slices

1 10¾-ounce can condensed tomato soup
½ cup chili sauce
¼ cup chopped green pepper
8 hamburger buns, split and toasted

In large skillet lightly brown meat and onion; pour off excess fat. Add chili, frankfurters (reserve a few slices for garnish), soup, chili sauce, and green pepper. Heat thoroughly. Garnish with reserved frankfurter slices and ripe olives, if desired. Serve over toasted bun halves. Makes 8 servings.

## QUICK TURKEY PIE

2 cups packaged biscuit mix
1 tablespoon instant minced onion
2⅔ cups milk
¼ cup chopped green pepper
2 ounces sharp process American cheese, shredded (½ cup)

¼ cup butter, melted
¼ cup all-purpose flour
½ teaspoon dry mustard
1 teaspoon Worcestershire sauce
½ cup shredded carrot
2 cups diced cooked turkey

Combine biscuit mix and onion; stir in ⅔ *cup* milk till mix is moistened. Pat into a greased 9-inch pie plate. Sprinkle with green pepper and cheese. Bake at 400° for 18 to 20 minutes or till golden. Meanwhile, blend butter, flour, mustard, 1 teaspoon salt, and dash pepper. Add remaining 2 cups milk and Worcestershire. Cook and stir till thickly and bubbly. Stir in carrot and turkey; heat through. Cut biscuit in wedges; top with sauce. Serves 6.

# CHEESE-NOODLES AND CHICKEN

6 ounces fine noodles
1½ cups milk
3 ounces sharp process American
 cheese, shredded (¾ cup)
3 slightly beaten eggs
½ teaspoon salt

½ teaspoon Worcestershire sauce
3 10½-ounce cans chicken a la
 king
¼ cup sliced pimiento-stuffed
 green olives

Cook noodles in large amount of boiling salted water till tender; drain. Combine with milk, cheese, eggs, salt, and Worcestershire. Turn mixture into well-greased 8x8x2-inch pan.

Cover with foil and bake in moderate oven (350°) for 1 hour. Uncover and bake an additional 15 minutes, or till set.

Meanwhile, combine chicken a la king and sliced green olives in saucepan; heat thoroughly. Cut noodle mixture into squares. Serve hot chicken sauce over. Serves 9.

# EASY CHICKEN DIVAN

2 10-ounce packages frozen
 broccoli
2 cups sliced cooked chicken or
 3 chicken breasts, cooked
 and boned
2 10½-ounce cans condensed
 cream of chicken soup

¾ cup mayonnaise or salad
 dressing
1 teaspoon lemon juice
2 ounces sharp process American
 cheese, shredded (½ cup)
1 cup soft bread crumbs
1 tablespoon butter, melted

Cook broccoli according to package directions in salted water till tender; drain. Arrange stalks in greased 12x7½x2-inch baking dish. Layer chicken atop.

Combine next 3 ingredients; pour over chicken. Sprinkle with cheese. Combine crumbs and butter; sprinkle over all. Bake at 350° about 35 minutes or till heated. Trim with pimiento strips, if desired. Serves 6 to 8.

# CURRIED CHICKEN BAKE

1 cup packaged precooked rice
1 10½-ounce can condensed
 cream of chicken soup
1 10½-ounce can chicken a la
 king
1 teaspoon curry powder

. . .

½ teaspoon Worcestershire sauce
4 ounces sharp process American
 cheese, shredded (½ cup)

. . .

1 10-ounce package frozen
 broccoli spears, cooked and
 drained

Cook rice according to package directions, *omitting salt in cooking water.* Combine soup, chicken a la king, curry, and Worcestershire. Heat. Add cheese and stir to melt.

In 10x6x1½-inch baking dish, place *half* the rice, then *half* the broccoli, and *half* the sauce. Repeat layers. Bake in moderate oven (350°) 25 to 30 minutes or till thoroughly heated. Makes 4 to 6 servings.

## CHICKEN 'N BISCUIT PIE

1 15¼-ounce can chicken in gravy
1 10½-ounce can condensed
  cream of chicken soup
1 tablespoon instant minced onion
½ teaspoon dried rosemary,
  crushed
1 8-ounce can peas, drained

1 3-ounce can sliced mushrooms,
  drained (½ cup)
1 5-ounce can boned chicken,
  diced
1 8-ounce package refrigerated
  biscuits (10 biscuits)

Mix chicken in gravy, soup, onion, and rosemary. Add drained peas, mushrooms, and chicken. Heat slowly, stirring occasionally, till boiling. Turn into a 2-quart casserole. Snip each biscuit in three wedges; arrange, points up, atop *hot* chicken mixture. Bake in very hot oven (450°) 15 minutes or till biscuits are done. Makes 5 servings.

## QUICK CHICKEN A LA KING

½ cup chopped green pepper
½ cup chopped celery
2 tablespoons butter or margarine
    . . . .
2 10½-ounce cans condensed
  cream of chicken soup

1 6-ounce can broiled sliced
  mushrooms, drained (reserve
  ¼ cup liquid)
2 cups diced cooked chicken
¼ cup chopped canned pimiento

Cook green pepper and celery in butter till tender but not brown. Blend in soup and reserved mushroom liquid. Add mushrooms and remaining ingredients. Season to taste. Heat. Serve over toast points. Serves 6 to 8.

## GOURMET DELIGHT

1 cup cold milk
2 teaspoons cornstarch
1 chicken bouillon cube
1 10-ounce can frozen condensed
  cream of shrimp soup, thawed

Dash nutmeg
2 cups diced cooked turkey
2 tablespoons dry sherry
¼ teaspoon dried parsley flakes

In saucepan blend milk into cornstarch. Add bouillon cube. Cook over medium heat until mixture is slightly thickened and comes to a boil. Add remaining ingredients; heat thoroughly, stirring occasionally. Serve over biscuits or in patty shells. Makes 4 to 6 servings.

## TEST KITCHEN TIPS

### Quick and easy meal endings

*Layer banana pudding, banana slices, and crushed chocolate wafers for parfaits.*

*Scoop ice cream ahead; then roll each scoop in crushed cookies; refreeze.*

## LAZY PAELLA

1 2½- to 3-pound ready-to-cook broiler-fryer chicken, cut up
2 tablespoons salad oil
½ envelope dry onion soup mix
1 13¾-ounce can chicken broth (not condensed)

1 cup uncooked long-grain rice
1 3-ounce can sliced mushrooms, drained (½ cup)
1 8-ounce can peas, drained
1 4½-ounce can shrimp, drained

In skillet brown chicken in hot oil. Season with salt and pepper. Combine soup mix, uncooked rice, broth, mushrooms, peas, and shrimp. Spread in 13x9x2-inch baking dish. Place chicken pieces atop. Sprinkle with paprika. Cover dish tightly with foil. Bake at 350° for 1 hour. Serves 4 to 6.

## TURKEY NOODLE CASSEROLE

2 slices white bread, cubed
1 10½-ounce can condensed turkey noodle soup

2 eggs
1½ cups diced cooked turkey

Put bread in a 1½-quart casserole. Pour soup over bread. Beat eggs well and pour over bread and soup. Stir in turkey. Bake in slow oven (325°) for 1 hour. Makes 4 servings.

## BEEF AND MACARONI

1 3½-ounce package sliced smoked beef, snipped (1 cup)
1 15-ounce can macaroni and cheese
1 3-ounce can chopped mushrooms, drained (½ cup)
2 ounces sharp natural Cheddar cheese, shredded (½ cup)
¼ cup chopped green pepper
1 hard-cooked egg, chopped
1 tablespoon instant minced onion
½ teaspoon Worcestershire sauce
½ cup soft bread crumbs
2 tablespoons butter, melted

Combine all ingredients except crumbs and butter; turn into 1-quart casserole. Combine crumbs and butter; sprinkle over top. Bake uncovered at 350° for 35 to 40 minutes. Garnish with additional green pepper rings or hard-cooked egg slices, if desired. Serve 4.

## BASIC GROUND BEEF

*Meat mixture to freeze in portions and use right from the freezer as the beginning for Quick Spaghetti, Quick Spanish Rice, or Barbecued Beef Burgers.*

1 cup chopped celery
1 cup chopped onion
½ cup chopped green pepper
2 pounds ground beef

Combine all ingredients in large skillet. Cook and stir over medium heat till vegetables are tender and meat is browned. Cool quickly. Freeze in two 2-cup portions in wrapping or containers which are moisture-proof. Seal to exclude as much air as possible. Makes 4 cups.

## QUICK SPAGHETTI

3 cups tomato juice
1 to 1½ teaspoons chili powder
½ teaspoon salt
¼ teaspoon dry mustard
2 cups frozen Basic Ground Beef
½ 7-ounce package spaghetti

In saucepan heat tomato juice, chili powder, salt, and dry mustard. Add frozen meat mixture. Cover; cook over low heat till meat is thawed, about 20 minutes.

Stir in uncooked spaghetti. Cover; simmer 30 minutes. Stir often. Serve with Parmesan cheese. Makes 4 to 6 servings.

# QUICK SPANISH RICE

4½ cups water
1 6-ounce can tomato paste
1½ teaspoons salt
  Dash pepper
⅓ cup chili sauce
2 cups frozen Basic Ground Beef
1 cup uncooked long-grain rice

In large saucepan combine water, tomato paste, chili sauce, salt, and pepper. Add frozen meat mixture. Cover and cook over low heat till meat is thawed, about 20 minutes. Add rice. Cover; bring to boiling. Reduce heat and simmer 30 minutes, or till rice is done. Makes 4 to 6 servings.

# BARBECUED BEEF BURGERS

In saucepan or deep skillet, heat one 10¾-ounce can condensed tomato soup, 1 teaspoon Worcestershire sauce, and dash pepper..

Add 2 cups frozen Basic Ground Beef mixture; cover and cook over low heat till meat is thawed and mixture is heated through, stirring occasionally. Serve over split toasted hamburger buns. Makes 4 to 6 servings.

# QUICK CURRIED TUNA

2 10½-ounce cans condensed
  cream of chicken soup
1 8¾-ounce can crushed
  pineapple
¼ cup chopped green pepper
1 tablespoon snipped chives
1½ to 2 teaspoons curry powder
2 6½-or 7-ounce cans tuna,
  drained and broken in
  chunks
Hot cooked rice

Combine soup, undrained pineapple, green pepper, chives, and curry powder in medium saucepan. Heat and stir to boiling. Add tuna chunks and heat thoroughly. Serve over hot cooked rice. Makes 6 to 8 servings.

# HADDOCK-SHRIMP BAKE

2 pounds fresh or frozen
  haddock or sole fillets
1 10-ounce can frozen condensed
  cream of shrimp soup,
  thawed
¼ cup butter or margarine,
  melted
½ teaspoon grated onion
½ teaspoon Worcestershire
  sauce
¼ teaspoon garlic salt
1¼ cups crushed rich round
  crackers (30 crackers)

Slightly thaw frozen fillets. Place fillets in greased 13x9x2-inch baking dish; spread with soup. Bake at 375° for 20 minutes. Combine butter and remaining ingredients; sprinkle over fish. Bake 10 minutes. Serves 6 to 8.

## CHOPSTICK TUNA

Combine one 10½-ounce can condensed cream of mushroom soup and ¼ cup water. Add 1 cup chow mein noodles, one 6½- or 7-ounce can tuna, drained and broken up, 1 cup sliced celery, ½ cup salted toasted cashews, ¼ cup chopped onion, and dash pepper; toss.

Turn into a 10x6x1½-inch baking dish. Sprinkle 1 cup chow mein noodles atop. Bake in a moderate oven (375°) about 30 minutes or till heated through. Makes 4 or 5 servings.

## TUNA CHIP CASSEROLE

1½ cups crushed potato chips
1 6½- or 7-ounce can tuna, drained and flaked
1 8-ounce can peas, drained

1 10½-ounce can condensed cream of mushroom soup
1 cup milk

Combine all ingredients *except* ½ cup crushed potato chips. Turn into a 1½-quart casserole. Border with remaining potato chips. Bake in a moderate oven (350°) about 50 to 60 minutes or till hot. Makes 4 servings.

## QUICK TUNA BAKE

1 7¼-ounce package macaroni and cheese dinner
3 tablespoons butter, softened
1 8-ounce can (1 cup) tomatoes
½ cup milk
2 tablespoons instant minced onion
1 slightly beaten egg

1 6½- or 7-ounce can tuna, drained and flaked
2 tablespoons snipped parsley
¼ teaspoon salt
Dash pepper
2 tablespoons cornflake crumbs

Cook macaroni according to package directions; drain. Add cheese (from packaged dinner) and butter. Toss to mix. Break up tomatoes; add with remaining ingredients, except crumbs, to macaroni. Pour mixture into 1½-quart casserole. Sprinkle with crumbs. Bake uncovered in moderate oven (350°) about 45 minutes or till hot. Makes 4 or 5 servings.

# DILLED SALMON STEAKS

Place 4 fresh or frozen salmon steaks in lightly greased baking dish (thaw steaks if frozen). Combine 2 tablespoons lemon juice and 2 teaspoons instant minced onion. Sprinkle over salmon. Season with ½ teaspoon salt and dash pepper. Bake uncovered in a hot oven (400°) for 15 to 20 minutes or till fish flakes easily. Remove from oven.

Spread ¼ cup dairy sour cream over salmon. Sprinkle with 1 teaspoon grated lemon peel and ½ teaspoon dried dillweed. Return to oven; bake 3 minutes longer. Serves 4.

# SHRIMP AND RICE SUPREME

In 2-quart saucepan gradually blend ½ cup milk and 1 cup water into one 10½-ounce can condensed cream of celery soup. Add one 7-ounce package frozen rice and peas with mushrooms, one 4½-ounce can shrimp, drained, 2 tablespoons snipped parsley, and ½ teaspoon curry powder. Cover and simmer gently 30 minutes. Stir occasionally. Transfer to chafing dish to serve. Garnish with toasted slivered almonds, if desired. Serves 4 to 6.

# SHRIMP AND RICE BAKE

| | |
|---|---|
| 2 4½-ounce cans shrimp, drained | ¼ teaspoon salt |
| | 1½ cups tomato juice |
| ⅔ cup uncooked long-grain rice | 2 tablespoons snipped parsley |
| ½ teaspoon instant minced onion | |

Combine shrimp, rice, onion, and salt in 1½-quart casserole. Combine tomato juice and ½ cup water; pour over mixture. Cover casserole tightly. Bake at 375° about 50 minutes or till rice is tender. Sprinkle with parsley before serving. Makes 4 servings.

# TUNA CHOWDER

In saucepan combine one 4-ounce envelope *dry* green pea soup mix, ⅓ cup uncooked packaged precooked rice, 2 teaspoons instant minced onion, and 3 cups cold water.

Cook, stirring frequently, till mixture is boiling. Cover;

simmer 3 minutes. Stir in one 6½- or 7-ounce can tuna, drained and broken up. Season to taste with salt and pepper. Cook till heated through. Serves 4.

# TRIPLE SEAFOOD BAKE

1 cup each milk and light cream
⅓ cup dry sherry
1 10½-ounce can condensed cream of mushroom soup
1⅓ cups uncooked packaged precooked rice
1 5-ounce can lobster, drained
1 4½-ounce can shrimp, drained and split lengthwise
1 7½-ounce can minced clams, drained

1 5-ounce can water chestnuts, drained and sliced
1 3-ounce can sliced mushrooms, drained (½ cup)
1 tablespoon dried parsley flakes
¼ teaspoon instant minced garlic
2 tablespoons toasted sliced almonds
2 tablespoons butter or margarine

Stir milk, cream, and wine into soup. Add uncooked rice, cut up lobster, and next 6 ingredients. Turn into 2-quart casserole. Sprinkle with paprika and nuts; dot with butter. Bake at 350° for 50 minutes. Serves 6.

# PRESSURE-COOKER QUICK

## INDIVIDUAL POT ROASTS

1 tablespoon shortening or
   salad oil
4 6-ounce pieces boneless beef
   chuck (1½ pounds)
Salt

Pepper
½ cup water
4 carrots, pared
2 medium onions, quartered

Gravy:

½ cup cold water
2 tablespoons all-purpose flour
1 teaspoon liquid beef-flavored
   gravy base

. . .

8 ounces medium noodles, cooked
Snipped parsley
Paprika

Set heat selector of 4-quart electric pressure pan at 400° and heat shortening; brown meat well on all sides. Turn heat selector to "off." Season meat with salt and pepper.

Add first ½ cup water to electric pressure pan. (*Or* add 1 cup water if using a 6-quart electric pressure pan.)

*Close cover securely. Place pressure regulator on vent pipe and set heat selector at 425°. When pressure regulator attains a steady, gentle rocking motion, turn heat selector to left till indicator light goes out. Cook 12 minutes. Turn heat selector to "off" and disconnect cord. Let pressure go down normally. After pressure has been completely reduced, remove pressure regulator and cover. Add carrots and onions. Repeat process beginning at*, cooking 5 minutes instead of 12 minutes. Remove meat and vegetables.

For gravy, blend remaining ½ cup water with the 2 tablespoons flour. Stir into drippings in pan along with gravy base. Cook, stirring constantly, till thickened and bubbly. Cook 2 to 3 minutes longer. Serve the individual roasts with gravy on bed of noodles. Garnish with parsley; dash with paprika. Makes 4 servings.

## JIFFY SPAGHETTI SAUCE

2 tablespoons shortening or
    salad oil
1 pound ground beef
2 large onions, sliced
2 8-ounce cans (2 cups) tomato
    sauce
1 6-ounce can (⅔ cup) tomato
    paste

½ teaspoon garlic salt
1 to 1½ teaspoons chili powder
1 teaspoon sugar
½ teaspoon salt
    Dash cayenne
8 ounces long spaghetti, cooked
    Grated Parmesan cheese

Combine all ingredients except spaghetti and cheese in 4-quart pressure pan. Cook at 15 pounds pressure for 12 minutes. Reduce pressure quickly under cold running water.

Serve over cooked spaghetti. Top with Parmesan cheese. Makes 6 servings.

## NEW ENGLAND DINNER

1 cup water
1 small clove garlic
1 bay leaf
2½ pounds corned beef

. . .

6 small potatoes, pared and
    halved

1 small rutabaga or turnip, cut
    in chunks
6 medium carrots, pared and
    halved
1 small head cabbage, quartered
4 peppercorns

Place water, garlic clove, and bay leaf in 6-quart pressure pan with rack. Place meat on rack. Close cover securely. Cook 45 minutes at 15 pounds pressure. Let pressure drop of its own accord. Open pan and add potatoes, rutabaga, carrots, cabbage, and peppercorns. Close cover securely and return pan to heat. Cook 6 to 7 minutes at 15 pounds pressure. Cool pan immediately by placing under cold running water. Serves 6.

## PORK CHOP SUPPER

2 teaspoons shortening
4 pork chops, ½ to ¾ inch thick
1 teaspoon salt
    Dash pepper
½ cup chicken broth

4 small potatoes, pared, and
    halved or quartered
4 medium carrots, pared, cut up
1 small onion, chopped
2 tablespoons all-purpose flour

Heat shortening in 4-quart pressure pan. Season pork chops with the salt and pepper; brown on both sides in hot shortening. Add broth. Place vegetables atop chops. Sprinkle with additional salt and pepper. Close cover securely. Cook 10 minutes at 15 pounds pressure. Cool quickly under cold running water.

Remove chops and vegetables to serving platter. Blend flour and ¼ cup cold water. Add to juices in pan. Cook and stir till mixture thickens and bubbles. Pass gravy with chops and vegetables. Makes 4 servings.

## SAUCY CHICKEN DINNER

1 2½- to 3-pound ready-to-cook
   broiler-fryer chicken, cup up
2 tablespoons shortening
1 teaspoon salt
¼ teaspoon dried basil, crushed
1 tablespoon instant minced onion

½ cup chopped carrot
1 8-ounce can tomatoes, cut up
1 2-ounce can chopped
   mushrooms, drained
1 tablespoon all-purpose flour
   Hot cooked noodles

Sprinkle chicken with salt and pepper. Heat shortening in skillet. Brown chicken; place on rack in 4-quart pressure pan. Add 1 teaspoon salt, dash pepper, basil, onion, carrot, and tomatoes with juice. Close cover securely. Cook 13 minutes at 15 pounds pressure. Cool pan at once by placing under cold running water. Add mushrooms; heat in open pan about 1 minute. Remove chicken to platter. Mix flour and 2 tablespoons cold water. Stir into liquid in pan and cook until thick and bubbly. Serve over chicken and noodles. Makes 4 servings.

## SPEEDY CHOP SUEY

1 pound beef, pork, or veal, cut
   in ½-inch cubes
2 tablespoons shortening
1 cup water
½ teaspoon salt
   Dash pepper

   • • •

1 cup sliced celery
1 cup sliced onion

1 6-ounce can broiled sliced
   mushrooms, undrained
   (1⅓ cups)
¼ cup soy sauce
3 tablespoons cornstarch
1 1-pound can bean sprouts,
   drained
4 cups hot cooked rice

Brown meat slowly in hot shortening in 4-quart pressure pan. Add water, salt, and pepper. Close cover securely. Cook at 10 pounds pressure for 10 minutes. Reduce pressure under cold running water. Add celery and onion. Cook at 10 pounds pressure 2 minutes longer. Reduce pressure under cold running water. Remove cover. Add mushrooms with liquid. Mix soy sauce and cornstarch; slowly stir cornstarch mixture into hot liquid. Cook, stirring constantly, till thick. Add drained bean sprouts. Serve over rice. Serves 6.

## QUICK RIBS AND KRAUT

2 pounds pork spareribs, cut in
  serving pieces
½ cup tomato juice

1 1-pound 11-ounce can (3½ cups)
  sauerkraut
2 tablespoons brown sugar

Brown ribs on both sides in medium skillet. Combine sauerkraut, tomato juice, and brown sugar in 4-quart pressure pan. Top with browned ribs; season with salt and pepper. Close cover securely. Cook at 15 pounds pressure for 15 minutes. Cool pan immediately by placing under cold running water. Makes 4 or 5 servings.

# GUIDE TO COOKING GEAR

A casserole dish is a covered utensil in which food may be baked and served. Yet there are casserole mixtures that can be baked in almost any kind of baking utensil.

What if you don't have the right size utensil for the casserole recipe? Use the recipe anyway following these simple guidelines. Remember to adjust time and temperature when interchanging deep casseroles with rectangular utensil. Container sizes may vary among manufacturers. If the volume is not marked on bottom of utensil, measure the volume this way: Fill a cup or quart measure with water; pour into utensil. Repeat till full. If a covered casserole is not available, make a cover of foil.

To compare the surface of two pans, measure the length and width from the inside edges. Multiply width times length to determine each surface area in square inches.

A baking pan or a baking dish? There is a difference: A *pan* is metal; a *dish* is glass. The recipe is tested for only that which is stated. The baking time must be reduced 25° when substituting glass for metal.

A general guide to the amount of servings for a casserole:

| | |
|---|---|
| 1 quart | 4 to 5 servings |
| 1½ quart | 6 servings |
| 2 quart | 8 to 10 servings |
| 3 quart | 10 to 12 servings |

## CONTAINERS TO USE

*Covered baking dish:* Known as the classic casserole. Usually a deep dish with a lid and one or two handles. It may be round, oval, rectangular, or square. Common sizes are 1-quart, 1½-quart, and 2-quart.

*Shallow rectangular baking dish:* Some of the common sizes for this basic glass dish are 10x6x1½-inch (1½-quart), 12x7½x2-inch (2-quart), and 13x9x2-inch (3-quart). Utensil sizes may vary among manufacturers. Refer to volume or dimensions on bottom of utensil, or refer to guide above.

*Round ovenware cake dish:* Trivets, cradles, or made-to-match holders take these dishes to the table. This straight-sided glass dish is 8¼x1¾ inches (1½-quart).

*Fondue pot:* The continental choice for cheese fondue is an earthenware casserole. Meat fondue calls for a deep metal one-pan chafing dish. Both are used over heat such as denatured alcohol or canned heat.

*Glass-ceramic skillet:* Will withstand sudden temperature changes; can go from freezer to oven. Some handles are detachable to turn a skillet into a casserole.

*Cast-iron skillet:* This is especially practical when dishes cook on top of the range, then bake in the oven. Look for porcelain-enameled cast-skillets and casseroles—all make handsome servers, too.

*Electric skillet:* Can be used as a chafing dish. Lets you cook at the table, on the patio, or in the living room.

*Omelet pan:* Any heavy skillet with sloping sides can be used. For French omelets, a small 8-inch skillet is best. Avoid scouring.

*Electric pressure pan:* Cuts cooking time and holds pressure automatically.

*Pressure pan:* Use on the top of the range. Tops for less-tender meat cuts.

# EARTHENWARE CASSEROLES

Earthenware (terra cotta) "stockpots" are also available for stewing and braising. Do avoid sudden contrasts of temperature or heating baker when empty.

# SOUFFLE DISH

Straight-sided, especially designed to help souffle rise to puffy heights. For single servings, or for eggs en casserole, choose ramekins or individual souffle dishes.

# BAIN-MARIE CHAFING DISH

This dish contains two pans which serve several uses. Cook directly over the heat in the blazer pan or double-boiler-style over the water bath. Or use as a warmer.

# PORCELAIN-ENAMEL ON STEEL

Can be gay and fun as well as practical. Casseroles are available in bright colors and designs. Surface resists stains, scratches, and is easy to care for.

# DUTCH OVEN

These utensils have side or bail handles. They're equipped with tight-fitting covers which are essential for long, slow cooking jobs. Sizes usually are 4- to 6-quart.

# INDEX